Blind Expectations

C.D. HAMILTON

This is a work of fiction. Names, characters, businesses, events and incidents are the products of the author's imagination. Any resemblance to actual persons, living or dead, or actual events is purely coincidental.

Copyright © 2021 by C.D. Hamilton

All rights reserved. No part of this book may be reproduced, transmitted, or distributed in any form by any means, including, but not limited to, recording, photocopying, or taking screenshots of parts of the book, without prior written permission from the author or the publisher. Brief quotations for noncommercial purposes, such as book reviews, permitted by Fair Use of the U.S. Copyright Law, are allowed without written permissions, as long as such quotations do not cause damage to the book's commercial value. For permissions, write to the publisher, whose address is stated below.

Printed in the United States of America.

ISBN   978-1-955363-46-4   (Paperback)
ISBN   978-1-955363-47-1   (Digital)

Lettra Press books may be ordered through booksellers or by contacting:

Lettra Press LLC
30 N Gould St. Suite 4753
Sheridan, WY 82801
1 307-200-3414 | info@lettrapress.com
www.lettrapress.com

For Erinn

1

Stepney Green College belonged in a picture book. Nestled among the Appalachian Mountains in northwestern New Jersey, it was every student's dream. Here, one could achieve higher learning on a secluded, intimate campus towered by breathtaking forestry. Magnificent evergreens surrounded the college like a fortress and blessed its grounds with heavenly aromas of pine. The serene atmosphere made studying tolerable, even easier, for the several hundred students enrolled here.

Peter Michael Webb still couldn't believe he was one of them. Even now, nearing the end of his second, and final, transfer year. It was already April. Not much longer before graduation in late May.

In the open common area outside his dormitory—a grassy field where students lie on beach towels to relax on sunny afternoons, much like this Wednesday one—Pete took a break from studying to reflect on his life. He closed his textbook, turned over on his back, slid down his sunglasses, and gazed into the springtime sky of wondrous blue.

He considered himself one lucky guy to attend the prestigious Stepney Green. It was, quite literally, a whole different world from the tough working-class neighborhood where he was raised. The college's Tudor buildings alone reminded him daily. These awesome structures—white with dark-brown wooden slabs—were nothing like the mundane, old-brick townhouses lining his street back home in west-central New Jersey.

Indeed, the 23-year-old transfer student prized his efforts to come here. His hard work to achieve good grades at the community college had really paid off. All the studying and research—while holding three part-time jobs to pay for books and tuition—led to a transfer scholarship. Studying diligently to renew it was an absolute must. He would do whatever was necessary to earn a degree here, one of America's most reputable education institutions. And in less than two months he would accomplish this extraordinary goal.

But there was something else he craved even more.

Still gazing into the spring sky, Pete thought back to his community college days, how his class schedules and long work hours had left very little time for a social life. But despite the hectic pace, he pursued a girlfriend. To his surprise, he was able to meet women on the job at the cinema, grocery store, and hospital. Moviegoers and shoppers, even hospital employees… Girls were everywhere.

Whenever he went to work, he made sure his short brown hair was combed and gelled to perfection. His clothes were always clean and ironed, and his face freshly shaven. Neatly groomed, coupled with a naturally tan complexion, he attracted a number of female admirers. Sometimes he caught girls secretly glancing at him, which he found flattering. He dated some of these young ladies, but no steady relationships evolved. They just couldn't give him what he wanted: a commitment.

Now, nearing his mid-20s, a saddened Pete wondered why he never found the woman of his dreams, even during his four-semester tenure at Stepney Green.

But was all this about to change?

Pete turned over on his side, smiled, and let out a hopeful sigh. Even this close to graduation it may not be too late. Yes, she could very well be the one!

Pete's gloomy outlook had disappeared one Wednesday night in early March, at a prayer group session inside the college chapel. It was there that he first laid eyes on 20-year-old newcomer Brandi Sparks. The more weekly gatherings he attended, the more desirable she had become. She was perfect! Brandi had everything he was looking for in a woman. She was pretty but not glamorous. She dressed well, too. Her outfits were neither conservative nor revealing, and she always wore just the right amount of makeup. Not that she needed any. Her beauty was natural; no need to cover it with a bunch of cosmetics. Pete also loved the sound of Brandi's voice. Its softness echoed in feminine soother. His heart fluttered like a lovesick seventh grader whenever he heard her speak or laugh.

He often glimpsed at the corner where she huddled with her friends. That smile of hers definitely enhanced her aura of warmth. Daylight wasn't the only thing that could illuminate the chapel's majestic stained-glass windows. Brandi's smile easily surpassed their peaceful array of yellows, blues and greens. In fact, it was so bright it could have lit the entire hexagonal chapel.

Tonight would be no exception.

Pete's own smile widened as he thought this. He then sprung up from the beach towel, collected his belongings, and happily strode across the common area to his dorm. Indeed, another exciting Wednesday evening was in store.

Tonight was the first prayer group gathering of April. Once again, Pete spotted his dream girl across the room frolicking with a few girlfriends. He wanted to join in on their fun, figuring it was a good way to learn more about her. But he was hesitant.

"Come on, man, just go up there and talk to her," said Todd, sneaking up from behind.

Pete flinched anxiously.

"Keep it down, will you?" he said.

Pete's friend, the lean and lofty Todd Galloway, knew of his secret crush on the girl with the lovely smile. He enjoyed teasing him about it.

"Shame on you, Pete."

"What?"

"You're such a naughty boy. Here we are in the chapel, and you're sitting there checking out the babes."

Pete knew full well Todd was right, although not quite like he put it.

"I am not," he said anyway.

"Peter Michael Webb, you will be punished for that lie," Todd said facetiously, "especially now during this most sacred gathering."

"Yeah, yeah, whatever… So what's up, Todd? What have you been up to?"

"No good," he answered, taking his seat next to his pal.

"Why am I not surprised?"

"You know, Pete, you really should go over there and talk to Brandi. She doesn't bite, you know."

He had a point. There was no harm in talking to her. There was nothing to lose. The hard part was over. Pete was no stranger to Brandi because Todd had introduced him a few weeks ago. Striking up a conversation with her would be easy. After all, they already had one thing in common: prayer group.

Pete wondered if Brandi might be different. Maybe she, as a member of this fellowship, was raised with good values. Perhaps she would treat him better than the other women he had dated.

Especially on this revered campus.

2

Liz Dabney was the last girl Pete courted. He actually had his eye on her during his first year at Stepney Green. Just when he coughed up the courage to ask her out, he discovered she was involved with someone else: Gareth Baker.

The following year they split up. Pete was delighted.

He held two jobs on campus: a resident assistant—RA for short—and library desk clerk. Two months ago, on a frosty Saturday afternoon in February, he spotted Liz inside the college library. He smiled and said hello as she passed the front desk. She gladly reciprocated and even stopped to talk to him. She remembered Pete well. He was a good friend of Corinne's, her roommate from last year.

Corinne Aldrich was also an RA. As such, they were assigned their own private rooms. But due to a housing crunch last year, a number of them had to share their living quarters. Pete was one of the lucky ones who didn't … Corinne not so much … and in more ways than one. She was no fan of Liz Dabney.

Unlike her fellow RA who had a major crush on her.

Liz remembered this all too well.

"So how are you?" Pete asked, his smile turning flirtatious.

"Just fine, thanks," she replied, returning the gesture. "And you?"

She knew he was still interested in her. His grin was all the proof she needed.

"Just fine," he said, "now."

Liz almost blushed from the flattery.

"So what are you up to?" he asked.

"Nothing much, just trying to get some research done."

Pete felt his heart racing. It was time to make his move. But how? He didn't want to appear overeager, that was certain. He had to be calm, cool, and no matter how nervous he was, he didn't want his voice to crack.

Pete breathed deeply through his nose, releasing his anxiety. This is nothing, nothing, he told himself. He'd been through this sort of thing dozens of times, right? He could get through this just fine, rejected or not.

"So what's up with you?" asked Liz.

Perfect! He did not have to word his way to asking her out. Her question created the ideal setup.

"I'm on duty tonight, RA duty that is," said Pete. "Too bad you're busy. I was hoping you could drop by and keep me company."

Did I really just say that?

He was never so forward.

"I'm not that busy," said Liz. "I could come over around midnight. Is that too late?"

Pete was thrilled but contained his excitement.

"No, not at all," he said, "I'll see you then."

After exchanging cellphone numbers, and after Liz exited the library, Pete leaned back in his chair and gazed at the ceiling. He could hardly believe what just happened: *the* Liz Dabney was coming to visit him tonight. He pinched himself to make sure this was no dream.

Pete was the on-duty RA for the Rockford Hall dormitory, while Corinne was on duty for Blake Hall. The two met in the gazebo outside for rounds sharply at 11 p.m. It was a chilly winter night.

"Hi, Corinne," he said.

"Hi," she replied cheerfully. "How are you?"

Pete couldn't help but smile. Corinne knew something was up.

"Okay," she said, "what's her name?"

"You already know her," he answered, walking out of the gazebo.

"I do?"

Pete nodded.

"And very well I might add."

"Well, who is she?" Corinne asked, intrigued.

"Liz," he replied, "your roommate from last year."

Corinne was stunned. She thought Pete's feelings for Liz had died down.

"Really?"

"Yeah," said Pete. "In fact, she's coming to my room in an hour."

"Oh."

Corinne didn't quite know how to take this news. In a way, she was pleased for him, but something disturbed her. To her, Pete was the sweetest guy in the world. He was bright but sensitive. He could be easily hurt. Corinne remembered Liz's mood swings all too well and wondered if Pete could handle them.

Not wanting to dampen her good friend's spirits, she decided to keep Liz's mood swings to herself.

"Well, good luck, Pete," she said as they entered Blake Hall.

He needed all the good luck he could get. He'd been hurt enough. Corinne knew he was no champion in the romance department. Pete had told her all about his past relationships, not that there were many. Corinne was truly sympathetic to his heartache and was glad to listen. She was also honored, as Pete was the kind of guy who valued his privacy. His love life was off limits to everyone but a select few. Even his mother was clueless.

His failed relationship with Dana O'Brien stood out the most. Corinne couldn't believe how badly he was treated. Nevertheless, he allowed himself to be used. He genuinely—and naively—saw the good in people. He never realized there were women out there who flaunted their charm for their own advantage, to make other men jealous. Dana O'Brien was certainly one of them. Corinne knew her type and figured that Dana would break his heart. There was nothing she could say or do. Pete was determined to stay in the relationship no matter what. He saw it through to the end.

Just as she expected, he did not leave the relationship unscathed. Corinne admired her friend's determination to heal the relationship's wounds, but his naiveté aggravated her. Still, she had no choice but to stand back and let Pete learn for himself—the hard way.

And she had to let him learn the hard way all over again.

After 11 o'clock rounds Pete returned to his room on the top floor in Rockford Hall. Fortunately, the campus was relatively calm. This was most unusual for a Saturday night. But the night was still young.

Expecting Liz shortly, he set up his room to reflect a romantic mood: dimming his lamp and turning on the music from his mini-stereo, keeping the volume low. The station, his favorite, was tuned to one that played nonstop love songs. He then straightened the navy quilt on his bed, cleaned up the desk clutter, and sprayed on his best cologne. Everything had to be perfect.

Liz arrived promptly at midnight. Her presence brightened the dim room the moment she entered. Pete loved how her curly blond hair draped down her body, the way her locks glistened against her pale-blue sweater, the same color as her haunting eyes.

He was mesmerized; he could hardly believe she was here. His waiting was over.

Liz had her backpack with her.

"I hope you don't mind that I brought my books and things," she said. "It'll give me something to do when you're on rounds."

"Not a problem."

Pete could not believe his luck. This meant she was planning to stay a while.

With 1 o'clock rounds coming up in less than an hour, he figured he should wait until later to make his move. So they talked in the meantime. Pete was surprised to learn that her major was biology. Her dream was to find cures for diseases. This really impressed him, but he learned that Liz's dream was very different than his own: to become a distinguished writer. Still, their life's goals had one thing in common: many people were striving to accomplish the same things.

The time went by quickly. It was nearly 1 a.m., and Pete had to meet Corinne for final rounds.

"Well, I have to go now," he said, "but feel free to watch some TV in case you get bored doing homework."

"Thanks," said Liz. "See you later."

"Bye."

Pete left the room with a starry smile. It stayed with him all the way outside to the gazebo, where Corinne waited.

"So, how's it going?" she asked curiously.

Pete blushed in glee, his face reddening despite the outdoor chill. Corinne nodded. She could definitely tell his date was going much better than expected.

One o'clock rounds ran smoothly, much to Pete's surprise—and relief. Now he could spend quality time with Liz without interruption. He had no incident reports to write. Only an emergency could distract his attention. Fingers crossed the night would remain trouble-free.

When he entered his room, he saw Liz lounging on his bed watching TV. She looked incredibly sexy.

"Oh, you're back," she said, switching off the small, 12-inch flat-screen television as she sat up. "That was fast."

"Yes, but I'm not complaining," said Pete, turning back on the music.

He then sat down beside her.

"So… Anything interesting on while I was gone?"

"Not really," she said, "I just didn't feel like working on my research project. I should've left my books back in my room."

"What's it about?" asked Pete, stretching his arm around her back.

"That makes me feel uncomfortable."

"What does?"

"*That*," she answered, removing Pete's hand.

"Oh … that."

"I'm not ready for that yet."

When he asked why, Liz explained she was just coming off her relationship with Gareth. They had been together since the beginning of the fall semester last year. Pete knew this, of course, but let her carry on anyway.

"I'm really sorry he hurt you," he said, resting his hand on hers.

She smiled, barely, and turned her hand upside down to squeeze that of her suitor.

"Thanks," she said.

"For what it's worth, I think Gareth was crazy to let you go," said Pete, again resting his hand on Liz's back.

She didn't remove it this time. She sensed his compassion, his sincerity. He only wanted to console her, she thought.

Pete was about to draw her closer when reality set in.

"Sorry," he said, whisking away his arm, "I just remembered you weren't ready for that yet."

He sat at the bed's edge and slouched forward, propping his elbows on his knees. His head then slumped into his hands. He knew he blew it this time.

"Don't worry about it," said Liz. "It's okay, really."

It's okay?

Pete perked up right away. Maybe he didn't blow it after all. But he had to act fast if he were to get a kiss from this girl. It was already 2 o'clock in the morning, and she would probably leave soon.

Because time wasn't on his side, Pete grew frustrated. He collapsed backward onto his bed, sighing heavily on the way. Flat on his back, he came up with an idea. He opened his dancing brown eyes and stared at Liz flirtatiously.

"What?" she said.

"Come lie down next to me," he answered, tapping the mattress.

Pete couldn't believe his boldness, more so than Liz. He figured he had nothing to lose.

"Why?" she asked, a bit hesitant.

"Nothing, I just want to hold you," he said. "No harm in that, is there?"

Liz found the good-looking guy too cute to resist. She smiled and snuggled next to him. As he put it, there was no harm in doing this.

Pete was enthralled, hopelessly infatuated. After a year and a half of secret glances and daydreaming, Liz Dabney was lying next to him—in his room, on his bed. And she seemed to enjoy it.

Pete stroked her arm tenderly. She did not flinch or remove his hand. Quite the contrary, she liked being held. She enjoyed feeling wanted again.

"Liz?" Pete said tenderly.

"Yes?"

Instead of answering verbally he kissed her cheek. The moment was perfect. Liz stared at Pete seductively, signaling her approval. She did not resist when he kissed her again. Pete then kissed her neck, several times, and eventually, her lips. She kissed him back and embraced him tightly. The pair made out for hours, caressing each other's bodies hungrily. Pete's shirt had become unbuttoned and was gradually taken off. So was Liz's blue sweater.

Shortly after 4:30 a.m. the couple lay holding each other. Their eyes closed, Pete wondered if Liz were asleep. Even though he'd been awake for more than 20 hours, he was far from drowsy. He tried to doze off, but his excitement kept his conscience stirring. He could do nothing but think about the wonderful night he just had. He relived its events over and over in his mind, especially the passion.

Pete had fallen "in like" pretty deeply this time. He was dangerously close to the edge of love and did not want to trip into it. It was definitely too soon for that.

Liz's eyes fluttered open.

"You awake?" she whispered.

He most certainly was.

"Uh-huh," he said, opening his eyes and cracking a smile.

"I better go."

"Why don't you just stay here? It's really late. In fact, it'll be dawn soon."

"Thanks, but I can't," she said, rising from the bed.

Pete sat up and watched his girlfriend-hopeful slip into her sweater and pick up her backpack.

"I wish you'd reconsider," he said. "If I weren't on duty, I could walk you to your dorm myself."

"I'll be okay."

Pete met Liz at his door and gazed into her eyes adoringly.

"Thanks," he said, "I had a really nice time tonight."

She didn't say anything; she only smiled politely. Pete invited her to the movies. He'd been thinking of checking out a Sunday matinee. Liz thanked him for the invitation but declined, explaining there was schoolwork to do before Monday's classes. Pete said he understood and kissed her goodbye.

As soon as she left, he crashed onto his bed, elated. Finally, he had found a girlfriend, or at least a very likely girlfriend. Liz was exceptionally attractive, smart and fun. And from her actions tonight she must have felt the same about him.

With these pleasing thoughts Pete fell asleep. His smile never left his face.

When Pete returned from the cinema early Sunday evening, he received a call from Corinne, who asked how his day was going—and how his date went last night. He was glad to hear from her but disappointed that Liz never phoned or texted. Nevertheless he shared with her the exciting news.

Pete considered 21-year-old Corinne Aldrich his best friend at Stepney Green. He could tell her anything, anything at all, and she would keep his confidence. Likewise, Corinne trusted Pete totally, without measure. Students on campus often wondered if they were more than just friends. They hung around frequently and even ate together in the cafeteria. Everyone knew they worked as RAs, too. They seemed to have so much in common—except chemistry. Pete viewed Corinne as a friend, a very close friend, like a sister. However, there was a slight physical attraction when he first met her. He found her shoulder-length brown hair, Mediterranean blue eyes and cute figure rather appealing. But this feeling diminished the deeper his friendship with her developed. Pete was fine with this. He liked having a female friend. He could get the woman's perspective on things like romance and relationships. Similarly, Corinne could get a man's opinion if she needed it. He was always willing to return the favor.

Corinne was equally content with the status of their relationship. She thought Pete was a cute guy but was drawn to his personality more than anything. His sincerity and compassion endeared her. He was also intelligent, but he had this little-boy-lost quality about him. Corinne adored this; somehow it conveyed a sense of innocence. She felt protective toward him, like a kid sister sticking up for her big brother.

This protective instinct flared when Pete explained how Liz left his room early this morning. Corinne feared that her "best friend on campus," a term she employed to describe her unique relationship with him, was heading for heartache—again. She deduced that Liz had her way with him to escape her own heartache caused by Gareth's breakup.

Blind Expectations

As was the case with Dana O'Brien, Corinne had to keep her mouth shut. Pete was too smitten with Liz to take her words of caution seriously. It was history repeating itself all over again.

"So why hasn't she called or texted?" Pete said.

"Just give her time," said Corinne. "Maybe she'll contact you later tonight."

"I hope so."

Pete thanked Corinne for listening and said goodbye. He decided to stay put in his room the rest of the evening, all the while hoping Liz would call—a sure indicator that she wanted to see him again. They could talk either briefly or at length, even throughout the night if she wanted, it didn't matter.

The working-class native had subscribed to a limited usage wireless phone plan. Given his low-income background, Pete considered his mobile phone and laptop computer prized possessions, luxuries even—a complete contrast to the wealthy students at Stepney Green, to whom high-tech devices were everyday items with unlimited usage plans. He'd worked damned hard to pay for his communications gadgetry as well as their associated bills—and he'd gladly work even harder to pay for the extra minutes to chat with his dream girl tonight.

But there would be no need.

As the hours waned so did Pete's wish of having Liz Dabney as a girlfriend. At 11 o'clock, he'd had enough. He picked up the phone, went to his contacts list, and pressed the call button below Liz's name. After four rings her voicemail activated. He did not leave a message. Frustrated, he hung up in haste and went to bed for the night.

Monday and Tuesday dragged. Pete kept waiting for Liz to call or text. It was all he could think about. But she never did either. He didn't even pass her by on campus like he usually did. The library, cafeteria, hallways, the gym … she was nowhere to be found. Perhaps that was how she wanted it.

Corinne sensed her friend's dismay. His glum expression at dinner

Tuesday evening said it all. She wanted so much to boost his spirits but was unable to help.

The next day Pete decided to phone Liz one last time. This way he could make peace with himself. He could honestly say that he did his best to form a relationship, to make whatever it was he had with her work.

Pete took a deep breath and picked up the phone. As he made the call, he felt his heart pounding ferociously. Even though it was a cloudless night, a storm brewed in his conscience. Anger and despair erupted simultaneously. He was mad at Liz for avoiding him and despondent because he didn't know her true feelings. Yet a speck of hope dangled inside. Although tiny, this feeling was the most powerful. As long as there was a shred of hope, a positive outcome could not be totally ruled out.

Liz answered after the third ring. Pete's anxiety immediately ceased. The blustering storm within his psyche had breezed abruptly to a halt.

"Hey there," he said calmly.

Liz knew exactly who it was.

"Oh ... hi," she said.

"You okay?"

"Uh-huh," she answered—coolly.

This tone began to sink Pete's hopes. She was obviously not pleased to hear from him. He knew what was coming: rejection. He carried on nonetheless.

"I was thinking... How would you like to go out for dinner this weekend?"

"I'm busy," she replied.

"Oh... Look, Liz, are you avoiding me? Why haven't I heard from you since we got together Saturday?"

"Because you're *not* what I'm looking for," she answered sharply.

Pete's last iota of hope dissipated at that very moment. Her voice was so cold. And the way she stressed "not" was particularly harsh. Pete kept asking himself how she could be so heartless. He genuinely cared for Liz, but she acted as if he were the most hated man on the planet. He wondered why she lost interest in him so quickly. Deep down he didn't want to know.

Pete felt it best to just let her go. He was too tired to fight for another Dana O'Brien. The same story was unfolding again—boy pursues girl; boy thinks he has girl; girl dumps boy for no good reason.

"Well, I'm sorry you feel that way," he said, barely getting out the words. "Bye."

A devastated Pete hung up and plopped onto his bed. He tried so hard to suppress his hurt, but it lingered the rest of the night. Endless guessing plagued his mind. He kept asking himself why he wasn't what Liz was looking for. Perhaps he came on too strong or too fast. Maybe she, like Dana, had used him to make another guy jealous, namely Gareth.

Pete folded his fingers into fists and pounded the mattress. His bottom lip uncurled for a moment to let out a steaming sigh.

"Damn," he said, fighting tears begging to boil over.

By dawn Pete had made peace with the situation. He realized Liz was *not* the one for him. She was the one letting a great person slip through her fingers, not the other way around. And as for her reasons behind the rejection, Pete discovered he was actually better off not knowing them than knowing them.

3

Yes, dating a member of prayer group could be just the change he needed. Surely Brandi Sparks was no Liz—and a universe away from Dana. She would never make him feel unworthy like they did.

Todd, with his elbow, nudged Pete in the ribs. He figured it was the most discreet way to snap his friend out of his trance.

"Are you going to talk to Brandi, or are you just going to sit there drooling?"

"Huh?" Pete replied, a bit dazed. "Oh, yes, Brandi. Yeah, I'll talk to her."

"Well, what are you waiting for, man? Go on over there."

"Maybe later, after the meeting."

Todd rolled his eyes in frustration—but not for long. Brandi was on her way over. Pete's mouth nearly dried out in anticipation. Nevertheless he stood up and smiled warmly as she arrived.

"Hi, guys," Brandi said cheerfully.

"Hey, Brandi," said Todd, rising from his chair, "what's up?"

"Nothing much," she replied. "How are you two doing?"

Pete gulped.

"Just fine, thanks," he said in a miraculously clear voice. "And you?"

Brandi said she was doing great, and her radiant smile proved it. Pete was awestruck. He always knew her smile lit up the chapel. But tonight, being so close to her, he believed it could ignite the whole campus.

Todd sensed Pete's growing attraction to Brandi but also his hesitation. As the three of them conversed he wondered why his pal was being so passive. The Liz fiasco was over. It was time to move on, not the time to give up. He'd told Pete the best way to get over a relationship was to start a new one. Todd quickly devised a plan to help his friend, to give him the push he needed.

"Pete," he said, "did you know that Brandi loves to rollerblade?"

"No, I didn't," he replied, intrigued.

Pete enjoyed the sport as well. He was delighted. Now he had two things in common with the lovely Miss Sparks: prayer group and rollerblading.

Brandi told the guys she could hardly wait to get back into the sport. In fact, she was planning to go rollerblading in the park Saturday. The weather forecast called for sunny skies and mild temperatures.

This was it, Pete thought. He had to make his move. His buddy Todd had created the perfect setup. The plan was masterful. Todd's spontaneity and cleverness never ceased to amaze.

"Sounds like fun, Brandi," said Pete, who then smiled amorously. "May I join you?"

Todd was pleased; his friend had taken the bait.

Brandi answered with an energetic and resounding "Sure." She seemed pleasantly surprised, flattered even. Her face beamed.

But not nearly as much as Pete's.

Pete woke up Saturday morning smiling. Not only was today the big day—his first date with Brandi—but sunlight had speckled into his room. He took this as a good sign of things to come.

Excited, he bounced out of bed, hurried on his robe, and rushed to the window. What a sight. A regal sun was enthroned amidst a tranquil blue sky. Without a doubt, a beautiful April day had dawned.

Pete opened the window and whiffed some fresh air. Four stories high, the air was slightly more invigorating. Its temperature was just right, cool but not cold. And it could only grow milder as morning turned to afternoon.

Indeed, the weather was ideal for rollerblading.

And whatever else may follow.

Corinne could hardly wait to see her best friend on campus. She wanted to wish him luck one last time before meeting Brandi this afternoon. She waited excitedly at a petite corner table in the dining hall's sunroom, an annex where students ate in a naturally lit setting. It wasn't very crowded, and Corinne loved how the incoming sunshine enhanced the room's solace.

Pete arrived for breakfast a few minutes after 10. The foods on his tray would impress the most fanatic of fitness freaks. Orange juice, unbuttered wheat toast, and fresh pineapple slices nobly complemented the main course: a yolk-free omelet folding over green peppers and mushrooms.

"Well, good morning, Mr. Health Nut," said Corinne, smiling facetiously.

Pete returned the gesture as he sat down.

"Ha-ha-ha, very funny," he said.

Corinne had never seen her friend so willing to impress a girl, and so early. He hadn't even gone out with Brandi, yet here he was altering his diet. She found this amusing more than anything. Corinne wasn't worried about Pete's feelings this time. She liked Brandi. Although she wasn't her friend, she knew her casually. Both were social work majors and had a number of classes together. Brandi seemed sweet and well-liked by her peers and professors.

"I must say," said Corinne, "Brandi must be one special lady."

"She sure is," Pete agreed, his face blushing.

He could not hold back his smile, either. The mere mention of her name sent him on a daydream flight into the clouds. He fought to drift into "the like zone" so soon, but it was no use. Although he feared getting hurt, part of him didn't care. He felt she was worth the risk.

Corinne was impressed. She admired Pete's willingness to take another chance, especially on someone so pleasant like Brandi.

"Well, let me know how everything goes, okay?" she said, finishing her breakfast. "I'm so thrilled for you."

"Thanks, Corinne," said Pete, wiping his mouth.

The two friends rose from the table and picked up their trays. As they exited the sun room, Liz arrived suddenly. Pete froze. He was not expecting to see her.

"Hi, Corinne," she said cheerfully.

An awkward pause polluted the air. Corinne expected Liz to say hello to Pete as well, but she did no such thing. She was solely focused on her former roommate. She refused to unglue her eyes or tilt her head. Corinne returned the hello but with far less enthusiasm. Her salutation was, at best, cordial. Liz's ignorance was not only immature, she thought, but cruel.

Although uncomfortable, Pete wasn't about to let his past love intimidate him. He forced himself to stay put by Corinne's side and not retreat to a corner. He also held his head up high, refusing to look down in humiliation. Becoming one with the bleak gray floor was out of the question. There was no reason to feel guilty. If anyone should be ashamed, it was Liz. After all, she was the one behaving childishly, not him.

As she conversed with Corinne, Pete wondered how he could have fallen for someone so shallow. He once thought Liz the most beautiful girl he had ever seen. Now, the ugliness inside her had crept out and covered her entire body.

"Oh and guess what?" she said, her eyes widening in bluish jubilation. "I met the most wonderful guy in the world. He's a real man, not like Gareth … and those others."

Corinne grew increasingly agitated. She knew Liz only said this to rile Pete. But her friend's rigid expression remained unchanged. She was so proud of him, and so glad her ex-roommate failed as miserably as she did.

"Really," Corinne said, struggling to be sincere. "Well, I only hope he knows what he's getting himself into."

A burst of laughter almost escaped Pete's mouth. When it exploded inside, his neck and head flinched. Corinne, barely maintaining her friendly smile, gently kicked his ankle. This nonverbal communication exclaimed "Stop!" quite well.

While Pete chuckled to himself, Liz laughed out loud. Little did she know that Corinne was only half joking.

"You know," said Liz, "not being roommates this year, I almost forgot how funny you can be."

Corinne, sensing more laughter about to blow up beside her, again kicked Pete's ankle.

"Those were really great times," Liz added, sincerely.

"Well, they certainly were something else," said Corinne, oblivious to the reddening face beside her.

Liz smiled.

"You're sweet," she said. "Thanks for the chat. It was really great to catch up with you."

Corinne widened her costumed smile as she replied, "Always a treat for me."

Pete could take no more. He hurried out of the cafeteria, laughing the whole time. He had held in his mirth long enough. Corinne, on the other hand, politely bid Liz goodbye and took her time leaving. She did not want to exit quite so hastily—and so obviously.

Outside the dining hall Pete managed to compose himself. But his grin reemerged as soon as Corinne arrived. She paused for a moment then shook her head in amusement.

It was a breakfast neither would forget.

By noon the temperature outside had warmed, just as Pete hoped it would. The sun was exceptionally bright, as were his spirits. He smiled at the irony. Standing outside his dorm, he slipped on his slick sporty sunglasses and gazed into the sky of perfect springtime blue, hoping this day would be as special for Brandi as it was for him.

Pete was pleased. He was already claiming the day as special, despite the Liz episode hours ago. In the past a bad experience like that would have ruined his whole day. Now, though, he had the strength to move on. The incident with Liz hadn't dampened his mood. That nightmare was shelved as quickly as he left the cafeteria.

It was time to focus on the present—and future.

Brandi was due to arrive any moment. As he waited, Pete donned his protective gear: wrist guards, kneepads, elbow pads, and helmet. He was taking no chances of falling. The last thing he wanted was for Brandi to see him cut up or bruised. His gear came in a matching set, gray with white trim. This set tastefully complemented his black shirt and shorts, which he hoped she would notice.

Suddenly, the concrete path nearby rumbled. The sound was all too familiar. Rollerblade wheels, spinning rapidly, were grating their stony surface. A smile splashed across Pete's face, and it widened significantly as he turned to the young lady approaching. Brandi looked incredible. It wasn't because her navy sportswear revealed an attractive physique. Nor was it the alluring crimps in her sandy-blond hair breezing away from her face. Rather, it was the glow from below her helmet.

That face. How beautiful.

Brandi's cheekbones seemed slightly elevated. Pete figured it was to make room for her expanded smile. Just above its rims lay adorable dimples. They were tiny but noticeable, and were the perfect complement to an already lovely face.

Brandi's arrival was a spectacle, at least to Pete. He was impressed by her eloquent swerve as she met him face to face.

"Whoa," he said, "I thought you were just an amateur."

Brandi, flattered by the compliment, smiled even more radiantly.

"Thanks, Pete," she said, her brown eyes dazzling with perkiness. "I thought the same about you, but not now."

His heart was fluttering again. It happened every time he heard her sweet soothing voice. He told himself to relax over and over, but it was no use.

"What do you mean?" he asked, clearing the schoolboy nervousness in his throat.

She explained how his protective gear made him look like the ultimate professional. Then she said something even more surprising. She told him how awesome he looked in his black shirt and shorts.

Pete was tickled. Not only did Brandi notice his outfit, she flattered him. A simple "great" or even "cool" would have sufficed. Instead he got an "awesome." It was just the encouragement he needed. Now he could pursue her freely, without any hesitation. He no longer wondered if she were romantically interested in him. She had to be at least curious. After all, she could have cancelled their plans. She had most of the week to make up an excuse not to get together. But she did no such thing. She showed up for their date and was on time. She was ready to rollerblade, not to admit she'd made a mistake in allowing him to join her. Brandi had only been in his company for a few minutes, and already she was complimenting his appearance. Indeed this was an "awesome" development.

"I'm so glad it didn't rain today," she said.

"Me, too," Pete said with newly restored confidence. "The forecasters were right on." He then smiled flirtatiously. "It truly is gorgeous out here today."

Brandi just about blushed, much to his delight.

"Smooth, really smooth," she said. "Now let's see how smooth you are on those skates, shall we?"

At that moment she whisked down the concrete path.

"Hey!"

Pete was both surprised and amused. He liked her playful streak. It was yet another attractive quality—and a turn-on.

He zoomed after her, passing the Rockford Hall dormitory and a few students who kindly stepped aside. The paved slope to the college's pedestrian exit wasn't difficult to navigate. It was curvy, but its descent was gradual. Several evergreens had been planted intermittently on each side, emptying pockets of pine into the neighboring air. The aroma was particularly strong throughout the half-mile stretch, but pleasant nonetheless. Piney air like this was most refreshing to Stepney Green students, especially rollerblade enthusiasts. Every time they skated down the pathway, their senses ignited. The fragrant breeze against their face and body created the perfect pick-me-up.

Pete didn't need any such stimulant today. He was alive as never before.

Near the end of the path Brandi glanced over her shoulder. Her suitor, eager to impress, had gained on her. He was determined to beat the charming Miss Sparks at her own game. Increasing speed, he caught up and eventually passed her. Brandi's mouth dropped in astonishment.

"How's that for smoothness?" asked a playful, triumphant Pete.

"Yeah, pretty smooth," she replied, accepting her imminent defeat with grace, "pretty smooth, all right."

She knew she deserved to lose the unannounced contest, especially after giving herself a head start. Pete's victory was well-earned, she concluded. His rollerblading skills were most impressive.

The arch at the end of the concrete path lay just a few feet ahead. It was quite a monument. Its huge stony chunks piled nine feet into the air. Connecting overhead, they formed a meticulous oval archway above the pedestrian path—or in Pete's case, the rollerblade runway. Intermingled with a whitish grout, the stones encompassed an array of luminous earth tones. Some people thought the monument stood as a testament to the college's natural surroundings. Others simply admired its supreme height, thickness and architecture. The president of the college went a step further. The arch, he said, was Stepney Green's "gateway to education excellence."

Pete liked this assessment most, given how hard he worked to meet the school's high enrollment standards.

He reflected on the president's symbolic quote as he skated through the archway, counting his blessings once again. He loved attending Stepney Green College, high in the picturesque mountains of Sussex County. The education he was receiving was invaluable. Pete felt he could achieve almost anything here. Although proud of his accomplishments, he was careful never to show it. He hoped his humbleness would impress Brandi—in addition to his polished rollerblade maneuvers, of course.

Outside the archway he curved sharply to the right, semi-circling to a halt. He stared in awe at the sight that was once behind him: the most amazing woman he ever met entering the archway.

Nearing the end, she suddenly lost her balance. Fortunately, Pete reached for her, resulting in a gentle crash into his arms.

"Thanks," she said, laughing relentlessly. "I'm so embarrassed."

As Brandi laughed off her clumsiness, Pete cherished the warmth pressed against his chest. Holding her was something he longed for since that initial prayer group meeting a month ago. But he was careful not to get his hopes up. He knew she didn't fall into his arms on purpose, even though deep down he wished she had.

He raised his arms to Brandi's shoulders and gazed into her eyes.

"Are you okay?" he asked softly.

"Yes," she replied, "thanks to you."

Pete smiled. Although she may not have known it, she was quickly learning how to tug his heartstrings.

"Ready to go to the park?" she said. "I promise to be a good girl from now on."

"Darn," said Pete, feigning disappointment. "Now you've really let me down. First I beat you to the arch and now this good-girl pledge. You're no fun."

"Oh, you," Brandi said, smacking his arm playfully.

Pete laughed. He delighted in making her smile, bringing out her best, which made him enjoy her company more and more. He hoped she felt the same, that she was being more than just polite.

After checking traffic the pair skated across the two-lane roadway, keeping inside the lined crosswalk. Stepney Green's community park lay just ahead. It was every bit picture-perfect as the college itself.

The park reflected the essence of springtime. Conifers weren't the only trees spread throughout. Budding maples, oaks, dogwoods, and others in the deciduous family bordered the park's skyline with wondrous greens, yellows, whites and pinks. Whenever a breeze rustled their colorful blossoms, it produced a kaleidoscopic spectacle. The grass below was seasonally fresh, as was the man-placed lake in the heart of the park, having recently thawed from March's chills. Songbird echoes unclogged ears blocked by the deafness of winter. Pete and Brandi, skating on the park's paved footpaths, took pleasure in these natural tunes.

"Listen to that," she said. "Isn't it beautiful?"

"It sure is," he agreed, "but it's definitely not the only thing."

Brandi smiled and changed the subject.

"So where are you from?"

Pete gulped. He was dreading this question. Nevertheless the truth would have to come out about his lower-middleclass roots. He felt he owed it to her to be honest. Ordinarily his background wouldn't have bothered him, but he was a little insecure about it on campus. Stepney Green was one of the costliest institutions of higher education in the state—and nation. The vast majority of students came from very affluent families. His friend Todd, heir to the Galloway Hotel Towers chain, was undoubtedly one of them. Corinne's family was wealthy—although she never flaunted the fact—and Pete figured Brandi's was as well.

"Woodlake Square," he said. "What about you?"

"I'm from Mantoloking."

Pete was right. She had to be from an affluent family. It was common knowledge that Mantoloking was one of New Jersey's most expensive places to live. With a prime location on the shore, the cost of homes ranged into the millions. Brandi said she was born and raised there her whole life. She lived on a beachfront estate, where her parents employed a housemaid and groundskeeper. She even had a nanny when she was younger.

As she described her upper-class upbringing, Pete breathed a sigh of relief. He was glad she didn't press him for further details about Woodlake Square. The less she knew about the Trenton outskirt the better.

Approaching the wooden bridge overlooking the lake created the perfect opportunity to get off topic. Pete suggested skating to the top to check out the view. Brandi agreed and led the way. With light swings of the waist and arms they made their way up the bridge's arch to the peak. The rainbow-shaped bridge was easy to skate on. It was like a boardwalk along the shore but with modest inclines on each side.

Leaning against the railing the pair relished in nature's awesome phenomena. The indigo lake's gentle waves below were as serene as the flowering baby leaves high above the ground. The atmosphere was just right for romance, Pete thought. Even the birds seemed to be playing love songs. Despite the moment's amorousness, he resisted his urge to rest his hand on Brandi's shoulder. He did not want to scare her away too soon, like he did to Liz. They should get to know each other better first, he reasoned. She may even respect him for this.

"So Bran—"

"Pete, can I—"

Speaking simultaneously made them laugh.

"I'm sorry," said Brandi. "Go ahead."

"No, you first," Pete insisted.

"I was just going to ask you about Corinne."

"What about her?"

"Please tell me if I'm being too personal," she said, "but are you two dating?"

Her question aroused his curiosity. Of course, other people on campus wondered the same thing about Corinne and him. This was annoying sometimes, but not when Brandi asked. She was special, and Pete wanted to be totally honest and upfront with her.

"No, we're not dating," he said, setting the record straight. "We're just friends … like brother and sister."

"That's really sweet," said Brandi, seemingly satisfied with his explanation. "So what were you going to ask me?"

He inquired about her family. She told him she was an only child and dreaded it, as her parents doted on her constantly. Pete thought she was lucky in a way. He and his older brother did not get along at all. Their mother often said they were as different as night and day. Although she never admitted it, Pete knew he represented the latter.

"What about your family?" she asked. "Are you an only child, too?"

Pete sighed. Given the friction with his brother, he should have known better than to broach the subject of family. But it was too late. The topic was already out there. And when it boomeranged it hit him hard. He mentioned Adam nonetheless but did not disclose the animosity between them.

"Are you close?" Brandi asked.

Pete sighed again.

"Not really," he said, "but who knows, maybe that'll change."

He wished he could believe what he just said. Still, it wasn't an outright lie. He hoped his optimistic words were enough for Brandi to drop the subject. This was neither the time nor place to talk about family squabbles.

"Sounds like you have the right attitude," she said.

Pete thanked her and suggested they carry on rollerblading. Skating off the bridge, the pair reentered the park's winding nature paths. Their pace was slow and relaxed. There was no need to rush through the park on a Saturday afternoon. Also, they didn't want to miss out on the springtime paradise surrounding them. Every colorful budding tree was a natural wonder this time of year. In a couple of weeks the blossoms would break off and forever drift away into the atmosphere. Now was the time to cherish this beauty, as it would only return in 50 weeks.

During their rollerblade stroll Brandi revealed her social work major. She wanted to contribute to society, she explained, and help those less fortunate. Pete admired this and described juggling his double major in both communications and English.

"It's a heck of a lot of work," he said, "but I'm having the time of my life. I love all the writing."

"Really," Brandi said, intrigued.

Pete expressed his desire to be a renowned novelist someday, even though achieving this level of fame was highly unlikely. However, he was a firm believer in the "you'll never know unless you try" philosophy—and not just about his writing. He passionately applied this principle to his courtships as well. Dana, Liz and other heartbreakers all had their share. Now it was Brandi's turn.

"So," he said, "what are you doing later? Any plans tonight?"

"I'm not sure," she replied. "Why?"

"I'm thinking about catching a movie in Vernon and was wondering if you'd like to come along."

"Sure," she said enthusiastically. "I'd love to."

She'd love to? Her upbeat response further boosted Pete's spirits—and confidence. As they neared the park's exit he reached for her hand. She did not yank it away. In fact, she smiled warmly. She must have welcomed the gesture, her admirer thought. He was most pleased with his progress.

As Brandi and Pete left the park two little boys on rollerblades were on their way inside. One looked to be about eight years old, and the other slightly younger. The sight of the big boy and girl holding hands disgusted them.

"Yuck!" screeched one of the kids.

"Gross!" cried the other.

As the children whizzed past, the college students turned to each other and busted out laughing. Crossing the street toward campus, Pete remarked how the kids' attitudes were bound to change in a few years. Brandi quite agreed.

Once through the archway the couple's hands unlocked. Skating their way up the concrete path, they discussed plans to meet this evening. Pete would pick her up at 9 sharp, as the movie started at 9:45 p.m. This left ample time for the drive to Vernon and a chat in their seats before show time.

"Well, thanks for a really fun time," he said, stopping outside Rockford Hall. "I'll look forward to seeing you later tonight."

"Sounds good," said Brandi, her eyes twinkling. "And thank *you* for your charming company this afternoon."

She said everything he wished to hear. Pete wanted to whisk her into his arms and kiss her at that very moment. But now was not the time. He was determined not to repeat the Liz fiasco. So instead he placed her hands into his and squeezed them tenderly. This made her smile yet again.

"See you later," she said, her voice swimming in sweetness.

"Bye," said her infatuated suitor.

As the lovely Miss Sparks skated away to her dormitory, Pete approached his. Inside Rockford Hall, he slipped off his rollerblades and toddled upstairs leisurely. A smile as big as the sun relaxed on his face all the way up to his room on the top floor. Once there he collapsed onto his bed and unleashed a sigh of euphoria. Lying sedately on his back, he gazed at the white ceiling. It used be dull, but this afternoon's events made it, and everything else in the room, sparkle. Brandi's jubilant smile flashed continuously in his mind, as did her crash into his arms outside the arch on the way to the park. Their joining of hands and the laughs they shared also entered his daydream. Even their familial discussions were tolerable. He loved every moment with her.

Pete tried to nap, but sleep was impossible. He hoped to catch some Zs before picking up his special lady friend tonight. But he was just too excited. The thrill of seeing Brandi again, so soon, kept him awake the entire afternoon. He didn't mind at all. This kind of insomnia was actually enjoyable. Nevertheless he stayed put in bed and rested. Feeling his best for tonight's movie date was a must.

Pete fought hard not to get too ahead of himself, to keep his emotions intact, but deep down he knew he was fighting a losing battle.

6

Although he had no appetite, Pete met Corinne for dinner at 6 o'clock. They sat at the same table they had this morning. Overhead fluorescents had replaced the sunroom's natural lighting from outside, which was diminishing by the minute. This excited him, as the darker it got outside the closer the 9 o'clock hour neared.

His joy was hardly inconspicuous. As he discussed the day's events, Corinne noticed a special sparkle in his eyes, a brown that never stopped dancing. And he had this unique blissful glow about him that permeated the entire sunroom. She had never seen her friend this happy. Brandi must have made quite an impression. Corinne was glad they planned to see each other again.

"Well, keep me posted," she said.

"Will do," said Pete, elatedly.

"I hope things work out for you two."

"Thanks, Corinne, so do I."

The two friends left the sunroom and dropped off their trays. Corinne's was empty, unlike Pete's. He barely touched his meal. Stomach jitters prevented any real nourishment this evening. Not that he minded. Tonight's movie date with Brandi, not food, was all he could think about right now.

Heading toward the exit, they noticed an elongated table crowded with chatty prayer group students. Brandi, immersed in conversation, was among them. So was Todd, who sat several seats away. He grinned mischievously as he spotted his pal about to leave.

"Why's he smiling like that?" Corinne whispered.

Pete was just as puzzled.

"Search me," he said, shrugging his shoulders.

Their confusion cleared when Todd discreetly flashed the okay sign with his long curly fingers. The gesture produced a smile on his hopeful friend's face. Pete now had proof that Brandi enjoyed their time together. She and Todd must have talked afterwards, he concluded, and it was all good news.

Pete spent the next two hours in his room dressing and grooming himself. He felt like he was preparing for his wedding instead of a date. That scenario would have been easier. At least then he would know what to wear. His dry-cleaned tuxedo would be ready to put on right away.

He had never taken so long to get ready for a date. But Brandi was special, really special. Of the women he had dated she was the one with whom he felt most connected. They seemed to understand each other. She laughed at his jokes, and he liked her playful streak. And of course they enjoyed rollerblading.

Was she "the one?" He still wasn't 100-percent sure, but the figure was definitely in the 90-something range. It could edge up farther—maybe even reach the 100 mark—if all went well tonight, if he received a sign to continue the pursuit.

Pete decided to dress casually but neatly. He took out his favorite rayon short-sleeved shirt and ironed out each petty wrinkle. Its deep red color, he figured, would set off his naturally tan complexion. He then selected his best pair of blue jeans and black dress shoes.

Standing in front of the rectangular ankle-to-head mirror, he sprayed on some cologne. He also applied a light coating of gel to his hair, combing his scalp until each strand rested in its styled position. The mirror's reflection afterwards was most welcome. Defying his modest nature, Pete told himself to be proud of how great he looked. He added that Brandi may become the envy of the ladies in Vernon tonight. But deep down he sensed the opposite to be true. All the guys would be jealous of him instead.

With just five minutes to go before the 9 o'clock chimes, Pete left his dormitory. He strolled across campus to Whitman Hall, where Brandi lived, clutching a smoky-black lightweight jacket over his shoulder.

Outside the residence hall's main entrance, Pete took out his phone to text Brandi that he had arrived. But as soon as he typed the first letter, the lovely Miss Sparks opened the door. Her stunning beauty left him spellbound—and for a moment, speechless. She looked sensational inside those figure-snug black jeans and slinky pink sweater.

"Wow," he said, slipping the phone back into his pants pocket. "You look great."

"Thanks," she said. "So do you."

Pete was entranced. He could hardly believe what he just heard. He kept telling himself it was true, she indeed found him attractive. All that grooming was worth it. More importantly, she confirmed the physical chemistry between them.

Suddenly, Brandi cleared her throat. It was her kind way of snapping her would-be boyfriend out of his daze. She looked on amusingly as Pete regained his senses.

"Sorry," he said, his face blushing in teenage embarrassment. "Shall we go?"

Brandi nodded sweetly and strolled alongside her date to the student parking lot behind Whitman Hall. Pete wished it were farther away so he could display his lovely escort across campus. But those curious eyes would have to wait for another time.

His used compact car sat at the end of the row, opposite Whitman Hall. Its fading white exterior appeared rusty underneath the amber streetlight. The overhead lamp also exposed several ugly brown spots, chips of white paint that had peeled off over the years. Embarrassed, Pete always parked far away from the lot's superior, more pristine automobiles. It was his saving grace. The number of comparisons would be minimal, ones that would obviously disfavor the compact carcass he and Brandi were about to board.

She winced at the unflattering sight, just as he figured. For once he did not panic. A wave of optimism crashed on top of him and rinsed away his shame.

"I know I don't have the greatest car in the world," he said, opening the passenger-side door, "but at least I have one."

Brandi smiled as she hopped inside, a pleasing image indeed. She had to be impressed by this blunt admittance, Pete thought, and his grateful attitude. Not everyone owned a car, and not everyone worked as hard as he did to purchase and upkeep it. Being thankful for what we have was a code Stepney Green's prayer group always emphasized.

To Brandi's surprise, the seat's spongy gray upholstery was rather comfortable. And when the engine started it turned over right away. Moreover, it purred not roared. The interior sound system was also excellent.

"Getting a new paint job is next on my list," said Pete, pulling out of the student parking lot. "But first things first, I had to get a new stereo. That's the important thing, right?"

Brandi chuckled but wondered why he didn't have everything fixed all at once—or why he just didn't get a new car instead. Pete admitted, reluctantly, that he couldn't afford to buy one. Besides, the car had been with him since his community college days. It had sentimental value. He knew one day he would have to part with it, but not until after graduation. A full-time job's salary was necessary to make the monthly payments. In the meantime, the clunker, with all its faults and flaws, would have to do.

On the road to Vernon, Brandi asked if his parents would contribute to his new car's purchase. She broached the subject of family again, twice in one day. Pete wished she had left that can of worms inside the tackle box. He preferred to talk about other people's family lives instead of his own. It was certainly easier that way. Still, part of him felt she deserved his honesty. She was special enough to allow inside his protective shell, a place only a few had entered. Corinne knew all about his tough childhood. And now Brandi would. It was risky discussing this part of his life with her this soon into their relationship. She could be scared away and end everything instantly.

It was a chance he had to take. If their relationship did work out, she would eventually find out about his familial struggles—in addition to his working-class background, to which he earlier hinted.

Preparing his response, he took in a deep breath.

"Well," he said, exhaling, "to be quite honest with you, I really never knew my father."

Brandi was shocked.

"Oh, I'm so sorry," she said. "His death must have been really hard on your mother."

Pete stirred uneasily in his seat. His father did not die, he explained, but left the family home a year after he was born. He never came back. His mother had to raise him and his older brother all by herself.

"That's what was so hard on my mother."

"I see," said Brandi, staring motionlessly at the dashboard.

A reflective silence simmered. Before it boiled into tension, Pete turned up the stereo. His favorite program, *Under the Stars with Evangeline*, was on the air. It always made him smile. To his delight it made his date do the same.

"I love this show!" she said exultantly. "Evangeline's the best. Nobody does it like her."

Pete quite agreed. The disc jockey's sultry voice romanticized the New York City radius, and beyond, almost every evening. The hours between 9 p.m. and 1 a.m. were hers. Evangeline's program garnered the highest ratings of any radio station in that timeslot. Listeners from New York, New Jersey and Connecticut called in to share their stories of love and heartbreak. As they dedicated love songs to their special someone, Evangeline shared in their emotions. Her voice rose in exhilaration when callers had found the love of their lives. And it sank into compassion toward those who hadn't. Her audience adored her. Any out-of-town listener could tell. People talked to her like a good friend, someone they had known for years. Pete believed that this was the reason her program was so successful, in addition to her naturally sexy voice.

Incidentally, her program was the same one he had on when he first—and last—dated Liz. He didn't let that little-known, insignificant fact stop him from listening to it. Quite the contrary, *Under the Stars with Evangeline* remained his favorite. It actually rescued him tonight. Talk of his father's abandonment had crammed the car with seriousness. Now it was gone, overrun by romance. Pete was glad. The lovely lady next to him was still there. She didn't bolt out of the car after his revelation. Evangeline deserved big-time kudos.

Her program kept them company the rest of the way to Vernon.

The historic theater rested inside the quaint downtown district among sprawling antique shops and cafés. The cinema's features encompassed a rich blend of both the past and present. Its petite size allowed for only one movie to be shown, although there were several show times. Posters, cardboard cutouts, and other relics of the featured film decorated the lobby and snack bar.

So did Brandi. Pete was so proud to have this striking young woman by his side.

"Would you like something to drink or a snack?" he asked.

"No, thanks."

"Neither do I."

This was true. Food was the last thing on his mind, just like earlier at dinner. His appetite had not returned. He could only smile at his stunning escort.

She smiled back and reached for his hand.

"Come on," she said.

Her soft touch, just the gesture itself, made Pete's heart pounce. His joy stuck to him as heartily as her hand did.

Entering the auditorium, the couple made their way to the back row. This part of the theater represented the present. Plush, red, modern-day stadium seats had been installed during the cinema's massive renovation some years ago. As a result, the audience no longer had to stretch their necks between people's heads for a perfect view. The audio system was also updated. State-of-the-art surround-sound speakers plastered themselves high on the sides and back wall. An enlarged silver screen rested in front. Although new and modern, it was covered by an elaborate red velvet curtain.

In front of this grand backdrop sat a shiny wooden stage with a microphone to the side. This facet embodied theaters of the past. Nostalgic moviegoers loved this treat. Moments before a film started the theater manager walked onstage to welcome the audience and describe the movie's background. After thanking the audience for their patronage, he or she left the stage. The houselights dimmed, and the curtain draped away in two.

This had not yet happened tonight. The 9:45 p.m. show was running late. Some of the audience sighed in frustration. Others squirmed restlessly in their seats. Not Pete. He enjoyed the extra time next to the lovely Miss Sparks. He could gaze at her beautiful face for hours.

At 10 o'clock the theater manager announced the picture would begin in 5 to 10 minutes. Everyone needed to finish their snack-bar purchases before starting the film, he explained. Boos hissed toward the stout, bushy-mustached man. Despite the ruckus his composure did not crumble.

"Ladies and gentlemen," he said, silencing the impatient crowd, "the ticket proceeds don't go into our pockets, okay? But those from our snack bar do. The money we get from that snack bar is what keeps this historic theater in business, so let's show our appreciation by waiting for them to take their seats. Thank you."

The audience exploded into cheers and applause.

"That was awesome," said Pete, clapping his hands. "He sure told them."

Brandi agreed, saying the speech was really cool.

It was also the perfect remedy to alleviate the auditorium's migraine. Now the thrill of movie watching could resume its prominence in the air.

Moments later the manager returned to the stage to talk about the film. When he left, the theater blackened and the heavy red curtain parted in half.

Twenty minutes into the movie, Pete placed his hand on Brandi's. It was the second time he did this. Her reaction was the same as when they left the park this afternoon: she didn't remove it. Like then, she must have welcomed the gesture, possibly as much as he did hers at the snack bar. Pete did his best to conceal his joy over his progress. He wondered if Brandi noticed. The theater was dark, but any moviegoer walking up the aisle could see it effervescing around him.

A half-hour later, he flung his arm over her. Again she did nothing. Emboldened, he fingered toward the edge of her seat and rested his hand on her shoulder. Brandi did not flinch or wiggle it away. Unlike Liz, she expressed no discomfort. She even held his hand on their way out after the movie ended.

Pete's dream of finding love seemed to be materializing, albeit steadily. This was fine with him. A relationship's natural, slow pace was a refreshing change. He hoped he could maintain that pace and not jump ahead too quickly. This was extremely difficult. He had never been this attracted to a woman. Everything about her endeared him, including her affectionate side. The moves she made tonight were really special.

The journey back to Stepney Green was a joyride. Love songs and dedications from *Under the Stars with Evangeline* showered inside the car. Brandi sang along to a number of tunes, her voice sweeter than those of the artists. It was magic, heavenly. Pete was mesmerized.

"Wow," he said, "that's some voice you have."

Pausing from her recital, she turned to him and smiled.

"Thank you."

Evangeline's program was almost over. Pete thought it ironic, and fitting, as he pulled into the student parking lot. Her show would end the same time his date would. The timing couldn't have been more appropriate, considering their love of the program.

Parked in the same space earlier vacated, Pete secured his car and ran to the passenger side.

"Allow me," he said, opening the door gentlemanly.

Brandi thanked him.

"Looks like the age of chivalry isn't dead after all," she added flirtatiously.

Her escort's face reddened like a schoolboy.

"Peter Webb, are you blushing?" she asked, knowing full well he was. "Are you actually blushing?"

"What can I say," he replied, "you bring out the best in me."

"You're sweet," she said. "Listen, thanks for everything tonight. I had a fun time."

"Good, I'm glad. I did, too."

They embraced warmly.

"I better go," said Brandi. "It's late."

"I'll walk you to the door."

"No, it's all right," she said, explaining she had a friend to see in Blake Hall before turning in for the night.

"How about I walk you there instead?" he suggested. "Like you said, it's late."

"I'll be fine," she said assuredly. "It's practically next-door. You go on ahead."

"Okay."

"Thanks again for everything," she said, kissing his cheek. "Good night."

Brandi smiled one last time, turned around, and faded into the April night.

Pete, electrified, leaned against his car underneath the amber streetlamp. He could hardly breathe.

"She kissed me," he said to himself, "she kissed *me*."

This must be the sign to continue the pursuit!

"Wow, she really is the one."

He was now 99.9-percent sure that Brandi Sparks was the woman who would make him happy the rest of his life. He vowed to always remember this day, the best he ever had.

Or so he thought.

8

Every weekday morning for the past 22 years Janice Webb woke at 4 a.m. She never once complained. She simply did what she had to do. Her survival, and those of her two children, depended on it. She had to work for a living. And she had to hold more than one job.

Janice worked full time at a service-station restaurant on the New Jersey Turnpike, just south of Exit 7A, midway through the Garden State. She'd been employed there since her husband left her, which was more than two decades ago. Peter, her youngest son, was only a year old at the time. Her eldest, Adam, was 5. It was the most difficult time of her life. Not only did the 25-year-old woman have to raise two little boys, she was cast into the role of breadwinner. She never received a cent from her runaway husband. He could have died for all she knew. Welfare was out of the question. Janice refused to accept any government handouts. With one parent out of the picture she had to set a good example for her children, one that rewarded hard work.

She was promoted in no time. After six months of cashiering she became frontline supervisor. She did such a good job the restaurant owner promoted her further years later, to morning-shift manager. Janice was really proud of herself and rightfully so. She hardly missed a day of work and never griped or grumbled. The staff, no matter how many times it turned over, enjoyed working with her. But most importantly she exemplified that hard work led to success, at least on a personal level. She may not have raked in the big bucks, but she had her independence. No one could take that away.

The service station was an easy 20-minute commute from Woodlake Square. Driving north on Route 206, Janice hopped on Interstate 195 east to the Turnpike. Her part-time job in downtown Trenton was closer to home. There in the state capital she worked as a cocktail waitress 7 p.m. to midnight Thursday through Saturday. Fridays, needless to say, were the most tiresome. Working the restaurant's early-morning shift with less than four hours of sleep, she returned home exhausted and went straight to bed. She needed the sleep. In a few hours she would be back on her feet at the bar.

The generous tips she received made working there worthwhile. Every bit of that income helped keep a roof over her children's heads, food on the table, and clothes on their backs—even presents underneath the Christmas tree. Still, there were times she wanted to quit. Over the years a number of drunken men hit on her. A few actually asked for a lap dance, and more. She wanted to slap their faces on the spot but could only decline their indecent proposals—politely. She needed their money. Sad but true, her livelihood was at stake. Her salary at the service-station restaurant wasn't enough to support her family. It barely paid the mortgage.

The come-ons occurred less frequently the older she got. Decades of laborious work stole years off her face and the shimmer from her long auburn hair. Janice did not age well, and she knew it. She was an overripe 47. Lines under her dark-brown eyes had widened into bags. No amount of makeup could cover up their uncomplimentary purple. The skin around her eyes and mouth pruned no matter what emotion she experienced. Her customers assumed she was much older than she was. This bothered her at first, but after a while she got used to it and let it pass. Janice preferred, instead, to focus on the positive effect from all her arduous work: she maintained a lean, fit figure.

Monday mornings were easiest to get out of bed for work. They fell after Sunday, her only day off of the week. But this particular Monday morning was a bit easier. Janice was excited. Her 27-year-old son had an interview at a clothing warehouse this afternoon. It was a great opportunity. Full-time work, a decent starting salary, benefits, flexible hours—the job had it all.

Janice so wanted Adam to succeed. She wished the best for both her sons. Peter worried her less, much less. He was the studious one, the one who worked three jobs to pay his way through community college. Now he studied at the highly acclaimed Stepney Green. Sometimes she could hardly believe it. Her little boy had come such a long way. And in less than two months he would graduate. The world of opportunity would seek *him*. Janice couldn't have been prouder. Indeed, Peter had learned that working hard led to success. He had heeded her example. Adam, unfortunately, did not. He barely graduated from high school and had trouble keeping a job.

She hated comparing the two. She loved them both very much, equally. But Adam concerned her. He needed direction in his life, a talent or trait to develop. It was there, whatever it was. He just needed to tap into his psyche and find it. He had to want to seek it out. Janice hoped this warehouse job would provide some stability in the meantime. At least he could earn a steady income and gain solid work experience. He may even like it. He could excel in that job and work his way up to management. His mother should know; a similar thing happened to her.

After slipping on her navy slacks and tucking in her white polyester short-sleeved shirt, Janice got down on her knees in front of the bed. A small crucifix hung on the wall above the plastic baseboard behind the pillows. She stared solemnly at it, shut her eyes, and prayed. It was a daily ritual. Janice asked God to watch over her sons and give her the strength to get through the arduous workday ahead. But today she added a special request: to help Adam land the warehouse job.

"In the name of the Father, and of the Son, and of the Holy Spirit," she said, handing her way through the Sign of the Cross. "Amen."

Janice opened her eyes, rose to her feet, and grabbed her purse inside the nightstand on the way out. Before going downstairs she paused outside Adam's bedroom in the teeny hallway. She reached for the doorknob, turned it, but did not enter.

Yes, yes, he is inside. He has to be. He wouldn't have gone out last night, he just wouldn't. He knows how important this interview is. I have to trust him.

Janice smiled, laying her doubts to rest. She had discussed the situation with her son yesterday. He assured her that he would perform his best during the interview. He said he really wanted this job. And she believed him. She had to. Adam was a 27-year-old man now. She couldn't keep babying him, making sure he behaved responsibly.

But that was exactly what she kept doing.

Downstairs in the kitchen Janice poured a second cup of coffee and drank it quickly. It was 5:30, and she needed to leave for work. Gulping down the last sip, she swiped her purse from around the chair and dumped her mug into the dishpan's sudsy water.

She headed to the front door, throwing on her coat on the way. There was some sort of commotion outside. She heard laughing, obnoxious laughing, a repugnant mix of cackling and snorting. It came from a woman, but its tone was anything but ladylike.

"Will you shut up?" Janice heard a familiar man say.

Oh no. Please, no.

Keys fumbled and jingled outside.

"Shit," said the man, "where the hell is it?"

The woman, amused, chortled.

Janice's face wrinkled in profound disappointment, then aggravation. She knew who they were and fought to keep her cool. Still, she flung open the door briskly.

"Oh ... hi Mom," Adam said awkwardly.

His sea-green eyes were bloodshot, his breath liquor infested. Somehow his words came out slur free. The chunky young woman by his side bowed her head—but not in shame. It was to tone down her irritating giggles. Catching the dismay on her boyfriend's mother's face would only intensify them.

Janice didn't utter a word. Her expression said it all. Adam knew she was mad as hell ... and that it wouldn't last. A few smooth pacifying words and everything would be fine. He knew exactly which buttons triggered her compassion, even when he was drunk.

"I'm sorry, Mom," he said. "It's just that..."

"Just what?"

Adam purposely gazed at the cracked concrete below. Not looking her in the eye would convey just the right touch of guilt and remorse.

"I lost track of time," he said, seemingly apologetic. "I only meant to have one drink. My nerves were on edge for today's interview. I couldn't relax."

He created a few tears and peered into his mother's eyes, which had become as sympathetic as her ears.

"I just had to get out for a while," he continued. "You can understand, can't you?"

Janice did not reply, but her face had mellowed. Concern replaced her anger.

Adam was delighted.

"The interview isn't until 1 o'clock anyway," he added. "I'll be just fine after I get a little sleep, I promise. That job means a lot to me, you know that. I would never do anything to jeopardize my chances."

Janice heard this tune before, way too many times. So did Pete—and Rae Jacobson, her best friend across the street. Those two saw right through Adam's act, and he resented them for it. But his mother was gullible, easier to dupe. She was susceptible to emotional blackmail. Tears worked wonders, as did a remorseful voice.

They certainly seemed to be doing their job right now.

"Well, just don't stand there," said Janice, gesturing her son inside.

His 26-year-old girlfriend, Belinda Price, followed. As the couple headed upstairs, Janice shook her head in disgust. Belinda said nothing to her as she passed, not even a simple hello. She was too busy containing her annoying giggles. Janice knew her son could do better—much, much better. He was tall, had a nice athletic build, gorgeous green eyes, and a clear olive complexion. What he saw in Belinda Price was beyond her comprehension.

"Get some rest, Adam," Janice said. "I mean it, I want you to look and feel your best for that interview."

"Yeah, okay, Mom," he said, entering his bedroom.

Belinda could no longer control herself. Her high-pitched, glass-shattering squeals burst from her diaphragm.

"What a bitch," she mumbled, slamming the door behind her.

What did she say?! What did she just call me?!

Janice was furious. Her first impulse was to jet upstairs, drag Belinda down by her bleached frizzy hair, and kick her fat rear end out of the house—her house—for good. But reality quickly set in and calmed her. She knew she couldn't do such a thing. Even entertaining the thought was wrong, no matter how good it felt.

Taking a deep breath, she sighed out all her negative energy.

"Belinda Price is not worth it," she said to herself.

Janice dreaded having to leave, knowing that repulsive young woman was upstairs. Belinda's presumptuousness annoyed her as much as her laugh did. She came and went as she pleased, as if she lived here. She slept over countless nights, bathed here, and helped herself to whatever was in the fridge.

The latter was especially obvious.

Janice left the townhouse and approached her ragged light-blue hatchback on the street. Across the road her 55-year-old best friend collected her morning paper on the doorstep, something she still preferred to do versus going online. As Rae picked it up, she spotted Janice getting into her car—and also her glum expression. Rae sighed. She knew something upset her. She could always tell when something was wrong.

The two women had been friends for ages, since becoming neighbors 23 years ago. When Janice's husband left home, Rae became her rock, the older sister she never had. Her kids called her Aunt Rae, though there was no relation by blood or marriage. Adam and Pete stayed over "Aunt Rae's" every day after school until Mommy came home from work, and also when she worked her other job at the bar.

Janice was ever so grateful. Rae babysat all those years for free. She never took any money from her, not one cent. She was just glad to help. Janice could only imagine how her life, and those of her children, would have turned out had she paid for childcare. There would not have been any Christmases. No tree, no decorations, and no presents. The cupboards would have contained a lot less food. No more biannual trips to the mall for clothes, either. Hand-me-downs from secondhand thrift shops would have had to suffice.

The Webb's were like family to Rae, as well as to her husband and children. She didn't mind watching Janice's kids at all. Not only were they well-mannered, they kept her three sons company. Rae really enjoyed watching her "nephews" grow up as much as her own children. Pete turned out to be a fine hardworking young man. He always helped his mother whenever he could, financially and domestically.

Adam, however, took a turn for the worse somewhere down the line. He started getting into trouble in high school—mouthing off to teachers, failing classes, smoking in the bathroom, and more. The police were called to the school on one occasion. Adam had been caught taking an odd purple-green pill. He swore it was a caffeine pill someone had given him. Turned out he was telling the truth, much to Janice's relief. Still, she warned her son never to take any pills from anyone. This person may have said it was a mere caffeine pill, but it could have been something far more potent, even fatal.

Unfortunately, Adam's deviant behavior continued after graduation. He could not control his temper. When something didn't go his way at work, he thought nothing of telling his boss and customers to go to hell. Janice lost count of how many fast-food restaurant jobs he quit—and lost—a long time ago. Nevertheless she kept excusing his behavior. His father left him when he was just 5 years old, she had said. It was too traumatic for him; she couldn't be there for him because she had to work so much; he didn't mean to act that way. The list went on.

Rae never bought any of it. She and her husband raised three boys of their own, and they never let their sons get away with such nonsense. They either had to shape up or ship out; it was that simple. Janice disagreed because Rae had a wonderful husband around to help raise the children. They had no paternal void in their lives, she explained, unlike Adam and Peter. True, Rae would retort, but then why did Pete grow up to become a responsible adult? After all, he was raised in the same household as his brother.

Janice knew Rae was right, deep down, but couldn't admit it. Adam kept making the wrong choices in life, even as an adult. Still, she never lost hope. She continued to see the best in her son no matter what. Naturally she had trouble seeing it sometimes, especially now. Unless, of course, he scored big points at today's interview and landed the job. Janice prayed Adam meant what he said about not jeopardizing his chances. She hoped he was serious this time.

So did Rae, who stared concernedly from across the street.

"Janice?" she called out.

Her friend waved.

"Morning, Rae."

Janice did her best to appear cheerful, but Rae wasn't convinced.

"You okay, honey?"

"Sure," said Janice, "why wouldn't I be?"

Holding the morning paper, Rae trotted toward the road but stopped suddenly.

Oh my.

She hardly looked presentable. Her dyed jet-black hair, knotted in rollers and hairpins, clung fiercely to her scalp. And her flamboyant pink dressing gown with matching slippers dulled the luminous sunrise in the horizon. She also had no makeup on.

Oh, the hell with it. This is Woodlake Square after all. Most of the neighbors aren't even up yet.

Rae approached the curb, squeezed through the row of paralleled parked cars, and dashed across the bumpy narrow street. She rested a consoling hand on Janice's shoulder and asked what happened *this time*. It had to do with Adam; that much she knew. It was almost always about him—or Belinda.

Janice shook her head in frustration.

"It's Adam … again," she said.

Rae was right.

"He went out drinking last night," Janice continued. "He's got a big interview today, the one at the warehouse, the one I told you about last week. What was he thinking, Rae? Doesn't he know how important this interview is?"

"Of course he does, honey," she replied bluntly, "but he still doesn't care."

Janice stood in silence as Rae's words sank in.

"Unfortunately, this job means more to you than to him," Rae continued, adding that Adam had his mother right where he wanted her. He could lead a life of leisure and do whatever he wanted, knowing full well he had a roof over his head. He knew his mother would never kick him out onto the streets. Surely she wouldn't want him to suffer another parental abandonment.

This was true. Janice could not erase from her mind little Adam's tears and shrills as Daddy walked out on him. To her, he was that same 5-year-old boy. Those tears of desertion still watered his sea-green eyes. And his voice continued to carry those painful shrieks. She couldn't bear to see him experience that anguish again.

"I hear what you're saying, Rae," Janice said. "But yesterday he went on and on about how much he wants this job. I really think he's serious this time."

"I know you do, honey," said Rae, "and I did as well. But think about it: if he were serious, then why did he go out drinking last night?"

"In two words: Belinda Price."

Rae was right again. Adam's girlfriend was trouble, pure and simple.

"She actually called me a bitch this morning," Janice added.

"What! The bitch called *you* a bitch?!"

"I couldn't believe it."

Rae was stunned when Janice said she let it pass.

"Honey, you can't let Belinda get away with that."

"Then what am I supposed to do?"

"Kick her fat ass the hell out!" said Rae, her eyes exploding in hazel incredulity. "Give her a piece of your mind, that's what you do."

Janice sighed.

"Hell if I'd let her into my home," Rae continued. "No wonder Adam still has problems. He'll never grow up with someone like Bulimia—I mean, Belinda—clinging to him."

Again, Janice knew she was right. But she could do nothing about it now. It was late. She had exactly 20 minutes to get to work.

"I just hope he does well at that interview, that he makes it there in time," she said, getting into her car.

"Me, too, honey," Rae said in a much softer tone. "I'll keep my fingers crossed."

Janice reached out the window and gently squeezed her friend's hand.

"Thanks," she said wholeheartedly, "for everything."

Rae smiled as the woman she considered a sister sped away on the rough blacktop, flanked by chipped brick townhouses. Before heading back inside, she stared at the Webb family home and shook her head. Despite her crossed fingers, Rae couldn't shake the feeling that Adam would let his mother down—again. Janice was in for a major disappointment, she thought. Heartache was inevitable.

On the way to work the Webb matriarch forced herself to think positively. She told herself that Adam would go to that interview looking and performing his best.

He promised me ... he promised.

As the morning sun brightened above I-195, so did Janice's outlook. Indeed, the power of positive thinking worked wonders.

At noon she called home to wish her son luck one last time—and, admittedly, to check up on him. To her surprise Adam answered the landline phone right away. He sounded alert, vivacious, and eager to impress Manning Outerwear.

"I plan to leave in a few minutes," he said. "Getting there extra early should be helpful."

Janice filled up. Her son's transformation from this morning was most admirable.

"Knock their socks off," she said.

"I sure will."

The rest of her workday ran smoothly. Her spirits soared. With his optimism Adam was bound to win over Manning Outerwear. His interview would be a success.

She visualized coming home to an ecstatic son running up to say how well everything went. She envisioned him thanking her for not losing faith, for believing in him when no one else did, including himself.

Janice could hardly wait to get home. As soon as the hands on the restaurant clock 90-degreed at 3 p.m., she was out of there.

Janice's excitement made the drive through Woodlake Square a lot less monotonous, even less depressing. She didn't grimace at the dilapidated townhouses this afternoon. Their hanging, dented drainpipes did not dent her mood. Neither did all the junk, trash and toys littering the yards.

The Webb townhouse stood out from these mini disaster areas. It was very well maintained, one of a select few. The Jacobson home across from it was another. Like Janice, Rae and her husband were hardworking people who took pride in their property. Both yards were never used for storing rubbish of any kind. Grass, trees and shrubbery covered them instead. Taking care of the house instilled a great lesson to the Webb and Jacobson children: their home's appearance reflected hard work; others around them, despair—and in some cases, downright laziness.

Janice smiled as she parallel-parked outside her house, her other pride and joy. Her sons, of course, were primary.

"Adam, I'm home," she said, entering the front door. "Adam?"

No answer. Janice hoped he would have been home by now, but maybe his being out was a good sign. Perhaps his interview lasted longer than expected. He may have even been offered the job! He could be filling out tax forms and other paperwork this very moment. Janice wished this were the case. She would find out soon enough.

After hanging up her coat she headed upstairs to rest. As she arrived, a casually dressed Adam exited the bathroom.

"Oh, hi," said Janice. "So how was the interview? I'm dying to know what happened."

Adam said he practically got home himself and that he didn't expect the interview to last as long as it did. He added how friendly everyone at the plant was, that he hoped he were selected for the position.

Janice embraced her son warmly.

"I hope you get it, too," she said. "I hope they call with a job offer really soon."

"Thanks, Mom, so do I."

She asked if there were something special he would like for dinner, even though it wasn't quite time to celebrate.

"I already made plans to meet Belinda at her house," he said, "but thanks anyway."

A shiver vibrated through Janice's bloodstream. Although the day turned out to be relatively pleasant, his girlfriend's "bitch" utterance had stained her memory. Nevertheless she wished her son a fun time. She then yawned.

"I'm going to lie down for a while, sweetheart."

"Yeah, you do that, Mom," said Adam. "Just relax and take care of yourself, okay?"

Janice, overwhelmed by his compassion, smiled adoringly.

"I will, son," she said, entering her room. "Thanks."

As soon as the door shut, a smirk plastered across Adam's face. He turned around and opened his own bedroom door, letting out Belinda.

"Come on," he whispered, "let's get out of here."

Belinda giggled; she couldn't help herself. Adam immediately slapped his open hand against her mouth.

"Shut the hell up, will you?"

Janice was about to get into bed. She had just put away her purse in the nightstand. Her shoes were off, and easy-listening music serenaded her room. But the distraction in the hallway aroused her curiosity. She could have sworn she heard Belinda's laugh. That snorted cackle could only come from her.

When she opened her bedroom door she found an empty hallway. No Adam; no Belinda. Janice figured she must have been hearing things and went back to bed.

She lay comfortably for the next hour. The radio's easy-listening music soothed her anxieties and helped her relax. She forgot all about Belinda's derogatory comment and Adam's interview. This was her "me" time. She wanted nothing to take it away.

But something did—a phone call. Janice turned off the radio and picked up the receiver on the nightstand.

"Hello?"

"Hello, I'm trying to reach a Mr. Adam Webb," said a woman. "Is he available please?"

She sounded very professional. Janice was thrilled. The woman must have been from Manning Outerwear's human resources department.

"Whom may I ask is calling?"

"This is Louise Burnett from Manning Outerwear."

"Oh, hello," said an exuberant Janice. "I'm sorry, you just missed him. This is his mother. May I take a message?"

"Well, we were wondering if Mr. Webb would like to reschedule his interview."

"Reschedule?"

"Yes, ma'am."

"There must be some mistake," Janice said. "My son interviewed today, this afternoon at 1 o'clock in fact."

"I'm afraid not, ma'am."

"Are you sure? Perhaps you have the wrong file or something."

"We're sure, ma'am," said Louise. "Adam Webb definitely did not show up."

Definitely did not show up?

"Could you please have him call me as soon as possible?" she continued.

Janice, devastated, nearly dropped the phone.

How could he? How could he lie to me like that? He promised me … he promised.

A tear of betrayal bubbled over and burned her pruning cheek.

No, not again.

"Hello?" said Louise. "Ma'am, are you there?"

Physically she was.

Emotionally, she could not have been any farther away.

9

Corinne Aldrich knocked on Pete's door a few minutes before midnight. By most standards it was late. But not according to college campus time. In fact, turning in for the night in the p.m. was a rarity. Most students went to bed past midnight. Dormitories were usually active during these late-night/early-morning hours, and Rockford Hall was no exception. Young lovers, free to release their rampant hormones, were at their most intimate. Friends visited, held study groups, worked on assignments, and just hung out. All the while RAs made their rounds.

"Come in," Pete called out.

He knew who it was. He'd asked Corinne to come over to get her opinion on his poem. Ordinarily he would have popped in Blake Hall to see her, but he was on RA duty this Monday night and couldn't leave his dormitory.

"Hey," she said, making her way to the desk chair.

Pete, lounging on his bed, smiled jubilantly.

"Thanks for coming over, Corinne," he said. "How are you?"

"I'm okay," she said, noting his beaming face. "But not nearly as much as you are apparently."

"Well, read this and find out why."

Pete handed over his latest poetry assignment. Considering its open subject matter, the poem was easy, and fun, to complete. Naturally he wrote about Brandi, the lovely Miss Sparks. She was his inspiration. Her face could not escape his mind since the weekend. In fact, he'd nearly forgotten about the poem's due date tomorrow. Fortunately, he completed his assignment in record time, about 20 minutes. The professor had only one stipulation: emphasize line breaks. Because the poem didn't have to rhyme, accomplishing this task was a cinch. He titled it *Out of Nowhere*.

Like winds of a storm electrifying
My senses,
She sparked into my life

Her natural, simple smile crumbles
My walls

Those joyous laughs of hers
Like songs from heaven
Soothing the aches in my heart

Her embrace jolts nerves
On seemingly endless journeys
Up and down my spine,
Chilling
The flesh of my back

Like a shock wave crashing
My shores,
A new reason for living arrived
From a place
Out of nowhere

As Corinne read, the blue in her Mediterranean eyes deepened in curiosity. For a moment she wondered if the poem could have been about her.

"Well, what do you think?"

Pete's question interrupted her silence. It also cleared the runway for reality's safe return. Of course, she reasoned, the poem described his feelings toward Brandi, not herself. She never should have pondered such a scenario—one that, if realized, would unhinge their deep, stable friendship.

"It's good, really good," Corinne said. "I like it."

Pete thanked her.

"I just hope you're not getting too ahead of yourself," she added.

"What do you mean?"

Corinne advised her friend to take his relationship with Brandi slowly. Although impressive, his poem conveyed rather strong feelings. He was just getting to know her, she explained, and vice versa.

"I'm sure you don't want to scare her away," she said.

"Of course not," said Pete, sitting up, "but Corinne she's the one, I know it."

"I hope you're right."

Her words of caution seemed to have exited his ears as quickly as they entered. Still, Brandi was a sweet girl. If she were to break up with him, she would do so as gently as possible, unlike Liz.

"You don't seem very optimistic," said Pete, who began pacing.

Corinne said she was sorry, that she was only looking out for his best interest.

"After all," she continued, smiling, "what kind of little sister would I be if I didn't nag you about such things?"

Hearing this, Pete's nervous march across the carpet came to a halt. It also made him smile.

"Thanks, Corinne."

"Anytime," she said, rising from the desk chair. "Just remember what I said about slowing down a bit, okay?"

"I will."

"Well, I better get back to my room."

"Already?" said a surprised Pete. "You just got here."

Corinne explained she had some studying to do. In actuality, she felt a little uncomfortable being here at the moment. Specks of shame had lingered inside her conscience. Second guessing the focus of her "friend's" poem was wrong, totally wrong. The guilt had to be cleared out, every trace of it.

Pete opened the door, saying he would keep her posted on whatever developed with Brandi.

"You better. Night, Pete."

"Good night."

As soon as the door closed, Corinne let out a deep breath, relieved to have made a hasty exit without suspicion.

Pete, in the meantime, swiped his poem on the desk and collapsed into bed. There, he read and reread his masterpiece until his eyes flickered shut. He slept so peacefully that night.

The next day Pete entered K.S.W. Hall to attend his 3 o'clock poetry class. He could hardly wait to hand in his latest assignment. It was definitely worthy of an A. He considered *Out of Nowhere* his best poem of the semester. Surprisingly, it took the least amount of time to complete. The words flowed from his heart and onto the paper effortlessly, like a stream cascading down a mountain.

As he walked upstairs to the second floor Brandi was on her way down. She appeared out of nowhere, ironically.

"Hey, Pete," she said.

"Hey."

It was all he could say. This was the first time he'd seen the lovely Miss Sparks since Saturday night, since their goodnight kiss. He dreamed of this moment, running into her again, but did not expect it to happen like this. He wished he were on his way out of class instead of in. That way he could suggest they head out to do something fun, to spend some time together.

"Heading for class?" asked Brandi.

Pete nodded slightly.

"Uh-huh," he said.

"Which one?"

His eyes twinkled like those of a movie star fan meeting his favorite actress. Decked out in off-white pants with a sky-blue blouse tucked inside, Brandi looked absolutely gorgeous.

"Uh…"

Stop stammering, you idiot!

In an instant Pete snapped himself out of his lovesick trance. He knew he shouldn't be this anxious around her. After all, they already went out together. Twice. And she kissed *him*. It was time to get confident.

"I'm off to my poetry class actually," he said, smiling. "So how are you?"

"I'm okay, thanks. Glad my classes are over for the day."

Pete's smile turned flirtatious.

"Wish mine were, too," he said.

Brandi returned the smile, much to his delight.

"Really," she said, her curiosity piqued. "And why's that?"

"If you kiss, I'll tell."

Brandi remarked how smooth Pete's comment was, just like his rollerblading skills he displayed Saturday afternoon.

"Speaking of Saturday," he said, "how would you like to have dinner with me?"

Again, pretty smooth, she thought.

"Oh, that would be nice," Brandi said, "but I'm going home this weekend to visit my parents."

Pete, disappointed, barely stopped his smile from frowning. He told himself to calm down, that this was not an outright rejection.

"So how about the following weekend?" he asked.

"Yeah, maybe then."

It wasn't the ecstatic reaction he hoped to hear. What happened to her trademark? Where was the enthusiastic, energetic "sure" he liked so much? Nevertheless she didn't turn him down. That was the important thing. The word "no" never crossed her lips.

Pete glanced at his watch.

"Listen, I better get to class," he said. "I have a poem, a really important poem, to hand in."

"Okay," said Brandi, "see you at prayer group."

Definitely! His hope restored, Pete winked goodbye.

The next prayer group gathering was held a little more than 24 hours later. Sitting inside the hexagonal chapel this Wednesday night, Pete stole glances at his sweetie huddled with some friends at the far corner. She laughed heartily at whatever they were talking about. There was such liveliness in her. It was a most attractive quality, one of her many. Pete knew he was falling for her, and fast. Despite Corinne's words of caution he couldn't slow down. He wanted Brandi—now.

"Shame, shame, shame," said Todd, surprising his pal as he took his seat.

"What?"

"Don't give me that. You're not as innocent as you look. I know what you're thinking about."

How did he know? How does he always know?

Todd handed over a handkerchief.

"What's this for?"

"To wipe your drool, of course."

Pete chuckled and flung it back.

"Very funny," he said.

Suddenly, Brandi left her circle of friends and was on her way over. Todd stood up and reoffered his handkerchief.

"Sure you don't need this?"

"Will you stop it," Pete mumbled.

Todd tucked away the hankie and slithered off just as Brandi arrived.

"Where's he going?" she asked.

He probably wanted to leave the two of them alone, Pete thought. Of course, he did not say this out loud.

"Well, gorgeous," he said instead, "looks like I'll have to do. Think you can handle that?"

An amused Brandi smiled.

"You and your smoothness," she said.

Pete wished her a fun visit home this weekend but added he would miss her, too.

"Aw," she cooed. "That is so sweet."

She went on to thank him for inviting her to dinner next Saturday and that she would let him know for sure soon, probably at next week's meeting.

Pete was fine with this. Actually, he was glad she brought up the subject instead of him. This had to be a good sign. It meant she'd been thinking about the invitation … and more importantly, about him.

10

While Brandi drove home to Mantoloking Friday night, Pete and Corinne worked their RA shifts. At 9 o'clock they met in the gazebo for rounds. The weather couldn't have been more pleasant. No jackets were necessary. It was warm enough to leave them behind. There was also a refreshing breeze, mild and piney.

As they left the gazebo for Blake Hall, Pete glanced into the nighttime sky. What a beautiful night. He wished Brandi were here to share it. The stars were especially bright. As they twinkled and basked against the dark backdrop, an idea entered his head.

Of course! It's perfect!

Here he was thinking about his dream girl *under the stars*. It was time to call Evangeline and dedicate a song. This would really impress Brandi. That is, if she were listening to the program. There was no guarantee she would hear the dedication. Still, it was a chance worth taking.

Some work lay ahead of him, though. Pete had to think of the perfect words to say. They had to come from the heart without being mushy. That should be easy given his love of writing. However, there was a hard part: getting through the busy phone lines to speak with Evangeline herself.

Corinne noticed Pete was awfully quiet tonight. He hardly said two words since leaving the gazebo. His lack of conversation was even more obvious when they arrived at Blake Hall's main entrance. When she opened the door her dazed friend stood at the threshold … and kept standing.

"Pete?" she said.

No reply.

"Pete!"

He flinched. Coming to, he wondered what had just happened.

"Sorry, Corinne," he said. "What is it?"

"We're here," she answered, looking on in amusement. "Gosh, what's up with you tonight? You're miles away."

"You got that right."

As Pete entered the residence hall, Corinne shut the door and smiled. She knew his absentmindedness had something to do with Brandi; that much was clear. It seemed she was all he could think about.

Corinne figured he was planning his next courtship move. Not wanting to intrude, she didn't press for details. He would reveal all when the time was right, she concluded. She needed to step back from the situation anyway, considering the spell of mixed feelings Monday night. Also, her words of caution were already out there. No need to repeat them. She wanted her friend to enjoy himself as much as possible. He deserved to have fun for a change, especially after the Liz fiasco.

As soon as 9 o'clock rounds ended, Pete raced to his room atop Rockford Hall. Panting, he took out his phone and dialed the toll-free number for *Under the Stars with Evangeline*. The line was busy, just as he expected. In a way this was good. He needed to relax and slow down his breathing before speaking with the popular radio hostess.

He brought the phone to his bed, where he lounged. Pressing the redial button, he again got the busy signal. This went on for at least half an hour. It seemed like ages, but Pete carried on. His resolve to contact the program and dedicate a song to his beloved Brandi outweighed his whim to give up.

His persistence paid off—finally, no annoying busy signal. The phone was ringing.

"Good evening," the radio hostess said sultrily. "You are under the stars with Evangeline. What can I do for you this lovely night?"

Wow, it's really her.

Pete cleared his throat. He wanted his voice to sound absolutely flawless.

"Hello, Evangeline," he said, "and how are you this evening?"

His voice was not only clear, it tinged with sexiness. He was most pleased. Evangeline seemed to like it, too.

"Well, hello there," she said. "I'm doing just fine. And from what I hear it seems like you are as well."

She's so cool.

"I sure am," said Pete, "and that's because I met the most amazing lady."

"Tell me about her."

"Her name is Brandi, and I really enjoy spending time with her. I think we could be great together and hope she feels the same."

"I hope so, too, sweetie," said Evangeline. "What is your name?"

"Pete."

"Well, Pete, I'll play something really special for you. I'm sure Brandi is the envy of all the single ladies out there right now."

"Thanks, Evangeline."

You totally rock!

"You're very welcome," she said, "and thank you for spending your Friday night under the stars."

"Thanks again," said Pete. "Have a great night."

"You do the same, sweetie. Bye now."

He could hardly believe what just happened, how perfectly it all went. Indeed, Brandi would be impressed. If she had on the program tonight, that is.

Pete turned up his mini-stereo as he waited for Evangeline to air his dedication. He hoped to hear it before he left for 11 o'clock rounds, which would begin in about an hour. Anticipating the broadcast, his adrenaline skyrocketed. He paced back and forth fiercely, as if he were in a hospital awaiting the birth of his child. The beige, flat, indoor-outdoor carpet thinned all the more with every fiery step. He paused only after each song and commercial break, careful not to miss a word of his dedication in case it aired.

Ten minutes before 11 o'clock rounds, it did. The broadcast was magical. So was the chosen song. Its mellow instrumentals, as well as the vocals, were very soothing to hear. There was nothing overly sappy about them—or the lyrics, which simply described a man wondering if he'd found his true love after a long search. The song could not have been more appropriate. For Pete it really hit home.

Corinne smiled puckishly as her best friend on campus arrived for 11 o'clock rounds.

"What?"

"Come on, Pete," she said, "you know what this smile's for."

Indeed he did.

"You heard?"

"I sure did," she said, exiting the gazebo. "That was a wonderful dedication."

She only hoped Brandi appreciated it. Even if she were nowhere near a radio, Corinne figured she would learn about it eventually. Surely others on campus heard the dedication, too.

When Pete returned to his room shortly after 11:30, four text messages arrived in quick succession. Was it Brandi? Could she have heard? There was only one way to find out. He retrieved the phone from his pants pocket and noticed the sender... Yes, it was she!

Hi, Pete. I just wanted to thank you for what you did a little while ago. I had the radio on while relaxing in the tub and caught your dedication.

It was really, really sweet, and I really appreciate it.

Anyway, I'm off to bed now, but I did want to at least say thank you before turning in.

Have a good weekend, and I'll talk to you later.

Pete saved these text messages, as he did all of Brandi's, but these instantly became his favorite ever. They were definitely worth reading again and again. Her words were tender, almost loving, and her gratitude sincere.

Her texts sprung directly from the heart—had to—just like his radio dedication. They also jolted him out of the like zone ... and into the lost world of love. No more 99.9 percent. Now he was totally 100-percent certain that Brandi was the woman for him.

Suddenly, his cellphone rang. Pete answered it right away.

"Hello?"

"Man, that was awesome," said Todd, obviously referring to his on-air conversation with Evangeline.

Whoa, a lot of people heard it.
"Thanks, dude."
"Brandi liked it, too, you know."
How did he know this?

She called him afterwards, Todd later explained. She wanted to share the news with a good friend.

Brandi seemed to confide in him quite a bit … a good thing actually. Because Todd was both their pals, he made the ideal matchmaker. He could easily exchange information between them, like he just did. Conveying her appreciation was a positive reinforcement.

Again, this was a good thing.

11

During Tuesday's poetry class Pete's professor handed back *Out of Nowhere*. To his joy he got an A. He wanted to give it to Brandi right away but hesitated. It was still too soon, despite having strong feelings for her. He figured he would be given a sign when the time was right, similar to the one after the movie date a couple of weekends ago.

Corinne was glad he decided to wait. She, too, felt more time was needed, much more than Pete would have liked. He wanted to share the poem within a week, while she advised to wait until graduation. Deep down she knew he could not, and would not, hang on to it that long. Graduation was next month, and he desperately wanted to be in a committed relationship before then. To him, that would be as huge an accomplishment as graduating with highest honors.

"Well, good luck, Pete," she had said to him … the same response the night she learned Liz Dabney had come over to his room.

Pete was tempted to bring *Out of Nowhere* with him to prayer group this evening, a mere day after he got it back. But he left it behind at the last minute. He was just too excited, as Brandi was to let him know about dinner this weekend. He knew she would say yes. The feeling was so strong his bones rumbled.

He arrived extra early for tonight's meeting, by 30 minutes in fact. No one else was inside the chapel, but the majestic stained glass windows were tilted open. Pete approached the one at the far-left hexagonal corner and slowly breathed in the fresh piney air. Peering outside, he watched all the limp tree branches rustling helplessly in the wind. The sight made him reflect on his two years at Stepney Green.

Where did the time go? It all went by so fast. College life would be over soon—no more classes, studying, or research papers; no library job or prayer group; no more bumping into friends around campus or hanging out in dorms; and no more RA duty. Meeting Corinne for rounds at the gazebo would soon end for good. Pete would really miss this, in addition to all the meals they shared inside the cafeteria. She was a terrific friend, as was Todd. Part of him wished he could stay an additional year just to be near them longer. This way they could all graduate together. And he would also have more on-campus time to see Brandi, before her own graduation a year after that.

The time had come to face reality. Graduation was a mere month away. Pete realized he had to get cracking on his résumé and cover letters. He definitely did not want to stay in Woodlake Square the rest of his life. His degree from Stepney Green College was his ticket out of there—and away from his troublesome brother.

As he took in another breath of fresh air, he once again thanked his lucky stars for being able to attend this prestigious school. And not just for academic reasons. Not only did he form close friendships, he'd found his true love.

Suddenly, the chapel doors flung open—and in she walked. A few girlfriends were with her. Nevertheless it got a little brighter inside.

Brandi spotted Pete by the window and waved. He waved back, smiling modestly. The passive look on his face suggested she need not come over.

But she did anyway.

"Hi there," she said, her voice dulcet as ever.

"Well, hello, gorgeous."

Brandi smiled, which lit up the chapel even more. Her brown eyes and sandy-blond hair sparkled just as luminously. Pete's attraction intensified. His body temperature actually went up a few degrees. He wanted to pull her into his arms and kiss her passionately right there and then. But he resisted. The chapel was definitely not the place for such moves. Besides, everything was going so well. Making a pass at her early on would only create another Liz fiasco. That had to be avoided at all costs.

"So what's up?" said Pete.

"Well, I wanted to get back to you about dinner Saturday," she said. "Are we still on?"

Her eager suitor answered with an amorous, "You bet." His intuition was right on: she agreed to go out with him again. He then added a dash of spice to his reply. "When a lovely lady wants to have dinner with me, I never cancel."

"Smooth as always," Brandi said. "Listen, I better get back to my friends."

"I understand."

Before she left to rejoin them Pete kissed her cheek. Like her voice, her skin was soft and sweet.

She was "the one," his soulmate, no doubt about it. Somehow he knew this since their first date in the park. That day couldn't have been more perfect—or more prophetic. Destiny had brought him to this college, Pete concluded. It led him to join this group and befriend Todd Galloway, who then introduced him to the woman of his dreams. All this had to be part of some divine plan. Everything was falling into place too seamlessly not to be.

Pete could hardly wait for Saturday to get here. He planned to pick up Brandi at 7 p.m. and take her to a classy Greek restaurant in the heart of town. Before leaving she would find a bouquet of pink roses waiting for her on the car seat. Pete looked forward to the grateful, radiant smile she would most certainly generate.

And maybe even a kiss, this time a passionate one.

12

The big day finally arrived. Overcast blanketed the sky, unlike two Saturdays ago. Today's dreary weather hardly defined Pete's spirits. Nothing was going to dampen them. They were so high, in fact, the cafeteria sunroom ignited as soon as he entered. He simply beamed this morning.

Corinne, seated at their usual table, couldn't help but notice.

"Someone's excited today," she said teasingly.

Indeed he was.

"I can't wait to see her again," said Pete, sitting down to eat his breakfast.

"You will soon enough."

Corinne was relieved things were progressing. Brandi must really like him. If not, then she would have declined tonight's dinner invitation. Also, Pete's radio dedication would have embarrassed, not humbled, her. Corinne was genuinely happy for her friend. He so deserved this kind of joy.

Pete thanked her for the sentiment. He also expressed his appreciation for all her support.

"Corinne," he said, "you're the best friend I ever had."

He then rested his hand on top of hers.

"I really mean it."

"Thanks, Pete," she said, deeply moved. "That means a lot to me."

It was a touching, solemn moment. Both knew their days of sharing meals inside the cafeteria were dwindling. They had vowed to stay in touch after graduation, but their friendship's strength and endurance would no doubt be tested. They could still talk virtually every day, just not in person. And what about Brandi? If she and Pete became a couple, would Corinne accept their special friendship? Would she grow jealous?

Now was not the time to think such things. Even though graduation was four weeks away, it was still too soon. Neither could say goodbye right now. Instead, they decided to cherish the semester's remaining days.

After their heartwarming meal Pete returned to his room. He had some schoolwork to do before his big date tonight, which would begin in about seven hours. But first he turned back on his phone, which had been turned off during his brunch with Corinne. To his surprise, he had two voicemail messages. The first was from Janice.

"Hi, Peter, it's Mom," she said. "I just wanted to see how you were doing, that's all. Take care, and I'll talk to you later. Love you. Bye."

It was good to hear from her. He felt like calling her back right away to share his Brandi news but decided against it. She would only get her hopes up and ask endless questions: What's Brandi like? How old is she? How did you two meet? When can I meet her? Do you want to bring her over sometime? Pete had enough problems keeping his own hopes grounded. After all, he was already in love. Mom would find out about her when the time was right, when he was ready.

The second message came from Brandi.

"Hey, Pete, it's me," she said.

Her voice sounded awful, like she was fighting to stay alive.

"Well, as you can probably tell, I'm not feeling very well right now. I think I have to cancel our dinner plans tonight. Hope you can understand."

Of course he could.

"I'm sorry, really sorry," Brandi continued. "I'm just going to spend the rest of the day in bed. Again, I'm very sorry."

So was he.

"Hope you can still have some fun this weekend. Bye."

Pete felt like slamming his phone onto the desk but rested it gently instead. He then plopped into bed, sighing angrily. He knew he shouldn't pout like this, but his disappointment got the better of him. He was really looking forward to tonight's dinner date, to spending quality time with Brandi. Now he had to wait—again. So would the bouquet of pink roses he planned to buy her. No beaming face as she picked them up inside his car. Not tonight at least.

Pete turned over on his bed and looked out the window. The gray and gloomy sky outside now reflected his mood. It was a drastic change from just minutes ago inside the cafeteria. He had to snap out of this depression. There had to be something he could do, but what?

Ah-ha!

Pete put aside his schoolwork plans and headed out to the local gift shop. There he purchased two boxes of mixed chocolates, the most expensive he could find. He also picked up an ornate gift bag in which to put them, one with intricate multicolored floral designs. Brandi was sure to like this surprise. It may even help her feel better; it certainly helped him.

Back in his room he composed a note.

"Just thought you'd enjoy this … when you feel better, of course," he said and wrote simultaneously. "Get well soon. Pete."

It was simple and perfect.

The gift stayed on his desk the rest of the day. He would deliver it later in the evening, after completing his work for next week's classes.

Normal dinnertime cafeteria hours ran from 5 to 7 p.m. But Pete decided to skip his evening meal tonight, choosing instead to nap.

At 8:30 he woke from a light sleep. His hair had remained ruffle free, much to his surprise. After slipping back on his blue jeans, he headed to the closet. There he took out a short-sleeve button-down shirt, used for either casual or semiformal occasions. Made of rayon and cotton, the shirt was among his most comfortable. Its striking aqua color produced a rather elegant contrast overtop his jeans. He wanted to look good in case Brandi spotted him delivering her goodie bag.

Pete called Corinne before he left. She was surprised to hear from him.

"I thought you'd still be out with Brandi."

"Change in plan," he said, explaining her sudden illness.

"That's too bad," said Corinne. "I know you were really looking forward to it."

He certainly was.

"Hey, if you're not doing anything tonight," she continued, "you can come over here and keep me company while I'm on duty."

Pete agreed but after delivering Brandi's surprise.

"See you probably around 10 o'clock," he said. "Thanks, Corinne. Bye."

After hanging up he reached into his desk drawer and took out a copy of his poetic masterpiece, *Out of Nowhere*.

"It's time," he said to himself, folding the paper neatly and tucking it inside Brandi's gift bag.

Corinne's advice to wait clearly had fallen on deaf ears.

13

There were no stars in the sky as the hopeless romantic left his dorm, not one. The overcast had festered into the nighttime heavens as well. The black clouds hovering above could unleash their torrents of rain any moment.

The impending storm was the last thing on Pete's mind as he neared Whitman Hall. His only concern: delivering Brandi's gift, hopefully without notice. Though seeing her in the hallway was entirely possible, he hoped that wouldn't happen. He really wanted to surprise her. It was more romantic that way.

Being an RA had its advantages, one of which was access to each of the dormitories. Pete inserted his master key into Whitman Hall's side door and entered. Technically he should only do this sort of thing for residence life purposes, such as making rounds or letting in a student who lost their key. But for the sake of romance he bent the rules a little. No harm in that. He had to cheer up the woman he loved during her bout of ill health. What better excuse could there be than this?

Pete rode the elevator to the third floor where Brandi resided. Another RA advantage was knowledge of students' room locations. A listing of them was issued to the resident assistants each semester. Todd, however, probably knew her room number and could have easily relayed the information. But he had done so much already—his introductions and all his support and encouragement. Strange but cool, Pete thought, that the Galloway Hotel Towers heir would befriend some working-class guy and help him sort out his love life.

Blind Expectations

Brandi's room lay on the right, a few doors before the hallway's dead end. It was silent inside. Pete figured she must be asleep, which was ideal. Now he could deliver her surprise without getting caught in the act. After placing the gift bag's handles around the doorknob, he tiptoed away in glee. He could hardly wait to find out her reaction. Visions of the lovely Miss Sparks wrapping her tender arms around him flashed continuously as he made his way outside.

This time Pete noticed the stormy nighttime sky. He had no umbrella, but Blake Hall was close by, just over the next hill. Fortunately, he made it there before any rain poured down. But it did start to drizzle when he arrived. His timing was perfect. Still, he was early. He had 35 minutes to spare before meeting Corinne at 10. He could drop by beforehand, but she was out on 9 o'clock rounds. She wouldn't return to her room for several more minutes. Todd lived on the second floor. Pete figured he could visit him for a while before heading up to Corinne's room, if he were there of course.

Turned out he was; his door was ajar.

Todd's room rested on the left side of the second-floor hallway, next to the stairwell. As soon as Pete arrived he heard his pal's voice trickling out the door. He was about to knock but stopped suddenly. He heard another faint—but familiar—voice. It was a girl's. She and Todd were both laughing.

Brandi?

Yes, it was she, had to be. He would know that laugh anywhere. But there was something different about it, something he couldn't put his finger on. And why, he asked himself, was she here in Blake Hall anyway? He thought she was sick, but her hearty laugh proved otherwise. Obviously she felt better, which was good news. But she never called back to resume their dinner plans.

"That car," Brandi said in between laughter, "I was so embarrassed."

What was that she said?

"And Woodlake Square … what a slum, a real slum."

I must be hearing things. This can't be her, not the lovely Miss Sparks from prayer group.

But it was.

"I have some really, really high standards," she continued, "and Peter Webb will just never meet my standards."

STANDARDS, STANDARDS, STANDARDS...

The echoing word pierced poisonous, reality-biting daggers into his heart. He so wanted to believe his ears had played a dirty trick on him, that none of this was real. Brandi was the one, his soulmate. She even kissed him. They had two wonderful dates together, and others were to follow. He was led to Stepney Green College to meet her. It was all part of some divine plan, right?

This wasn't supposed to happen.

STANDARDS, STANDARDS, STANDARDS...

The maddening echo continued its unrelenting, merciless campaign to slash open his heart. With no psychic walls protecting it, the mission was easy to accomplish.

Why is this happening? Why?!

Pete shut his eyes and leaned backward against the off-white wall. Standing like a zombie beside Todd's door, he fought to mask his hurt. But his lips trembled involuntarily. To deflect attention from any students passing by, he tilted his head up toward the ceiling. He wanted no one to see him like this. A couple of students did, though. Luckily they never stopped to ask what was wrong. Pete wouldn't have been able to answer them anyway; he hardly knew the answer himself. Plus he was in no condition to talk, especially after hearing more wicked laughter spewing out of Todd's room.

How can she laugh at me like that? I love her, damn it!

The laughter soon ceased.

"You're the one I want," Brandi said to Todd, "the one I've always wanted."

"I want you, too."

What!

Then silence. His curiosity aroused, Pete opened his eyes and stole a gander through the cracked door. The sight inside his pal's room boiled his blood: Brandi and Todd kissing and groping each other.

His stomach spun in directions he never knew existed. To keep from throwing up, he turned away hastily and re-closed his eyes.

This can't be happening. This just can't be happening. Todd is my friend!

He brought Brandi and me together. He encouraged me, kept cheering me on. He wouldn't do this to me, he just wouldn't.

But he did.

I must be seeing things. This is all a nightmare, some horrible dream.

No, everything was real, all of it.

"You're the one, Todd," Brandi said after their steamy kiss, "the only one who'll ever meet my standards."

STANDARDS, STANDARDS, STANDARDS...

Pete could take no more. He had to get out of here. Not only would his feverish head explode, his shattered heart had left behind a rising flood of tears—and there was no time to build a dam. Clutching his upset stomach, he rushed down the stairwell as quickly as possible. His vision clouded by the second, and wheezing had contaminated his lungs. When he arrived on the main level, he charged for the door. Fortunately, no one was in his way—for their sake. Those stupid enough to block his path would have found themselves lying on the floor facedown, thumped by an emotional, erratic cannonball.

Blake Hall's main door nearly unhinged from its frame as Pete crashed against it. He couldn't have cared less. Nor did he give the inclement weather a second thought. The only thing on his mind was getting the hell away from here.

Corinne, meanwhile, had returned from 9 o'clock rounds. Inside her room on the fourth floor, she grabbed a towel and dried her drenched hair.

"I knew I should've brought my umbrella," she said to herself, good-humoredly.

She needed to get out of her wet clothes and change, as Pete was due to arrive shortly. Before doing so, she approached the window. The rain outside, pounding the earth even harder, had seized her attention. It sounded like hail.

The view was spectacular from the top floor. Around the amber lampposts Corinne gazed at the trillions of heavy raindrops falling like meteorites. She then faced the gazebo in the near distance. A familiar figure in an aqua shirt was running toward it like a bullet.

Pete?

He did not rest or seek shelter inside. He simply shot through it—and kept running. Corinne squinted to get a closer look, but he vanished over the hill before she could lower an eyelid. She sensed something was wrong, something terribly wrong. There was more to his supersonic sprint than just escaping the rain. He would have stopped inside the gazebo if that were the case. So then why was he running so fast? And why was he running from Blake Hall instead of toward it?

Only Pete himself knew.

STANDARDS, STANDARDS, STANDARDS…

Brandi's favorite word gonged persistently inside Pete's head. Her voice, that sinister voice, wouldn't leave him alone. There was no place to hide. It would find him no matter where he went. Still, he had to get away.

All the water dumping out of the sky couldn't rinse the red from his face. Nor could it cool the hot tears bucketing from their ducts. It did, however, soak his hair and clothing. His shoes, and the socks inside them, were as saturated as the campus soil. Despite the added weight Pete dashed past Rockford Hall like a cheetah.

He headed toward the college's pedestrian exit, on the same piney slope he and the now lowly Miss Sparks once rollerbladed. Trudging down the half-mile concrete path, snippets of their date that day flashed before his eyes: the joyous glow on her face as she arrived; her gentle crash into his arms at the archway; overlooking the park's lake together atop the bridge; holding hands on the way out; and so much more.

Oh, God, make it stop! Please!!!

The nine-foot-high stone archway lay just ahead. Once inside the damp symbolic monument, a shivering Pete slumped to the ground. Slouching on the wet concrete, his waterlogged jeans moistened even more. He hardly cared—or noticed. His cold sodden legs had numbed during the torrential trek.

His heart, unfortunately, hadn't.

Dana O'Brien and Liz Dabney each had their fun ripping it out. The wounds took ages to heal. Now the pain was back, and more excruciating than ever. Brandi Sparks caused it this time. Pete wondered how she could be so kind and sweet to his face, but so cruel and heartless behind his back. He soon discovered the answer: like Dana and Liz, she had to steal his heart because she had none of her own.

Corinne repeatedly said to take things slowly, but he chose not to listen.

How he wished he had.

He also wished, for the first time, that he never stepped foot here. All this hurt could have been avoided had he transferred to another four-year college, one much less costly. Stepney Green's richer-than-life students were so fake, especially ones in prayer group—namely Brandi and Todd. Too bad they never practiced what they were preached. Both thought nothing of hurting him ... and playing him for a fool.

Pete had never felt so stupid in his life. How ironic to be sitting underneath the "gateway to education excellence."

To him, it had become the gateway to hell.

14

Corinne paced the floor of her room—all night long. She was worried sick. Pete never came over to hang out. And he never returned her voicemail messages. She must have left a dozen. She knew something upset him, and pretty badly. But what? And where was he now? Where did he run off? Corinne prayed time would move faster so she could find out. She was still on duty and could not leave her dormitory. Her shift would not end until 5 a.m. She had 20 minutes more to wait.

She approached the window and looked outside. Rain continued to fall out of the bleak sky, just not as hard. Corinne had listened to it throughout the night. Usually she enjoyed the soothing sound of raindrops splashing against the earth's surface. But it wasn't enough to ease her anxiety this morning.

Glimpsing at her watch, she noticed only a minute had passed.

"That's it, I can't wait any longer," she said, slipping on her boots and pastel-blue raincoat.

As she locked her room and made her way outside, Corinne, risking her job, believed she was doing the right thing by leaving. She had to help a friend in need. RAs were supposed to help fellow students anyway, including counseling. She figured she could use that as an excuse if caught by one of the residence life supervisors.

Outside Blake Hall, Corinne flipped up her hood and ran to the gazebo. Once there she thought of something: What if Pete left campus?

His car! If it were here, then so should he.

Corinne reversed out of the gazebo and ran to the back of Whitman

Hall, where the student parking lot lay. Her blue eyes widened frantically as she searched for Pete's rusty white compact vehicle. She found it, finally, underneath a dim amber streetlight at the far end. Corinne was relieved. He could not have gotten far. He had to be somewhere on campus.

Breathing heavily, and with thickening raindrops plopping on her covered head, she trudged across the grounds toward Rockford Hall, arriving shortly after 5 a.m. Her RA shift officially over, she no longer had to worry about a residence life higher-up spotting her. No students or campus safety officers could report her, either. Not a soul was about this early on a Sunday morning anyway. Most students partied Saturday nights. She assumed they conked out a couple of hours ago. Plus they wouldn't venture outside in such a rainy mess unless they absolutely had to.

Corinne certainly had good reason.

At the main door, in the alcove, she took out her mobile phone and dialed Pete's number once again, figuring she'd give it one more try. After the fourth ring his voicemail activated. Rather than leave another message, she hung up.

She then stepped back outside the alcove and looked up to Pete's bedroom window on the top floor. She wondered if he were inside but honestly didn't think so. He would have answered the phone if so. But something really upset him last night. His hurt could have formed a protective shell and sealed him inside his room, away from the world.

She had to find out for sure.

Corinne inserted her master key and opened Rockford Hall's main door. Once inside she torpedoed up four flights of stairs to Pete's room. She never even took off her raincoat or pushed back her hood. Finding her friend was all that consumed her.

Nearly out of breath, she knocked on his door.

"Pete?" she said softly, with a slight wheeze. "Pete, it's me, Corinne. Are you there?"

She knocked again, a little harder.

"Pete? Are you okay? Please say something."

Another spell of silence passed. Deeply concerned, Corinne keyed into his bedroom. She would never do this sort of thing ordinarily, but this was an emergency. Anything could have happened to him.

Upon entering, Corinne gasped quietly. Pete's bed was still made.

"Damn it, where are you?"

She left the room, locking the door behind her, and scurried back downstairs.

Outside, she scoped the area for possible clues as to where her friend may have gone. The rain, pouring everywhere, had intensified once again.

He's got to be someplace.

The gym, library, cafeteria and student lounge were all closed. She wondered if he had spent the night in a friend's room. But he would have called or texted to let her know. Pete always kept his word. If he said he was coming over at a set time, then he should have been there. It wasn't like him to renege without explaining why.

Think, Corinne, think.

She glanced around again, this time paying special attention to the pathway leading to the college's pedestrian exit. Thinking back, she recalled her last vision of Pete zipping out of the gazebo—on the same concrete path. Not only did it lead right here to Rockford Hall, it forked toward the archway monument. Could he have gone there? Maybe he left campus. It was entirely possible, anything was. But then why didn't he take his car?

Corinne sighed in aggravation. She kept shooting down the possibilities floating inside her head. And standing in the rain only added to her frustration. She had to do something, start looking someplace, *any*place.

She took off down the half-mile path, figuring she had nothing to lose. Perhaps there was a clue to Pete's whereabouts near the arch, she thought—and hoped.

15

Musty pine spoiled the usually fresh, invigorating air around the curvy pathway. Too much rain was to blame. Corinne hardly noticed as her boots splashed against the sheets of water covering the concrete.

After the last curve the magnificent stone archway came into view. So did a mysterious figure slumping underneath. Could it be? Corinne wasn't sure … until she ran closer.

"Pete!" she cried.

He did not reply or flinch. No response whatsoever. His eyes, though open, were empty of emotion. He barely blinked. Corinne was shocked at the state of him. With skin tinted in an eerie indigo, he looked like death, or close to it. She figured he had been out here all through the rainy night—in drenched clothes.

She bent down to stare inside his glassy brown eyes.

"Pete?" she said. "Pete, can you hear me?"

He nodded, ever so slightly.

"Oh, thank God," said a relieved Corinne. "Can you tell me what happened, why you were here all night?"

Pete was in no condition to answer, to get into all that now. He was so weak, physically and emotionally. He just wanted to forget everything, that he ever met Todd and Brandi. He fought like hell to erase their kiss of betrayal from his mind, but the image refused to go away.

STANDARDS, STANDARDS, STANDARDS…

The maddening echo was back yet again. Pete could no longer handle it. He reached out for Corinne and sobbed into her arms.

"It's okay, I'm here now," she said consolingly. "Everything's going to be all right, you'll see."

He wished he could believe that.

"I'll help you get through this, whatever it is," she continued. "I promise."

Pete latched on to his best friend more tightly.

"Thanks," he uttered through whimpers.

Corinne slowly stood up, lifting her fragile friend on the way.

"Come on, let's go," she said. "We need to get you out of the rain and into some warm clothes."

Pete was too exhausted to refuse, which is what he wanted to do. The thought of returning to campus sickened him almost as much as Todd and Brandi's duplicity. For the first time, life back in Woodlake Square appealed. He never thought he would look forward to going home, to the lower-middleclass neighborhood of chipped brick townhouses. Now, though, they seemed more familiar, more comforting than the college's faultless Tudor-style buildings.

The trek back to one of them, Rockford Hall, was arduous, especially for Corinne. Pete leaned against her all the way up the concrete slope, resting his weary head on her shoulder. Despite her own fatigue she didn't seem to mind. She was just grateful to have found her friend alive.

They spoke no words during the entire journey, including up the four flights of stairs to his room. Pete collapsed into bed as soon as he entered, instantly dampening the quilt. Corinne took off her raincoat and stood beside him.

"Listen, Pete," she said, "you need to get out of these wet clothes and hop in the shower, a very hot shower."

Pete sighed.

"I know it sounds like a strange thing to do having been out in the rain all night," she continued. "Come on now."

She lifted him up off the bed and led him to the closet, where she took out his robe and a fresh clean towel.

"Here you are," she said, handing them over. "Now go take a nice hot shower. You'll feel better afterwards."

"You'll be here when I come back, won't you?" Pete said, childlike.

His little-boy-lost quality was emerging, complete with sad puppy-like eyes. Corinne felt so sorry for him.

"Yes, of course I will," she replied, smiling assuredly.

He smiled back, as best he could. He then headed to the door, collecting a t-shirt and underwear from the dresser on the way. Before leaving he stopped. Turning to face Corinne, a tear bubbled out of his eye and slid down his cheek.

"Thank you," Pete said wholeheartedly. "Thanks for coming to find me, for being here right now."

She answered with a simple but important, "That's what friends are for."

A grateful smile creased his mouth as he left.

My God, what could have happened to him?

She knew he was down about Brandi canceling their date. But there had to be something more to his sorry state, a lot more. She had never seen her friend this depressed, not in the two years they'd known each other. Whatever the reason, it was definitely profound.

Corinne sat on the bed's edge and scooted backwards toward the wall. Leaning against it, she dared not close her eyes. She would fall asleep for sure if she did. But it felt great to get off her feet.

———◆●◆———

A freshly showered Pete entered the room moments later. The hot water appeared to have done some good. His skin, though still pruned, no longer contained that deathly indigo tint. The only blue on him now was his thick heavy robe.

After tossing his damp and dirty clothes into the laundry bag, he fell into bed. He rested his head on Corinne's lap, much to her surprise. He definitely needed to lean on her in more ways than one.

"Ready to talk about it?" she said, stroking consoling fingers through his drying hair.

Pete sighed in exhaustion.

"Don't fall asleep on me," said Corinne. "You need to let it out, whatever it is. Keeping it bottled inside doesn't do any good."

Pete sighed again.

"Is it Brandi?"

"I hate her," he answered, gritting his teeth. "I hate them both."

Corinne was shocked. Not only to hear the word hate coming from him but that there was another party involved.

"Both?"

"Uh-huh."

After gulping she asked who the other person was.

"My buddy," he answered scornfully, "Todd Galloway."

Corinne gasped silently.

"Oh."

The pieces of this puzzle were snapping together. Apparently Brandi and Todd had become a couple, or were all along.

"How could they do this to me, Corinne?"

"Do what?" she asked, knowing what was most likely ahead.

As Pete revealed everything—Brandi making fun of his car and where he lived; Todd's and her kiss of betrayal; and her demeaning "standards" comment—he shed no tears. No whimpers spat out, either. Stoicism pressed against his face the entire time.

"I'm so sorry, Pete," Corinne said tenderly. "I'm sorry they hurt you like this."

She added, in a much less gentle tone, how much she loathed that standards remark. She had thought Brandi a nice girl, someone genuine and compassionate. Her behavior reflected anything but. Corinne never dreamed she would hurt him like this.

"I'm such an idiot," Pete said, angry with himself.

"No, you're not."

"Then why do I keep doing this to myself? How come I never learn?" he said, referring to his past relationships.

"You're just a hopeless romantic, that's all," she said. "There's nothing wrong with that, really. It's just…"

"Just what?"

"Just a little naïve," she answered. "I think you've seen too many romantic comedies."

Pete chuckled, knowing she was probably right. He had worked at the Trenton cinema a long time—his junior and senior years of high school, all through community college, and even now between semesters at Stepney

Blind Expectations

Green. Watching films for free was supposed to be a perk for movie theater employees. Not so, apparently, in his case.

"Point well taken," Pete said. "It's about time I realized this is real life and not a movie."

"Things don't always go the way we want them to," said Corinne, "like in the movies, that's for sure."

She made a lot of sense. He'd been living in a dream world all this time, a flowery illusion that only Hollywood realized. His love life was anything but the fluff smeared across the silver screen. It contained heartache, real heartache. The pain did not fade away after two hours either. It lingered for weeks and months—and in the case of his high school sweetheart, years.

Mary Ann Tolliver was her name. Pete was a senior, and she a junior. She had enchanting blue-green eyes, medium-length golden-brown hair, and an amazing body: trim, athletic and toned. He literally saw stars when he kissed her, even in broad daylight. She was the first girl to show him genuine affection. She held his hand in the corridors and kissed him goodbye as she headed into class. Pete had longed for this kind of relationship since his freshman year. He desperately wanted it to thrive, to last well after graduation. He even dreamed of marrying her. Sadly, the all-too-short two-month relationship ended a week before he graduated. Mary Ann broke it off, saying it just wouldn't work. She would never see him. If he wasn't at the community college taking classes and working on research projects, then he'd be working one of his three jobs, including the one at the cinema.

Pete was devastated. He thought about her every day for the next three years, all through his tenure at the community college. He envisioned her calling to ask him back, even coming to his house. But she did no such thing.

Indeed he had watched too many romantic comedies, all with blissful—and unrealistic—finales.

Transferring to Stepney Green evaporated the dream of a Mary Ann reunion once and for all. The reason: graduate student Dana O'Brien, 3 years his senior, whom he had met at the college library. One day she asked for his help in locating a book, but their conversation soon took a personal turn. They started talking about what they liked to do in their free time, and eventually, dating and relationships. They seemed to click instantly, which Pete mistakenly took as a good sign.

It was another love story happening before his very eyes, just like on the silver screen. He found himself infatuated. Dana was outgoing, easy to talk to, and very attractive. Her long, iron-curled brown hair stopped ideally midway down her back. Her ample lips and haunting green eyes equally captivated him. She also had a gorgeous figure, thanks to all her vigorous country line dancing.

"Corinne, you remember Dana, don't you?" said Pete.

She certainly did, and not too fondly.

"Yes."

"I did so much for her," he said. "I even took line dancing lessons to impress her—I'm not even into country music—and she still broke up with me."

"I know," Corinne whispered.

Her consoling fingers moved out of his hair and down to his shoulder and arm. Her instinct to strum away her friend's pain simply took over. Pete felt like a baby cradled in his mother's protective arms. He definitely needed some tender loving care.

"She used me to make some 40-year-old guy jealous," he said, "that married man she met on the dance floor one night."

Corinne knew this already … and everything else about the Dana saga. She let him carry on anyway. If re-releasing this pain would help him, then so be it.

"The whole time Dana and I were going out she kept telling me I was too young for her," Pete continued, "and that she only went for older guys. Yet the moves she made on me said otherwise. I thought actions spoke louder than words."

"Try not to dwell on all that again," said Corinne. "You already learned from that mistake."

Did I? Did I, really? I wonder.

Pete sighed.

"If I really did learn from that mistake," he said, "then explain what happened with Liz and Brandi."

Corinne must have told him a thousand times not to jump into relationships too quickly. He would only get carried away, she warned, and drift into a storybook, a grim fairy tale where no one lived happily ever after.

So true. Too bad he realized this within the last 12 hours and not sooner. Still, better late than never, as the saying went. From now on things would change, Pete himself would change. No more daydreaming about girls he just met or started to date. He needed time, lots of time, to get to know them. That was the only way to find out if they were sincere people. Hazy daydreams of false love had to clear out—and end for good. So did watching romantic comedies. Those films only fed the daydreams, he concluded, and digested them into nightmares.

It was time to snap out of it once and for all. And get real. Graduation was a mere four weeks away. He had to pull himself together. He had come too far in his life to give up now. People like Brandi Sparks and Todd Galloway were not worth throwing away a college education. He would be leaving soon anyway, never to see their lying faces again.

I'm staying put ... and I'll be strong.

Corinne continued her hands-on approach to healing her friend's pain. Her patting had grown slower, gentler. Pete was beginning to feel uncomfortable, though he was careful not to show it. He let a moment pass before lifting his head off her lap.

"I think I'm going to be okay now," he said, hoisting himself off the bed and onto his feet.

"You're not fooling me, Pete," she said. "Brandi really hurt you. It's going to take time to get over this."

She was right, unfortunately. He really didn't hate Brandi as he earlier stated. It was a knee-jerk reaction. But one thing was certain: his love for the lowly Miss Sparks had disappeared—completely. No trace of the emotion lingered. Just hurt.

"Corinne, can I ask you something?"

"Sure," she replied. "What is it?"

"How do you do it?" said Pete, marveling. "How do you remain so strong all the time? What's your secret?"

Corinne smiled in both amusement and embarrassment.

"Well, there is no secret per se," she said. "When life's obstacles crash our way, we only have two choices: sink or swim. I just prefer the latter."

That sounded logical enough, but what Pete wanted to know was *how*. How did a person swim around the wreckage of obstacles blocking destiny's path? What exactly did one have to do? He remembered Todd telling him the best way to get over a relationship was to start a new one. But given his track record—the horrible events of last night—he probably lied about this, too. Easy for him to say anyway. Though his former friend's looks fell on the lower half of the average scale, he had money. Mountains of it, in the shape of crisp hotel towers spread across the globe. As an American golden child he could get any girl he wanted.

He sure got Brandi.

Or Brandi got *him*.

Todd would never really know if it were he she truly wanted or his mega-fortune. Pete thought it most deserving.

He also thought of what might happen the next time he saw him, he and Brandi both. Part of him wanted to tell them off. He certainly knew of an appropriate place they could stick their duplicitous faces. But that would be stooping to their level. Avoiding them as much as possible would be more dignified. Besides, graduation was four weeks away. He would be back in Woodlake Square in no time.

Nevertheless, Pete would have to face them. He didn't know where or when exactly, but he would have to see them again. He had a choice, though: sink or swim. He decided, proudly, on the latter.

"Corinne," said Pete, "I can't thank you enough. You've helped me more than you'll ever know."

She rose from the bed smiling.

"I'm just glad I was here," she said, taking his hands into hers.

"Me, too."

They embraced warmly, closeness Corinne secretly enjoyed. Closing her eyes, she wished she could hold him more tightly.

What am I thinking? This is wrong, so wrong. I shouldn't be thinking this right now. I'm here to help him. He needs my support.

Corinne's eyes flashed open, their Mediterranean blue highlighted in guilt.

We're friends, just friends.

"So," she said, freeing herself from the entanglement, "how about some breakfast?"

"Now?"

He reminded her that it was Sunday. Brunch was served weekends from 10 a.m. to 2 p.m. They had several hours to wait before the cafeteria opened.

"How about we get some shut-eye instead?" Pete suggested. "You must be exhausted, too."

Indeed she was. It had been quite a night—and morning. She even forgot which day it was. Corinne figured they should meet for brunch at noon instead of 10. Pete agreed. He was dreadfully tired as well.

"Well, I'll see you then, okay?" she said, heading to the door.

"Wait."

Pete asked her to stay. He still did not want to be alone. Gazing into his baby browns, Corinne easily gave in.

"You can have the bed, and I'll just sleep on the floor," he said, taking out an extra blanket and pillow from the closet.

"Are you sure you'll be able to sleep okay?" said Corinne, slipping underneath the bedcovers. "That floor must be hard as a rock."

Pete yawned and nestled into a fetal position.

"I'm so tired right now," he said, pulling the extra blanket over him, "I could actually sleep on a rock."

Corinne smiled.

"Night, Pete."

"Night ... and thanks for everything."

Seconds later the two friends conked out—and slept two hours longer than they had planned. They woke at 1:30 in the afternoon. They would have slept longer had it not been for the cafeteria closing in half an hour. Both were famished. Pete hadn't eaten a thing in more than 24 hours. Strange, he thought, that his appetite returned only after his interest in Brandi flushed out of his system.

16

Corinne stood solidly by Pete's side as they made their way to the dining hall. Although he had vowed to be strong, she knew he was still vulnerable. Part of her wanted to pluck out the crimps in Brandi's sandy-blond hair after what she did to him, something a protective kid sister would do on a playground. But this was a college campus.

Inside the sparsely populated cafeteria Pete put two plates on his tray and covered them in plateaus of food. He emptied the serving bar of sausage links, ham slices, scrambled eggs, home fries, and mini oat-bran muffins. Luckily for Corinne he left the blueberry pancakes and apple-cinnamon waffles. The two friends wolfed down their brunch in a record-breaking eight minutes, seconds before the cafeteria doors were to lock.

"I was so hungry," Pete said to Corinne on their way out.

"Really?" she said, feigning surprise. "I couldn't tell."

He laughed.

"It's nice to hear you laugh," Corinne said with a smile.

"It's nice to be able to laugh," said Pete, adding that after last night he didn't think it possible.

Outside the cafeteria he thanked his best friend one last time. He didn't know how he could have got through this nightmare without her.

"You rescued me," Pete said pointblank.

She actually trudged through heavy rain and mud to find him, he continued. She lent a shoulder and ear. And she gave him the pep talk he so desperately needed. Indeed, no one else on campus would have done all this for him. He was forever grateful.

"How could I ever repay you?" he asked.

"You already have."

"I have?"

Corinne nodded.

"How?"

"By thanking me the way you did," she said softly.

"You're amazing, you know that?"

Corinne was about to blush. To hide her reddening face she embraced Pete, patted his back, and told him to hang tough.

"Will do," he said. "I'll call you later, okay?"

The time had come to part for the day. Corinne had homework to do, and Pete wanted to catch more Zs. He certainly owed them to himself, as did Corinne. But she was too wound up to sleep. Or concentrate on her homework. As Pete ventured upstairs toward the north exit, Corinne opened the south door leading to Whitman and Blake Halls. Outside, under the overcast sky, she brought her hand to her racing heart and told herself to relax. She then shut her eyes.

What's going on? Why is this happening to me?

Deep down, she knew the answer: she was falling in love. Why now? She had known him for two years and was content with being just his friend. Was it because he was graduating next month and they wouldn't see each other on a regular basis? Could be. A number of things were possible. Pete's determination to be strong attracted her, as did his embraces. He had hugged her before, plenty of times. But today, for some reason, the gestures meant something more. She nearly melted in his arms, especially after he told her how amazing she was.

Corinne wasn't sure how to handle all this. One thing was certain, though. She needed time to reflect. Exhaling deeply, she left for Blake Hall to try and sort out her feelings. She had quite a task ahead of her.

And Peter Michael Webb had quite a task ahead of him—literally.

───◆●◆───

About to leave the building's north exit, Pete stopped suddenly. Several girls, at least half a dozen, breezed through the glass doors. He recognized them. They were from prayer group, friends of Brandi's. And they were laughing—at him, he thought, because he would never meet a certain member's high-and-mighty standards.

They can all get lost—and take their Standards Queen with them! Just where is she anyway? Shouldn't she be giggling and gossiping with her merry band?

Then it dawned on him: she was probably shacked up in the Galloway presidential suite on the second floor of Blake Hall.

But Pete was mistaken. Brandi was with them, at the back of the group—hiding, he thought, behind the taller girls so she could pretend she never saw him. Her plan backfired. The above fluorescent light had betrayed her confidence. Penetrating the giggly girls' line of defense, it produced a concert of sparkles on a stage of sandy-blond hair.

Pete grew nauseous. The sight of his former dream girl created boiling acid in his stomach, which ate at its four-layer walls.

The lowly Miss Sparks slithered to the front of the group and unleashed an oh-so perky, "Hi, Pete!"

Her voice, that sweet-turned-sinister voice, stunned him into immobilization. A brisk cold whipped into his body without permission, gusting through his organs and bloodstream like a merciless blizzard. His temperature dipped to a frosty area somewhere below normal, stiffening him into a corpse. His face froze without a trace of emotion—unlike Brandi's. Hers displayed a put-on smile with dimples and electrified eyes to match. At least his stoicism was real. There was nothing genuine about her joyous visage.

Dressed in a head-to-toe pink sweat suit, he figured she was on her way to the gym next to the cafeteria. Had last night's events not occurred, he would have asked to join her and her entourage. Now he wanted to flee. Twenty-four hours ago he would have relished in a chance encounter like this. Not anymore. If he could click his heels and magically disappear, he would do so in a heartbeat. Pete realized this time would come, bumping into her again. He just wished it hadn't come so quickly.

But he was prepared.

"So how are you?" she asked, smiling ear to ear.

How am I?! How do you think I am, you twofaced hypocrite! I want to throw up because you make me sick, that's how I am.

"Fine," he answered, his voice tingling with iciness.

Brandi was completely unaware of his ill feelings, and that was how he wanted it. For now, that is. It was time she got a taste of her own medicine. Now it was her turn to be on the receiving end of an emotional game.

Pete was all too happy to play.

He stood rigidly after his cool reply, which confused Brandi. Usually he asked how she was doing, too. But he said nothing. Little did she know just how uninterested he was.

"Oh, by the way," she said, her face exploding in feigned jubilation, "thank you for the gift bag.

I love chocolates!"

Oh no, the bag! I forgot to take it off her doorknob. How could I be so stupid? Anyway, that was then and this is now. I'll show her.

"Good," Pete said nonchalantly, "because those chocolates have high-quality … standards."

Man, that felt good.

Brandi remained oblivious.

"And I liked your poem," she said, continuing her charade of enthusiasm. "It was really good."

The poem! Shoot! I'm so stupid!!! Why didn't I listen to Corinne? Why didn't I wait? I know why. The reason is right in front of me. How can she stand there like that and act so fake? She didn't like my poem; she doesn't even like me. After all, I'll never meet her sanctimonious standards. Just look at her smiling like that—so insincere, so fake. Everything about her is. But I'm on to her now. She can't fool me anymore. That smile used to make me melt. Now it brings bile to my mouth. I should spit it on her face. Yeah, that'll wipe off that fake smile of hers. But I won't do it. I'm better than that, better than her at this game. It's my move now. She better watch out … I'm going to win.

"Really?" said Pete, feigning surprise but maintaining a rigid posture. "I wasn't sure if the poem would measure up to your standards."

That was the second time he uttered the word standards, which Brandi noted. Her phony wide and cheery smile shrunk to a bona fide nervous straight line. Her lips trembled ever so slightly, but enough for Pete to see—and savor. Spots of sweat suddenly condensed on her face, especially along the hairline, which also tickled him.

"Something the matter, Brandi?" he said, smiling to himself.

"No, not at all," she replied, choking on her words.

"You don't look so hot right now."

In more ways than one!

Brandi cleared her throat.

"I'm fine, really," she said.

"Well, good," said Pete, "because you sounded really sick yesterday, the way your words spewed out … yeah, really *sick*."

Wiping her sweaty forehead with her sleeve, Brandi grew increasingly anxious.

He meant the message I left on his voicemail, right? Yes, of course he did. He doesn't know about Todd and me; he couldn't possibly know … or does he?

"Heading to the gym, I see," Pete said, calm, cool and collected. "Wow, you must really be feeling better since last night … oh, I meant since yesterday, of course."

Ooh, I know that got her.

And it did. More and more Brandi struggled to maintain her composure. Wondering if he'd found out about Todd and her, she could barely stand erect. Adrenaline swished through her system with such force her entire upper body swayed like a pendulum. Her girlfriends noticed and looked on oddly. Pete sensed a few of them wanted to reach out and prevent her from tipping over. As delightfully entertaining the scene was, he fought his urge to bust out laughing.

Brandi stole a nervous glance at the girly groupie rainbow behind her, then faced her ex-suitor and excused herself. They should get going to the gym now, she explained.

"Okay," said an expressionless Pete.

That was it. No, "have a fun time," "see you later," not even a "bye." Brandi's concern deepened. She had never seen him so aloof. He used to light up like the sun on a cloudless summer afternoon when he saw her. Now he was this cold hard statue. Why? She prayed it wasn't due to her affair with Todd, anything but that. She wanted—and needed—to convince herself that wasn't the case. All this not knowing was doing her head in. Pete was clueless, she told herself continuously. He had to be. He was too naïve and childlike to play mind games. Besides, he would have confronted her if he knew of the affair. No man would stand idly by like that. She was getting worked up over nothing, absolutely nothing.

"Well," she said, desirous to part on a pleasant note, "see you at prayer group."

Oh, no, you won't!

Pete was flabbergasted. She had some nerve attending an organization like that after degrading him the way she did, that among other things. No way would the group condone her behavior, hers or Todd's. And no way would Pete step foot in that chapel. As far as he was concerned his membership terminated right here and now.

A drab, lifeless "Yeah, whatever" was all he could utter. Politeness was too good for her. She wasn't worthy of it. Besides, he would be acting fake just like her. The thought of any similarity with the lowly Miss Sparks repulsed him beyond disgust.

So he left, out the door to freedom just a footstep away.

He did not look back—but was tempted. The look on Brandi's face must have been priceless. He envisioned her jaw dropping to her ankles in humiliation; her brown, mortified eyes protruding from their sockets; and her pinkish face reddening with outrage. His curt reply and waltz out the door happened right in front of her beloved girlfriends, an embarrassing situation to say the least. But she deserved it. She deserved it all.

Outside, an enormous delightful grin smeared across Pete's face. He was so proud of himself. He did what he set out to do: he gave Brandi a taste of her own medicine.

And he was strong.

He only wished Corinne could have witnessed the encounter. No doubt she would have been proud as well. He wanted to tell her about it right away but decided to wait a while. She needed to catch up on her rest, much like he did.

17

Pete lay in bed the rest of the afternoon, reflecting on the extraordinary events of the last 24 hours. He'd undergone a remarkable transformation, having realized just how superficial some people could be. They were not all true to themselves—or to others—like he was. With him it was a case of what you see is what you get. And this was a good thing. He wasn't the least bit pretentious, unlike Brandi and so many others at Stepney Green.

He never should have been ashamed of his working-class roots. So what if his car was a clunker? At least he paid for it with his own money, hard-earned wages from three part-time jobs. He had no rich Daddy to write checks for luxury sports cars or whatever else his heart desired. In fact, he had no Daddy at all. He only had a mother, Janice, who was the kindest, most caring and hardworking person he knew. Thanks to her example he learned to appreciate what he had, to take nothing for granted. Raised by someone like her in a place like Woodlake Square was actually a blessing.

But his love life was not so blessed. In fact, he felt cursed. He truly believed he had been led to this college to find the love of his life. But Dana had rejected him, as did Liz and Brandi. Three strikes—now he was out.

Pete knew he should never question God, but he couldn't help himself. He wanted to know what he did that was so terrible. He had thought himself a good person for the most part. But he received such ill treatment, such ridicule. And he was girlfriendless. Always, it seemed. He wished he could understand. Was all this part of the plan? Everything happened for a reason, did it not?

Whatever the reason was, nothing could take away his newfound strength. He would never forget that miraculous moment during his encounter with Brandi: a tough, carefree mindset landing on the fields of his brain and rooting itself underneath. The old Pete would have just been polite and exchanged pleasantries to keep peace. But he had become a new man, one who no longer sat strapped in a highchair eating the feces dishing his way.

This surge of inner strength, from wherever it came, felt amazing. It liberated him from the confines of insecurity. The bars of this mental prison had been slashed, torn down, and burned into measly ash. Pete no longer cared what the lowly Miss Sparks thought of him, or anybody else for that matter. If they didn't accept him for who and what he was, then so be it. They were the ones who had a problem. Not him. And contrary to their belief their wealth did not make them better than other people. Everyone was created equally.

Still, Brandi could never meet his standards.

Encountering her this afternoon was only the beginning ... and what a beginning it was. Surely this newfound strength would help him overcome future obstacles as well. There would undoubtedly be more challenges ahead, including his troublesome brother back home. Adam's constant belittling, even at age 27, would be no match for the new, stronger Peter Michael Webb. Maybe that was why he was led here: to get strong.

Everything was going to be all right. Not having a girlfriend wasn't the end of the world. No more sulking in self-pity. Miss Right was out there somewhere. He just wasn't meant to meet her right now. Perhaps once he landed a good full-time job and was able to support himself independently. It was certainly possible. Whatever fate had in store Pete would be happy either single or attached.

Bachelorhood enveloped many positives: no relationship disputes and the freedom to come and go as he pleased, to name a couple. He would also have more money in his pocket—for himself. Now he could buy something that *he* wanted. Single life also meant added leisure time, with which Pete could discover even more about himself. He had learned so much already, especially within the last 24 hours. Finally, he was strong enough to swim around life's obstacles. It was one of the most important lessons he ever learned.

Corinne definitely deserved some credit, if not more. She saw the strength in him that he never could. She had truly become his best friend. Pete just hoped he were as good a friend to her as she was to him.

He knew he would miss her, terribly, after graduating next month. This was it; no coming back after summer break. He would see her much less frequently once he entered the full-time working world. And she would be even farther away after her own graduation a year later, though New York City was easily accessible by bus or train. Corinne's dream was to work there as a social worker, much to her rich family's dismay. They preferred she carry on the family business, Aldrich Enterprises. But Corinne wasn't the least bit interested in financial services. She wanted to get out there in the world and help people. Pete could personally vouch for her expertise.

His mother was also talented in this field. She always lent an ear or a helping hand whenever she could. Pete was grateful. At least he could count on her love and support once he returned to Woodlake Square, and she on him.

Suddenly the phone rang—and it was Janice.

"Hi, son," she said cheerfully.

"Hi, Mom," said Pete, having picked up the phone on his desk. "I was just thinking about you."

"You were? Well, isn't that nice."

Pete smiled, awed by the upbeat inflections in his mother's voice.

"So how are you?" he asked.

Janice said she was okay but wondered why yesterday's phone call wasn't returned. Even though she didn't ask him specifically to call her back, he usually did anyhow.

Pete sighed, having totally forgotten. He apologized and assured his mother that he was just fine, which was true as never before. He was also relieved. News of dating Brandi never transmitted to Woodlake Square. He didn't have to explain what happened last night. To her the lovely-to-lowly Miss Sparks never even existed. Perfect.

Janice changed the subject to Pete's graduation next month, saying how excited she was to attend. For once he shared in her joy. He could hardly wait to escape the college's stuffiness and return to the genuine lower-middleclass surroundings of his heritage.

"And Aunt Rae is coming, too," Janice added.

"Cool," said a thrilled Pete.

He just loved his mother's best friend across the street, the one who babysat him after school all those years.

"I don't know about your brother, though."

No surprise there. He knew Adam would not commit to going. His word was as corrupt as his heart. Besides, watching little brother walk across the stage to pick up his prestigious college degree would only create more resentment.

"I wouldn't count on it, Mom," said Pete.

Janice sighed. Deep down, she sensed the same. She couldn't force him to come along, no matter how badly she wanted to. He was a 27-year-old man after all. Still, she wished Adam could show some support, if only a little. His attendance at Pete's graduation would mean a lot to him, and to her. But Adam was not the selfless type. Lying about the job interview the other week was more than enough proof.

"Anyway," said Pete, "it'll be great having you and Aunt Rae there."

"We wouldn't miss it for the world."

Pete smiled.

"I'm proud of you, son," Janice continued.

"Thanks, Mom," he said, deeply touched. "That means a lot to me."

A silent, solemn pause followed. Somehow it strengthened their mother-son bond. Both Pete and Janice could feel it.

"Well, I should get going now and get dinner started," she said.

"Okay, enjoy the rest of your day off."

He so wanted her to. Like every Sunday today was the only day she had off. She worked so hard—always. The two jobs she held were quite laborious, and at times backbreaking. She was on her feet constantly. But she never complained about working at the restaurant and bar, not once. Pete really admired her for this. One day he would rescue her from this hard life. He didn't know how or when, but someday he would alleviate her adversity. It was the least he could do to pay her back for the decades of sacrifice she endured. Making sure her kids were fed, clothed and sheltered was her top priority. She gladly passed up buying herself an outfit if either of her sons needed something, like new shoes or a pair of jeans.

"I love you, Mom," Pete said with all his heart.

"I love you, too."

"Take care of yourself, okay?"

"You do the same," said Janice. "Bye, Peter."

"Bye."

As he hung up, he remembered the messages he had saved from Brandi, both texts and voicemails. Pete's smile instantly crunched into a scowl. It was high time to delete them.

He still could hardly believe what all had happened. Yesterday he would have moved heaven and earth for Brandi. Now he would move heaven and earth to avoid her. He wanted nothing more to do with her. Now that she got her just desserts outside the cafeteria, that is.

Todd was next.

Pete didn't know which was worse: Todd's false encouragement or Brandi's nasty standards comment. To him they were one in the same, along with their slobbering kiss of betrayal. They really deserved each other.

At least Corinne was true. Her friendship was the real deal. She was the one person on campus who cared, who actually gave a damn. She was always honest with him, too. Her spirit was genuine.

And she never even attended a prayer group gathering. How ironic.

———◆●◆———

Corinne was dealing with some irony of her own. Unable to focus on her homework, she instead spent the day lounging in bed listening to music—and thinking of her friend in ways other than amiably. For the first time in two years she wished she were the one he pined for. Part of her wanted to tell him just that, and that she would never hurt him like Brandi and the others did. She felt this urge to get out of bed and call him, to make that first move. But something else held her back. It was just too risky. She didn't want to ruin their rock-solid friendship.

It was that Monday night all over again, the one that aroused these mixed feelings in the first place, after reading Pete's poem. She realized then that they were better off as friends, so why not now?

Corinne knew this dilemma of hers would not resolve itself anytime soon. She had to push these feelings aside. Or at least try. It was the only way she could go on with her life. Plus she had Pete's complete trust. It would no doubt crumble if he discovered her true feelings. He would wonder why she hid them, why she wasn't totally honest. Dishonesty was something he could not, and would not, tolerate. Todd certainly could attest to this, she thought, or would in due time.

Suddenly, her phone rang. It was just the distraction she needed. Corinne hopped out of bed and answered it.

"Hi, it's me," said Pete.

The distraction didn't last long—at all.

"Hey, what's up?" she said, carrying on as if nothing special stirred inside her heart.

He mentioned he was skipping dinner tonight, having eaten too much at brunch. Corinne planned to do the same.

"So how are you?" she asked. "Are you all right?"

"Oh, I'm just fine," he answered with a devilishly delightful grin. "Guess who I ran into after brunch? Brandi."

"You're kidding."

It was no joke. Pete divulged all to his best friend, sharing every delicious morsel of his after-brunch treat. Corinne was astonished at how the encounter ended.

"You actually said 'yeah, whatever' like that and just left?"

He certainly did—and loved every minute of it.

"Good for you, Pete," she said. "Serves her right anyhow, given those awful things she said about you."

"And you know what else I thought of?" he said, having remembered something.

"What's that?"

"The night I took her to the movies in Vernon, she said she had a friend to see in Blake Hall before turning in for the night. Guess who that *friend* was?"

No need to guess. The answer was as transparent as last night's raindrops.

"I was so blind that night," said Pete, "but at least I see things clearly now."

Corinne did, too. Her friend was no longer that lost little boy she met two years ago. He was evolving into a man, grounded and strong. She was so proud of him.

And found him even more desirable.

I have to stop this now. I have to.

She forced these romantic feelings into a jar and tightened the lid vigorously. It was for the best. Two weeks of classes remained, followed by final exams and Senior Week. The semester's remaining days would be hectic enough. Pete more than anyone deserved a problem-free month. Revealing her secret would only burden him further. She vowed to wait until after he graduated.

Maybe, if she still had the nerve.

Oblivious to the sealed jar's contents, Pete continued to meet Corinne for meals inside the dining hall. They talked on the phone and hung out in each other's rooms like they always had. He was the most relaxed and carefree she had ever seen him. His mind, empty of relationship woes, must have been the reason.

Corinne was pleased, figuring she did the right thing by containing her feelings. Now his final days at Stepney Green could be his best.

And they were.

18

Like a schoolboy playing hooky Pete skipped Wednesday's prayer group meeting without explanation, avoiding—and confusing—his former friend. Todd left a voicemail message that night, one that wasn't returned. Let him squirm like the weasel he is, Pete thought, at least for a while.

Lying in bed, he plotted to toy with Todd's mind a little differently than he did Brandi's. With him he would pretend as if nothing were wrong, like Saturday night never happened. And when he and Brandi compared notes, their brainwaves would crash onto a shore of utter perplexity, maybe even panic.

It was a most gratifying scenario. Pete could hear them now: "Todd, I'm telling you he knows about us," Brandi would state emphatically, detailing his frosty exchange Sunday morning. Then Todd, who experienced nothing unusual, would retort, "You're imagining things. No way does he know about us. You need to chill out, okay?" And she would come back with something like, "Don't tell me to chill out! I *know* what I saw. I didn't imagine anything." Pete snickered as he visualized their conversation escalating into a full-blown argument.

A pleasing thought before nodding off into dreamland…

Operation Buddy Todd launched the next day. Pete could hardly wait to activate his plan. All day long he prepared himself, writing a script in his mind. The difficult part was acting it out convincingly. He knew he could do it, though. He had confidence and inner strength now. With these, he could accomplish anything.

When poetry class ended at 4:30, Pete exited K.S.W. Hall and spied Todd in the distance. His lean and lofty so-called friend—sporting designer jeans, sunglasses, and a brown leather backpack—was on the concrete path heading back to his dorm. This was his chance.

Pete took a deep breath and trotted toward him, calling out his name in a jolly tone. Todd flinched and swung around. Standing rigidly, he didn't know what to expect: a punch across the jaw, a vengeful shove to the ground, maybe even a flight across campus.

Pete sensed his anxiety, which delighted him to no end. He just wished he could see through Todd's chic sunglasses to view the nervous pale blue swishing in his eyes. X-ray vision sure would come in handy right now.

"Hey, man, what's up? " said a seemingly sprightly Pete.

A quiet, wary "hey" uttered back to him.

"I got your message last night, bud. Sorry for not calling you back right away."

Todd paused in bewilderment. Pete was his usual friendly self—and he just apologized! No way would he have done that if he knew of the affair. Brandi must have imagined things on the way to the gym the other day. His pal wasn't the least bit hostile.

"No problem," said a relieved Todd. "I just wanted to make sure you were all right, that's all. It's not like you to miss prayer group."

It is now.

"I know, dude," said Pete, who then raised his eyebrows to convey excitement, "especially with you-know-who there."

Todd masked his guilt with a smile, but Pete saw right through his facial costume. He knew he was getting to him—and could hardly wait to deal the game's next hand.

"You know something, you really are a true friend," Pete said, trying not to gag. "I really mean it, Todd."

"Come on, stop it."

"No, I'm serious, man. I mean, look at all you've done for me, convincing me to ask out Brandi and everything. I don't think I'll ever be able to repay you for all your encouragement."

Todd sighed out an uneasy breath of hot air.

"Pete, come on, man, stop it already," he said.

No way. His guilt trip had just begun.

"Since when are you so modest?" said Pete. "The Todd I know would've been like 'I know I'm great, but carry on if you must.'"

Todd chuckled awkwardly.

"It really is an honor to be friends with *the* Todd Galloway, heir to the world-renowned hotel towers," Pete continued. "I still can't believe how someone like you would go out of his way to set me up with a girl like Brandi—me, some working-class guy from Woodlake Square. But then again you never made fun of where I came from. You're not one of those multimillionaires who look down on us poor folk, are you? No, of course not. Prayer group taught you that much at least."

And with a slight glare he added, "I'm sure you would never consider Woodlake Square a slum."

Maybe not but Brandi certainly did. According to her, not only was it a slum it was a *real* slum. Like Pete, Todd remembered her description all too well.

"Uh, listen, man, I better get going," he said, struggling to conceal his discomfort. "Glad you're feeling okay. I'll catch you later, okay?"

"Sure, *pal*," said Pete, sprinkling sarcasm into his term of endearment. "Have a good day, okay?"

"Yeah ... you, too, man."

He already did. Operation Buddy Todd was a smashing success. Soon he would disclose all to Brandi, who would then compare her encounter with his. She would surely grow mad, wondering why Pete was so warm and friendly to Todd and so cold and standoffish to her. It was all going according to plan.

This was one game he would win ... and deserved to win.

Pete avoided Brandi every chance he got. Whenever he saw her inside a lecture hall he ducked into a classroom. Outside he would run in the opposite direction, pretending he never noticed her. If she entered the gym to work out, he finished his exercise and left. At dinnertime he rushed past her cafeteria table without any eye contact whatsoever. And he never texted or called. No more movie dates, dinner invitations, or rollerblading jaunts—nothing.

But he socialized with Todd all the while, feigning the perfect friendship. Pete sensed this would drive her nuts.

And it did.

19

The following Thursday Brandi and Corinne attended their last social work lecture of the semester. As soon as it ended, the rotunda classroom inside MacLean Hall emptied of students—except for them.

"Corinne," Brandi called out, "do you have a minute?"

She had several actually, just not for her.

"Well, I—"

"It'll only take a moment," Brandi said, cutting her off.

"What is it?"

Brandi closed the door, not wanting their conversation to leak out into the hallway. When she did this Corinne's guard activated, sensing an intense tête-à-tête underway.

"I was wondering if you knew what was up with Pete."

"What do you mean?" Corinne replied, knowing full well what she meant.

"He doesn't talk to me anymore."

"Really?"

She did her best to feign ignorance, but Brandi wasn't convinced. If anyone on campus knew what was going on inside Pete's head, it was Corinne Aldrich.

"And he missed last night's prayer group meeting, the last one of the semester—his last one ever."

Corinne kept up the appearance of innocence.

"Oh?" she said. "That's not like him at all."

"Do you know why he missed the meeting?"

Corinne shrugged. Although she knew the reason, she wasn't about to get in the middle of the Galloway-Sparks-Webb triangle. She was in too deep already.

Brandi's eyes squinted in skepticism as she studied the girl in front of her, someone who definitely knew more than she claimed.

"You really have no idea, Corinne?"

"Sorry."

"Like hell you don't," Brandi snapped, her pinkish face reddening.

"Excuse me?"

"You heard me. Just cut the crap, okay?"

Her hostile voice bounced off the classroom's round walls and stung Corinne's eardrums like a fireball.

"Everyone knows you and Pete are like this," Brandi said, flicking crossed fingers between their faces.

Corinne was having none of this tirade.

"What he and I discuss is between us," she stated firmly. "If you want to know why he doesn't talk to you anymore, then why don't you ask him yourself?"

Brandi scowled. Probably to mask her cowardice, Corinne thought. No way would she ask Pete why. She already knew the answer: that she was a twofaced reptile who led him on while bedding his friend behind his back. Now she paid the consequences, something she probably never had to do before. She did not hold all the cards in this game. This time she was the one being dealt a tricky hand.

Corinne wondered why Brandi even cared. After all, Pete could never meet her precious standards, right?

That bitch.

Recalling that cruel comment charred away whatever patience Corinne had left. The usual tranquil blue in her Mediterranean eyes bludgeoned in outrage.

"Better yet, Brandi," she said, her tone uncharacteristically shrill and bitter, "why don't you just look in the mirror?"

Dead silence.

"I'm sure you'll find the answer there ... as if you didn't already know."

Corinne stormed out of the room, nearly unhinging the door as she flung it open. The heat of the moment had got the better of her. She knew she'd gone too far. Her slip of the tongue, though deliberate, could not be withdrawn. Still, part of her was glad it was out there. It had to be said. After all, Brandi herself was to blame.

Now she had irrefutable proof that Pete knew of her affair with Todd.

By dinnertime Corinne had calmed herself. It was a good thing she did, too. She needed to explain what happened after her social work class in the most composed manner possible. She wondered how Pete would take the news. Would he be furious? Would he interpret her exchange with Brandi as a betrayal of his confidence? She definitely hoped not. But as his best friend she had to tell him. She had to be honest.

And, like Brandi, she had to pay the consequences.

Pete arrived at their traditional corner table inside the sunroom with a cheerful smile. But it shaped into a concerned straight line as he sensed Corinne's tension.

"You all right?" he asked.

She looked down and moaned at her untouched spaghetti dinner.

"Come on, Corinne, the food can't be that bad."

"Pete, I have to tell you something."

"Sure, what is it?"

She begged him not to get angry, took in a deep breath and let it out slowly, after which she spilled everything.

"I'm so sorry," she said.

"Sorry?"

He burst into joyous laughter, leaving Corinne stunned. His reaction was totally not what she expected.

"You're not mad at me for what I said to Brandi?"

"Don't be silly," Pete said in between laughing spurts. "How could I possibly be mad over something so awesome?"

The final hand in his game with Brandi had been dealt. And the outcome couldn't have made him happier: he was truly the winner.

Corinne was utterly taken aback. Her best friend on campus had become so laidback, so content. He was enjoying his life, not taking it so seriously.

She wondered if he would react the same way if she twisted off the lid to her special jar, the one holding her true feelings. Would he be so happy-go-lucky then?

Maybe.

Or maybe not.

Whatever his reaction, she had to wait until after his graduation—which, in 16 days, wasn't too much longer.

20

Final exams were held all of next week, after which Brandi Sparks left campus. She never bid Pete goodbye or good luck, just as he expected. She just packed her things and left—in humiliation, he thought, an emotion she truly earned. He was glad to see the back of her and hoped he never saw her again. She hurt him in ways like no other woman had. He would never forget her for that.

Still, she taught him an awful lot, lessons he could utilize the rest of his life. He now knew not to rush into any romantic relationships. If by chance they crossed his way. That was how it was going to be from now on: ladies had to seek him out, not the other way around. It was their turn to do the courting now, to make the first move. Pete had had quite enough. Whenever he initiated these gestures he ended up in the doghouse.

Plus he liked his new relaxed, easygoing self. He wanted some time to get to know him better. Ironically, these qualities reminded him of Todd.

The hotel heir was due to leave campus Saturday, the day after his lover returned to her Mantoloking mansion on the shore. Pete wondered if his supposed pal would ever confess his treason. Most likely not because it would take a lot of guts—and Todd had none to spare. Pete knew it since the day he launched his master plan. His "buddy" didn't even mention Brandi's name nor could he afterwards. The shame and guilt, gnawing away his usual cool self-assurance, would overpower him.

Pete never mentioned Brandi to him after that day either. He wanted Todd to think about why. So much so his stomach would churn.

And it did.

A scent of truth began to linger in Brandi's suspicions. She could be right after all; Pete may actually know of the affair. The clues were adding up: ignoring Brandi, the friendship praises, skipping prayer group. And who could forget what Corinne said inside MacLean Hall last week. The case definitely closed after that. Pete knew full well what was going on behind his back—and played them both for fools. The tables had been turned.

Todd knew he deserved this. He had betrayed his pal in the worst possible way. But Brandi was downright irresistible. Even though he encouraged her to date Pete, she never stopped flirting with him. She danced that seductive smile every chance she got. And flaunting her tits on that killer body ... what man could resist? Not him, that was for damn sure.

Todd realized he probably lost a friendship, a good friendship, over this. Still, he had to try and salvage it. No better time than now, the night before heading home to Upper Saddle River—and Pete's final RA duty shift. It was 10 p.m., a good time to call him. He made no rounds this hour. Todd reached for his phone on the desk and carried it to bed, where he sat tensely upright. Exhaling an uneasy breath, he called Pete.

"Hello?"

"Hey, it's me," said Todd, cautiously. "Just wanted to say goodbye before leaving tomorrow."

How big of you.

"And I hope we stay in touch after your graduation."

Pete wanted to say not to count on it but instead uttered, in a deliberately dispassionate tone, "Sure, whatever, man."

Clearly he couldn't care less about keeping in touch with the likes of Todd Galloway, especially now. He admitted no wrongdoing whatsoever, not even over the phone. Instead of heading over to Rockford Hall to face him like a man, he cringed in the safety of his locked bedroom. Coward! No apology for screwing Brandi behind his back. Not even one for standing by as she mocked his neighborhood and working-class roots. That was it, Todd's last chance to come clean. And he blew it.

Corinne wasn't surprised but was glad nonetheless. Her friend could truly move on with his life. Never would he have to set eyes on those two people again. He could let go of all the hurt they caused. Finally, there was closure.

But Pete reflected on this betrayal and more during Senior Week. While other graduating students partied in New York and elsewhere, he stayed put on campus. He chose instead to walk the grounds, taking in the green of spring. The emerald grass reminded him of the Yorkshire Dales he had seen in a travel brochure, the one displaying northern England's magnificent hillside. The college's greenery, including the towering pines, created a picture-perfect campus. Indeed, Stepney Green should be showcased in a brochure as well.

He had learned so much here, in addition to academics. He learned life, experiences that had shaped him into a man. This place made him strong. And this was a good thing. For this kind of education no price was too high to pay.

21

Now it was time to leave. Saturday had arrived. No coming back in late August. The world of opportunity lay just outside the gates—along with Miss Right hopefully. She certainly wasn't here. Dana, Liz and Brandi were anything but right for him. Neither was Woodlake Square. Though grateful to have a home there, Pete longed to settle elsewhere, where bigger and better things lay within his grasp. In a few hours, with college degree in hand, he could begin steering in that direction.

First things first, though. There was a graduation ceremony to get through. No problem on a day like this. The weather was absolutely perfect: a cloudless blue sky, sunshine, warmth, and no humidity. Definitely not too hot to flaunt navy caps and gowns outside.

Or dresses. Rae Jacobson was relieved. No sweat had blotted her orange two-piece suit with matching hat—big enough to shade three people. Nor did it drench her dyed jet-black hair, whose short strands had been fastidiously brushed and sprayed. But her caked-on makeup, faultlessly applied, pleased her most. No way would it melt in this kind of weather. Her aristocratic hand fan could stay tucked inside her black faux-leather purse. Pete got such a kick out of his 55-year-old "aunt" who always dressed to the nines, and then some.

His mother Janice dressed more comfortably, in a long white cottony gown with subtle turquoise flower prints. Rae liked this dress on her most. Janice's long auburn hair draping against it produced an elegant contrast with the garment's patchy aqua.

Their attire was the last thing on Pete's mind. He was just glad to see them in the stadium bleachers—along with Corinne, who sported a simple, but charming, yellow outfit. Her RA obligations had kept her on campus during Senior Week. But later today, after all graduates check out of their rooms, she would head home to Long Island. Even if she weren't a resident assistant, she would be here right now. Nothing could keep her from witnessing her special friend's magical moment—receiving his bachelor-of-arts degree with highest honors, something for which he worked so damn hard.

Corinne could not have been more proud. Pete epitomized the essence of accomplishment, having achieved success under incredible odds: raised in a one-parent household in a low-income neighborhood; working all those jobs to pay for community college; and all that studying to earn and renew his transfer scholarship.

Everything paid off in the end. Now look at him.

Pete's face beamed in laurels as he shook hands with the college president, who then handed over his prized B.A. degree. And when he rushed to his loved ones in the bleachers after the ceremony, his joy surpassed even that.

He embraced them all warmly.

"This is just the coolest," he said, smiling more radiantly than the sun. "My three favorite ladies, all here."

"Honey, we wouldn't miss this for anything," said Rae.

"Congratulations, son," Janice said as a tiny tear of happiness trickled down her cheek. "I'm very proud of you."

"Well, I'm proud to be your son."

Corinne looked on with an admiring smile. Pete had always spoken highly of his mother and how close they were. Never was this more apparent than on this day, the first she met Mrs. Webb—and secretly hoped that more interactions would come. She was a very warm person, Corinne noted, kind and friendly. Pete was fortunate to have had these traits passed on to him. And he possessed strength, another trait he most likely inherited ... but only recently discovered.

With these attributes he turned to his best friend.

"Well, Corinne, this is it."

"Yes, but remember it's not goodbye."

"Definitely not," he concurred.

Janice glanced at Rae, telling her telepathically what a wonderful couple this young lady and he made. Rae's smile said the same.

So did Corinne's.

Pete's, on the other hand, didn't. To him Miss Right was not to be found here, only strength and wisdom, which now he had. He vowed to carry these qualities into the future horizon, which could only brighten. The rest of his college experiences, namely the heartbreaking memories, would stay inside the Stepney Green diary. Tucking it high on a shelf, he promised never to open it.

But that would prove impossible.

22

Getting up early was going to be quite an adjustment—but well worth it. Life back in Woodlake Square had started off on a good note. Full-time job opportunities landed on Pete's lap in record time, often within 24 hours of interviewing. Indeed, a degree from Stepney Green worked miracles. Newspapers across the state sought his English-grammar and communication skills, verified by the esteemed college. But one job offer stood out the most. It was for a copyeditor at *Jersey News Central*, a highly reputable newspaper in the heart of downtown Trenton.

"Central" not only denoted its geography within the state, it signified an information hub where news from across the region disseminated. It also represented a balanced weight on the political scale. *Jersey News Central* endorsed no candidates running for public office, ever. The paper's motto: both sides of the story. All political articles contained an equal share of pros and cons. No bias was permitted.

Pete admired this motto and was eager to start working here, though he wasn't hired to copyedit the politics section. Entertainment was his department. Though not an on-the-field reporter, his job was exciting nonetheless. And it ranked high in importance. Correcting and editing articles on the world of showbiz, he ensured the works contained no errors, factual or grammatical. The position, he thought, perfectly complemented his part-time job at the movie theater, a job he continued to work after graduation. He still enjoyed watching movies for free—except romantic comedies. He stayed away from those at all costs. No way would he allow them to instill any more false hope. The kind of love those films displayed reflected anything but real life.

But his new job did—along with his alarm clock's irritating beeps at 4:45 a.m. Pete sighed as he reached to his nightstand to shut it off. After a wide and loud yawn, he sat up in his twin-sized bed and glanced around his rectangular bedroom. Such a tiny room, even smaller than the one he occupied at Rockford Hall. Still, it was his, his own private haven, an escape from the brotherly bothers elsewhere in the house. He could do anything he wanted within these four walls. And now that he graduated from college this was truer than ever. No more schoolwork. The miniature wooden desk in the corner could now be used leisurely, perhaps for creative writing projects. Fortunately, his laptop easily fit on the diminutive desktop.

Pushing back the lightweight blanket, a seminude Pete stumbled out of bed and opened his closet across the narrow floor. He took out a sky-blue dress shirt, black pants, and one of his new ties he had bought over the weekend. Having shaved and showered last night, he rolled on some deodorant and dressed himself right away.

Afterwards, he approached the window behind the nightstand. Staring at the predawn sky outside, he thought about the day ahead, wishing all to go well. This was it, a new start, the beginning of the rest of his life—one that, hopefully, would not include this demoralizing view much longer. His window overlooked a bleak back road, often mistaken as an alley. Its bordering boxed-in backyards had produced a foul décor. Chips of house brick, decrepit toys, junk, trash—and God only knew what else—piled messily into shameful outdoor furnishings.

"Welcome home, Pete," he said to himself, good-humoredly.

At least it was dark outside. Woodlake Square's lovely litter still hovered under the nighttime tarp of darkness. But it wasn't invisible. Some junk piles glistened off the amber streetlamps, while other unsightly heaps displayed a speckled lightshow, courtesy of back porchlights left on throughout the night.

This sure isn't Stepney Green College.

He had that right, and was glad. Though he could do without the horrid landscape, Woodlake Square definitely felt more like home. It was rough but warm. His neighbors may have had their issues, but they were always there for each other in the long run. Rae Jacobson certainly was for the Webb family. All in all, community spirit flourished in the multiethnic Square, but at a price: privacy. Everyone pretty much knew each other's business, but this was inevitable in a clustered community of slender townhouses.

A gentle knock at the door interrupted his train of thought.

"Peter, it's Mom."

"Come in," he said, turning away from the window.

Janice, dressed for work, entered with a proud smile. This was her baby boy's first big day at his first big job.

"My, don't you look handsome," she said.

"Thanks, Mom."

"Wish I looked as good so early in the morning."

"Of course you do," said Pete, reciprocating the compliment.

As he observed more closely, however, he realized he had stretched his words. His mother certainly had aged beyond her 47 years. But not without good reason, and Pete could think of no better one than working hard to make ends meet. In time he hoped she could quit her part-time job at the bar. His salary from *Jersey News Central* would more than replenish that income to pay the extra bills. Then Mom could rest, really rest, all day long if she wanted, on the weekends.

Pete was already contributing to the bills, donating hefty portions of the paychecks he received from the movie theater. Not that they were substantial. Still, he gave what he could, and Janice was ever so grateful—and proud. She never asked him for any money, not a dime, but his generous heart gave anyway.

She only wished Adam could be as charitable.

So did Pete. His brother's freeloading had really got to him this summer. And that was what he did—freeload—no matter how many times their mother said otherwise. As Pete labored long nighttime hours at the Trenton cinema, Adam and his pig of a girlfriend barhopped across the river in Philly. Daytime was no better. The youngest Webb child prepared résumés and went on job interviews during these hours, completing household chores all the while so his mother could rest after a hard day's work. The eldest, on the other hand, spent his mornings and afternoons sleeping off hangovers, often with Belinda Price slobbered by his side. How pathetic.

No wonder Woodlake Square had the reputation it did. Belinda and his brother blended in quite well with all the trash lying around.

Janice hated when he said these kinds of things. Still, part of her agreed with his assessment. She would never admit it, though, and didn't have to. Pete could read his mother's heartache in her saddened dark-brown eyes. But she was in such a good mood this morning. Now was not the time to get into the Adam mess.

"Off to work now?" said Pete, noticing the time edging closer to 5:30 a.m.

"I am, but I had to come by to wish you well one last time."

"Thanks, Mom," he said, followed by a yawn. "Gosh, I hope I can get used to getting up so early."

"Oh, you will soon enough," said Janice. "At least you can sleep in a little more than I can."

This was true.

"By the way," she added, "your friend Todd called again last night."

Friend? I don't think so!

"Did you get the message I left for you?"

He did but tossed it in the garbage can as soon as he got home from the cinema. Last night's shift was exhausting, and Pete didn't want to add to his fatigue by dealing with the likes of Todd Galloway. Not last night, not today, and probably not ever. He knew what he wanted—a resumption of their friendship—but that was out of the question.

He also knew that Todd realized his number had been blocked on his former pal's mobile phone. Obviously he was trying to reach him via the Webb landline, which Janice insisted on keeping during technology's ever-changing evolution. It was Todd's last resort, as Pete had no social media account and never replied to any of his emails.

"Anyway," said Pete, eager to drop the Galloway subject, "have a nice day at work."

Janice's proud smile returned as she wished him the same. She then stepped out of his room and into her own, where she retrieved her purse. Strange, her son thought, that she kept it inside her bedroom nightstand. There used to be a place for it inside the closet downstairs, on a nail next to the pole. The nail was still there, though. So then why was her purse no longer ringed around it? Even more mysterious was the indoor-outdoor knob on her bedroom door. Pete noticed it the day he moved back home but said nothing to his mother. She was just too happy on graduation day. Still, he wanted to know why this lock was installed. Mom of all people shouldn't have to key into her own room in her own house. Something must have happened while he was away at college this spring; that much was clear.

Okay, brother of mine, what did you do this time?

After a hearty breakfast of eggs, sausage, toast, and orange juice, Pete brushed his teeth and turned on the living room's 26" TV. The flat-panel television, which Janice had purchased used, was getting up there in age, much like the rest of the house fixtures. But it kept on kicking, bless it. Janice almost didn't go through with the digital upgrade; paying a cable bill, another monthly expense, was the last thing she needed. But with the end of analog, it was either upgrade or no television at all.

The traffic and weather report aired first thing on the 6 o'clock morning news. Pete sighed as he heard the three dreaded Hs: hazy, hot and humid. With no air conditioning in his car he figured he was in for a steamy commute. But if he left early enough, under a non-blazing sun, he could avoid those nasty sweat drips. Better to have them after work than before, he realized, especially today. Meeting new people, it would be a day of first impressions. Pete was determined to convey one of professionalism. A neat, non-sweaty appearance would help him do just that.

Adam's appearance was anything but as he staggered into the house all of a sudden. Naturally Belinda Price was by his side—and she looked no better. It didn't take a genius to figure out where they'd been all night. Once again the city of Philadelphia had those two to thank for keeping alive its nightlife.

When will you ever grow up, Pete wanted to tell his brother. But it would do no good, especially in his drunken state.

Although inebriated, Adam was well aware of who was in the vicinity ... all dressed up. Daggers of envy zapped out of his whirling green eyes. He could not hold them back, despite his best efforts.

"Well, well, well, what have we here?" he said, spraying liquor fumes into the petite living room. "Sweet Pete's all decked out in his Sunday best on a Monday morning."

Here we go again.

"If Mommy could see her little angel now ... big man on campus all ready for his big-shot newspaper job."

His tone was deliberately sarcastic. Pete knew it all too well, having been on its receiving end more times than he could count. Odd, though, that Adam's mocking occurred more frequently the older they grew. He had thought just the opposite would happen. Then again this was his brother, a man who really never matured.

And how could he with the Belinda beast constantly clinging to him. As usual she found her boyfriend's belittling remarks highly amusing. Burying her cackling snout into his shoulder, she at least spared Pete the putrid full-front view of herself: a flabby physique coated in bar sweat and morning dew. Why on earth, he wondered, did she wear tube tops that exposed such nasty midriff ripples? Did she want all of Woodlake Square to know she had more rolls than the corner bakery? Whatever her reason, Pete was grateful for the limited view. After all, he had just finished his breakfast. To keep it down he resisted guessing the contents a snorting Belinda could be leaving on Adam's shirt.

Ignore them. Ignore, ignore, ignore.

Determined not to dignify his brother's juvenile comments with a response, Pete did just what the voice inside him told him to do.

"What's this?" said Adam, feigning over-the-top surprise. "The high-and-mighty graduate from Stepney Green College is speechless? Say it ain't so!"

Pete remained silent—unlike Belinda, whose obnoxious giggles deflected off her boyfriend's snot-covered shoulder.

"All that college sure did you a lot of good, didn't it, Sweet Pete?"

Yes, as a matter of fact, it did. He learned how to be strong most of all, which was why he turned off the television, grabbed his backpack, and headed out the door.

Adam wasn't about to let him leave so easily.

"Too bad it didn't teach you how to get laid."

Pete braked at the threshold, his hand so filled with raging adrenaline he could crush the metal doorknob with a single squeeze.

Damn him.

He knew just the button to press. He also knew which one triggered Janice's emotions. But unlike her, Pete refused to demonstrate its effect. He remained straight faced, focused, and most importantly, tightlipped. Adam wanted him to react, he realized. He wanted to dig under his skin using a razor-sharp shovel.

It wasn't about to happen, not with the tough epidermis Pete had formed during his final weeks of college. So instead of slamming the door on Adam and Belinda's faces he simply closed it. Trash like them, he concluded, wasn't worth the effort.

Outside, he released his tension in the form of a protracted exhale. It had been quite a day so far. And it was only 6:10 a.m.

23

Normal work hours ran Monday through Friday from 7 a.m. to 4 p.m., with an hour-long lunch break. Today, however, Pete would arrive extra early for orientation—and to get away from Adam and the Belinda beast.

His supervisor had warned during the interview that "normal" work hours applied only on "smooth-sailing" days, ones when the paper could be "put to bed" by 4 p.m. Asked how he felt about mandatory overtime, time for which he would not be financially compensated, Pete had responded with an emphatic, "Not a problem."

Managing editor Vito Caparelli not only liked this reply he liked how he said it. It came across as both relaxed and sincere, along with all his other answers. Two very important qualities in this line of work, essential for a highly reputable newspaper like *Jersey News Central*. His mind had pretty much settled after this interview. Peter Michael Webb, who was polite, flexible and hardworking—evidenced by his employment history and graduating with highest honors from Stepney Green College—was the best candidate for the job. To Vito's delight he accepted the offer.

The job seemed to have everything Pete was looking for: editing for an esteemed publication close to home; an excellent benefits package, including healthcare and paid holidays; and a more-than-reasonable starting salary. The fact that he was no longer paid hourly tickled him. No more punching a time clock or jotting down work hours in a log. Now he was a salaried employee.

Pete also liked his supervisor. From the moment they met he insisted being called by his first name. "Mr. Caparelli" was too formal, Vito explained, and made him sound much older than his 36 years. With a rapidly balding head and ever-expanding Italian waistline, he said he needed no help accelerating his age. His candor—and the way his brown eyes energized as he spoke—made Pete want to laugh. Vito sure did tell it like it is, he thought. And he respected him for this.

Orientation lasted a little more than three hours. Pete was glad when it ended. Never in his life had he filled out so many documents. Tax forms, emergency contact information, a media ethics affidavit, to name just a few. He also had to watch a lengthy documentary on what is expected from *JNC* employees. But he loved collecting his badge afterwards. He felt like a true employee, an official staff member of a remarkable newspaper.

After orientation he knocked on Vito's door.

"Hello, it's only me."

He was hesitant to say even this. His supervisor's office looked like the remnants of a New Year's Eve confetti bomb. Piles upon piles of papers and files lay scattered on his desk and floor. Above them, large windows, tinted just enough to block out the sun's sweltering rays. Somehow a three-story cart managed to fit itself in the office corner. Its top shelf held an enormous coffee pot and two small bowls, one containing sugar packets and the other, creamers. Two large coffee cans rested below, along with filters, stirring straws, napkins, even a box of doughnuts. The cart's bottom shelf, Pete noticed, housed columns of paper cups plus the tallest and widest travel mug he had ever seen.

"Hey, guy!" Vito said perkily, a greeting obviously of high caffeine consumption.

As he rose and scuttled over to greet his new employee, Pete contemplated the meaning behind his jovial tone. Was he glad to see him or relieved to take a break from all the paperwork? Perhaps a little of both.

"Welcome to my pig pen," Vito said with a natural, good-humored smile.

Pete returned the gesture as he replied, "Well, thanks for inviting me."

This produced a hearty laugh from his boss.

"Dude," he said, shaking his new employee's hand vigorously, "you're going to blend in just fine here."

Dude? Pete found this quite amusing coming from a suited 36-year-old man—and his superior. Still, he welcomed the term of endearment. It softened the first-day-of-work butterfly flaps in his stomach. It also provided the perfect pick-me-up. Vito's warm, witty greeting was just what he needed after the Adam episode.

He relaxed even more as the morning evolved. Instead of getting to work right away Pete spent the remaining a.m. hours in his supervisor's office. They did not talk shop. Vito simply wanted to get to know his new employee better. Chatting with him like an old friend, he conveyed a sense of approachability. Pete appreciated this and was amazed at how well they seemed to be connecting. Somehow the conversation shifted to children. Vito asked if he had any.

Kids? I can't even get a girlfriend!

Adam had made that fact gallingly clear this morning.

Pete decided to keep his dating status to himself, answering instead with a direct, "No, do you?"

Vito and his wife of nine years, Carla, had three: a 4-year-old son and identical twin daughters, born seven months ago.

"Wow, that's awesome," said Pete, figuring the adjective was safe enough to say after the "guy" and "dude" uttered by his boss. "I bet they keep you hopping."

They certainly did, including most of last night.

"Needless to say," Vito continued, grabbing the humongous travel mug off the cart, "this is what keeps me going around here."

He filled it to the rim with steaming coffee then held it up, as if toasting to good health.

"Especially today," he said most proudly.

Pete chuckled as he watched the overtired father of three guzzle several long sips.

"Oh, I'm sorry, man," Vito said afterwards. "Can I offer you some?"

"No, thanks, I'm fine."

You probably need it more than I do!

Besides, Pete was not a coffee drinker. He preferred tea but only drank it occasionally. With so many new things going on, today wasn't one of those days. He was wired enough already.

"Anyway, bud," said Vito, stepping around folder and paper piles while circling the office, "I apologize for the mess in here. It's not normally like this, believe me."

"Not a problem."

Impressed, Vito cracked a smile. Whether he knew it or not, Pete had just uttered the same reply during his interview. His tone was also the same: relaxed and sincere.

And it resonated in his offer to help.

"Is there something I can do? Sorting? Filing?"

The managing editor shook his head—in amazement. He could not get over how genuine this young man was. Such a rarity in today's world. And Vito knew a lot about this world. After all, his paper reported on it daily. Plus he considered himself an excellent judge of character, and this Webb guy was definitely unique.

"You're one of the good ones, man," he said matter-of-factly. "We need more people like you in this office, that's for sure."

Wow, what a cool thing to say.

"Thanks."

"No," said Vito, "thank *you*."

He extended his hand, and Pete shook it meaningfully. Both men couldn't help but think a sound working relationship was underway.

And maybe even a friendship.

24

A public library sat alongside the main road home, a mere two blocks from *JNC* headquarters. Pete decided to walk there after work, which turned out to be a "normal" day. He could have driven, but with no air conditioning inside his car the three dreaded Hs would still make him sweat. Besides, walking was good exercise. Nevertheless he was glad to enter the air-conditioned library when he did. The hazy, hot and humid weather—with no thanks to a relentless sun overhead—would have roasted him to a breathless crisp.

Inside, he dashed to the computers. He could hardly wait to email Corinne about his first day at his new job. He could have easily done so via his mobile phone, but after this morning, he was in no hurry to get home.

Pete wished he could tell Corinne about his experience at *JNC* in person, but that wasn't possible. As glad as he was to have graduated, part of him longed for a meal with his best friend back at the college. Describing his workday at their traditional corner table inside the dining hall's sunroom would have made the ideal meeting place. But this computer terminal had to do.

He considered calling her, which he did numerous times already this summer. He just felt uncomfortable cutting short the conversation, sometimes after only a few minutes. Corinne didn't mind in the slightest. Even though she had unlimited minutes on her wireless plan, she was well aware the Webb budget was a whole lot tighter than hers. But most importantly—and unbeknownst to Pete—she relished hearing his voice, no matter how long, or short, the conversation lasted.

In his email Pete described his fantastic first day at *Jersey News Central*: how cool his supervisor was; the staff's warm welcome; and how much fun he had editing his first article—after, of course, helping Vito organize the mounds of paperwork inside his office.

He also mentioned Todd's phone message last night. He thought he'd heard the last from him after final exams but apparently not. Pete asked his best friend for her opinion. What would she do in his position? Continue to ignore the messages or call him back? And if the latter, what should he say?

He would find out soon enough, all on his own.

25

A classy sports car in Woodlake Square? Yes, it was, Pete realized as he parallel-parked behind it outside the Webb townhouse. He did not know its manufacturer, much less its model. Living in the Square all these years, he never really paid attention to car brands. As long as it ran and got him where he needed to go, that was the important thing. Still, whoever owned this radiant red beauty better have a good insurance provider. No telling what could happen to it in this neighborhood. It definitely stood out from the other vehicles around, including his. Pete chuckled as he recalled a similar situation at Stepney Green College. His white compact car, in all its rusty glory, throbbed like an eyesore in the student parking lot. But here it blended in quite well.

Pete got out of his car, secured it, flung his backpack over his shoulder, and lumbered to the front door. He was practically panting. Despite taking off his tie and unbuttoning the top buttons of his shirt, the three dreaded Hs had made his commute home excruciating. Trenton's snail-paced rush-hour traffic was to blame. No breeze had entered his car, only stagnant air. One of these days he would get a brand new car with air conditioning, definitely by next summer. Also by then, if not sooner, he could finally afford to upgrade his wireless phone plan, with unlimited minutes and messaging.

Cool air refreshed his body as he entered the front door. It felt positively sensational. What a relief to have on the air conditioner. So rare, as his penny-wise mother only turned it on when absolutely necessary. He could understand her frugal nature, needless to say, given her limited income.

Blind Expectations

"Hi, son," Janice said cheerfully, entering the living room from the kitchen.

When she embraced him he apologized for his sweaty state. But at least he was cooling down now.

"I'm so glad you turned on the a/c," he said, taking off his backpack. "I felt like I was driving through the center of the earth … in an oven."

Janice cracked a smile and asked how his first day went.

"Awesome," he replied. "It was just—"

"Honey, don't you dare start without me," said Rae, exiting the kitchen with a proud smile.

She kissed his cheek, but only barely. Pete knew the reason: she did not want to smudge her rosy-red lipstick, something she applied meticulously. Even in this dreadful heat, Aunt Rae, for whatever reason, felt the need to dress up, to keep up some sort of glamorous appearance. He and Janice found this amusing more than anything. They never doubted Rae's love for them, not for a moment. She may prefer air kisses and hugs that didn't wrinkle her apparel, but her heart was golden.

"And don't start without me either."

Pete could not believe his ears—or eyes—as Todd Galloway followed Aunt Rae into the living room. Suddenly the air conditioning became less cool.

"What are you doing here?"

His tone was not exactly friendly. But it wasn't rude, either. Stunned was more like it.

"I came to see you, of course," Todd answered, curiously upbeat.

Why? What the hell for?

Pete stood in silence, a quiet that bore tension. Janice and Rae picked up on it instantly. So did Todd, who actually felt it seeping into his skin.

"So, Pete," he said, anxious for a distraction, "your mother tells me you work for *Jersey News Central*."

"Uh-huh."

"And today was your very first day on the job."

"Uh-huh."

This time the utterance carried a warning: stop this charade *now*. Todd had no right to be here, and he damn well knew it. Not after the Brandi disaster. How could he carry on as if nothing ever happened—and in front of his mother! Pete could just imagine how his former friend charmed his way into the Webb home. "You're his mother?" Mr. Smooth Talker would begin. "No, you can't be. That's impossible. You're so fit!" Of course, he would overlook all the wrinkles in her face. The compliment farce would continue by telling her what a lovely home she had and what a great job she did raising a nice guy like Pete. And to top it off, how grateful he was for his friendship.

The feeling was mutual ... once upon a time.

Rae nodded at Janice, letting her know she would clear the room's friction.

"Pete, honey," she said, starry eyed, "you never told us your friend was Todd *Galloway* of the Galloway Hotel Towers."

"That's right, I didn't," he said, and with a steely glance toward the man in question, added, "Obviously it wasn't that big a deal to me."

Rae's idea barely got underway before it backfired. So Janice, with honesty as her policy, took her turn.

"All right, Peter," she said firmly. "There's obviously something wrong here. I thought you'd be happy to see your friend from college. Clearly you aren't."

You got that right. And for the last time he is not my friend.

"So I'm going back to the kitchen so you two can clear up your little misunderstanding."

Little misunderstanding? This was the last thing he needed today. The number of events kept mounting, even now into the evening hours. Adam's smart-ass remarks; starting a new job; meeting fellow employees; the stifling drive home; now this.

Rae bid everyone goodbye. She had to get home herself. Part of her wanted to stay, though, the part that relished in juicy gossip. Yes, darn it, she loved every bit of tittle-tattle that simmered in the Square. And what was brewing here could very well boil into classic tabloid fodder! Too bad she had to miss it.

"It was nice to meet you, Todd," she said, shaking his hand excitedly, believing he was the closest thing to a celebrity she would ever encounter.

"Same here."

Leaving was the right thing to do, Rae concluded. Whatever happened between Pete and his friend was none of her business. Still, Janice may dish the dirt later. The sooner she left, the sooner she could get the lowdown.

"And honey," she said to Pete at the door, "I'll find out how everything went later ... your first day at work, of course."

Nice save, she told herself on the way outside. At least to her it was. The Webb family knew better, as did anyone else who was close to Rae Jacobson. Even with a treasure of a heart she couldn't resist sinking her teeth into a luscious gossip sandwich.

Janice flashed a cast-iron glance at her son before exiting into the kitchen. The look on her face was clear: he had better behave himself. Todd, no matter what, was still a guest in their home.

Maybe to you he is.

The living room now theirs, Pete asked the "guest" how he found out where he lived.

"You're the only Webb's in Woodlake Square," Todd explained. "I got your address off the Net. And your home phone number, too. For some reason I couldn't reach you on your cell. I called and texted but never heard anything."

Gee, I wonder why. Could it be because you're blocked?

Pete approached the window and pulled open the curtain, revealing the red sports car outside.

"It's pretty risky driving something like that in this neighborhood," he said. "Don't you think?"

"What do you mean?"

"I mean, driving a fancy sports car in a slum," he answered, releasing the curtain. "And not just any slum, a real slum."

Todd's head sunk in disgrace.

"I'm sorry, man," he said, recalling Brandi's not-so-flattering description of Woodlake Square.

"Damn right you are."

Todd looked backed up at the alien face in front of him, so cold and stern, and with eyes blistering in contempt. He longed for the familiar expression—the friendly, smiling one—that had greeted him on campus. But it was long gone.

"You could've defended me, you know," Pete continued. "But you didn't. You said nothing. Instead you stood there and laughed—you laughed at me! And you call yourself my friend?!"

The guest of dishonor turned away. The guilt was unbearable.

It was about to get even worse.

"I heard everything that night," Pete revealed with great pleasure. "I stood right outside your door and heard it all."

Todd froze in shamefaced silence.

"So, *pal*, tell me, how did it feel banging Brandi behind my back?"

He did not answer. He couldn't, even if he had tried.

"Did you enjoy it, Todd? Huh? And did you enjoy cheering me on all the while? Telling me how impressed she was, how much she liked me?"

Again, silence.

"Yes, of course you did," Pete answered for him. "And you want to know why? I'll tell you why: because you're a liar … and a coward."

Todd's pale blue eyes began to water, but nothing leaked out. He stopped it just in time. The guilt escaped down his throat instead, in a gulp of bitter saliva. Turning to Pete, he again apologized. What he did was wrong, he said. He didn't expect to fall for Brandi himself. He'd wanted to come clean before but needed time to think of the best way how.

Pete was far from impressed.

"You're breaking my heart," he said without a trace of sincerity.

"Come on, man, can't we be friends again?"

"No."

"Why not?"

"It's just not possible," Pete told him. "In order to have a friendship there must be trust."

And it was gone. Forever. It would never return. Their friendship could never be what it was.

"How you can possibly think otherwise boggles my mind," Pete added. "Everything's changed … everything."

"So I drove all this way—halfway down the state—for nothing?"

"No, not really," Pete said, opening the front door. "Kicking your fake sorry ass out of here is worth a lot to me."

Todd took a moment to collect his thoughts. Only until now, this very moment, did he realize the severity of his actions. The incident with Brandi was one thing he could not laugh off. For the first time in his life his charm and charisma had failed him. He couldn't spread them, no matter how thickly, to smooth things over. A friendship, a good friendship, had truly ended. And it was his fault.

With a somber downward gaze Todd slowly made his way to the threshold. As soon as he crossed it the door crashed shut behind him. It was the most thunderous slam he had ever heard. And it carried an unmistakable warning: do not come back.

Back inside, Janice stormed into the living room. She demanded to know what that door slam was all about. Pete wasn't about to go there. He had quite enough for one day. All he wanted to do now was hop into the shower. The confrontation with their "guest" had left him with a soaring body temperature. The air conditioning may as well have been turned off for all the good it did keeping him cool.

Pete picked up his backpack and headed upstairs.

"I'm waiting for an answer to my question, young man," Janice said, irked.

Her son paused midway up the steps. He then shut his eyes and sighed. The hot breath he let out reeked in utter exhaustion. He was just too tired to get into all this now. The explanation had a long history attached to it—a history that, at this time, required a sizeable trim. So Pete decided to put his editing skills to use here at home. Janice would indeed find this version short, but not so sweet.

Opening his eyes, he shot a glance over the banister.

"All you need to know, Mom, is that Todd Galloway is not my friend," he said. "He's not the nice guy you think he is."

"He's not?"

Pete shook his head weakly.

"And did I ever find out the hard way."

26

Corinne sure did miss her best friend on campus. Stepney Green just wasn't the same without him. Two months into the fall semester, however, she felt differently. The reason: homecoming. The second Saturday of October had finally arrived. And Pete was due to visit.

She could barely contain her excitement. She had to force herself to eat all week, as lovesick jitters kept filling her stomach. This month marked one-third of a year since she last set eyes on him. Pete was just too busy to get together this summer, he had said. Working two jobs—one full time, the other part time—took up virtually all his time. Corinne respected him for working so hard but thought of another reason behind his hectic schedule: the more he worked, the more he avoided dating. She knew how hurt he'd been, how badly he was treated. She also knew that she could change all that—if he gave her a chance.

Convincing him just to come here was a big step. It took a lot of work. He did not want to step foot on campus soil again. Too many hurtful memories would surface. But he had vowed to be strong. He shouldn't let those recollections bring him down, she stressed. The good ones should triumph. She reiterated their talk about choosing to sink or swim—and how the latter was essential. In the end Pete agreed. But Corinne also had to insert the key of compromise—he did not have to come up for the football game and parade; arriving later, after sundown, would suffice. No chance of running into Todd or Brandi then. No witnessing the two walking hand in hand outside during the festivities, a gesture they now proudly displayed around campus. In addition, the pair resided in Blake Hall, a separate dormitory from Whitman, where Corinne now lived.

Pete agreed to spend the night in her room. It would be like old times, he thought, ones when they talked and laughed the time away. But for Corinne it represented the chance for which she'd long been waiting: to finally make her move. Yes, homecoming night was going to be *the* night.

She had waited a long time for this, four months to be exact. Back home in Long Island for the summer, her parents wondered about the guy who called so frequently—and whom their daughter called, too. So did Corinne's three younger sisters. Whoever he was he had to be someone special. She was quite particular about whom she pursued.

A number of admirers, she found, were only after one thing: sex. Although Pete wasn't an admirer—yet, she hoped—he definitely stood out from those other guys. With his handsome looks he could have traveled that route had he wanted. But his heart constructed a roadblock. It would not allow him to pass, to venture the path that hurt innocent young women. That, she realized, was what made him so special. His heart was genuine. There was nothing phony in his words or actions. Sincerity, coupled with strength, resonated throughout his being. He had become the perfect man to love. And Corinne was ready to let him know just that.

Pete would make the ideal boyfriend to bring home. His politeness and respect toward others would win over her parents in no time. And she was eager to impress them. The eldest of four daughters, she felt tremendous pressure to succeed. Her sisters would always look up to her, they had said. She had to set a good example. And not just by getting a college education at Stepney Green. Dating the right kind of man would impact them as well. He should be someone her sisters would admire. He should possess decent qualities, ones to seek in their own romantic relationships.

Corinne accepted this duty rightfully. She loved her sisters very much. And she wanted to make up for not carrying on the family business, Aldrich Enterprises. Though disappointed, her parents supported her social-work aspirations. They admired her desire to help those less fortunate. But most of all they wished their daughter to find true love and happiness.

Corinne believed Pete was the gentleman who could make this dream come true. Their times together at the college, and subsequent phone conversations, text messages and emails, revealed the most decent guy she had ever known. Now, finally, the time had come to show this wonderful person how special he was.

When the 7 o'clock hour arrived she began grooming herself. Sitting in front of the mirror, she applied her makeup, a little more heavily than usual. She was painstakingly precise. Looking her absolute best was vital tonight. Her mindset reflected that of someone preparing for a formal. But instead of a flashy gown she slipped on a more casual outfit, a cream-colored cottony dress that draped down to her knees. She fixed her hair afterwards, brushing out every knot, and ensuring every brown strand cascaded in perfect elegance. She wondered if Pete would like its new length, not that it was significant. It now extended past her shoulders instead of curling up just above them.

Spraying on her favorite perfume and inserting a breath mint, she waited patiently for her best friend's arrival. He was due any minute now.

Shortly after 9 p.m. a text message arrived. Pete was here, downstairs waiting to be let in. Corrinne could hardly believe it. All these months of waiting were over. She texted back, letting him know she would be right down. Before leaving, she glanced one last time at the mirror. This was it, she told herself. It was now or never.

Choosing the former, she strolled downstairs with a confident smile to greet her best friend—and hopefully, after tonight, her boyfriend.

Holding an overnight bag, Pete waited anxiously at the main door to Whitman Hall. Here, outside in the cool mountain air, he couldn't help but think of the time he picked up Brandi for their movie date. He was so different then, so misguided about love—and very naïve. But that lost little boy had found his way into manhood. Just coming here proved this. It took a lot of strength to drive up to Stepney Green. But he had gained this strength on this very soil. Therefore, he had nothing to fear during this visit. The good times on campus far outweighed the bad. Meeting Corinne, his best friend in the world, topped the list. She had done so much for him. Spending time with her was the least he could do to pay her back. He didn't want to let her down. It really had been ages since they last saw one another.

The door opened suddenly, revealing Corinne's angelic smile—and beauty.

What the...?

Pete froze in mesmerized shock. She looked amazing. He had never seen her so glamorous. More makeup, perfectly styled hair, and a sexy dress that revealed a knockout figure. Its off-white color, he noted, contrasted nicely with her Mediterranean blue eyes.

Corinne took his stunned silence as a good sign, that he must have liked what he saw. All that sprucing up was worth it.

"So do I get my hug or what?"

"Huh?" Pete said, coming out of his daze. "Oh, yeah, of course."

They embraced warmly, though her squeeze was noticeably tighter. It had been a long time since she last felt him in her arms. She didn't want to let go.

"It's so good to see you," she said, breaking away reluctantly.

"Same here."

And it was, it really was. Seeing her in person did not compare to email, texts, or telephone talk. Corinne agreed. She loved having her best friend on campus *on campus.*

They headed upstairs to her room, which she had left dimly lit. A 25-watt bulb emitted the room's only light, from a small lamp atop the dresser.

"Have a seat," she said to her special guest.

As Pete sat at the foot of the bed, Corinne pressed a button on her laptop, shuffling into action a handful of digital songs on the balladic playlist. She had selected them carefully, ones that undoubtedly reflected her amorous mood.

"So," she said, taking a seat on the bed's sunny yellow comforter, "how does it feel to be back?"

Despite the dimmed light, Pete clearly saw the twinkle in her eyes as she spoke. He began to wonder about his *friend's* intentions. The room's atmosphere seemed a little too welcoming, as did her outfit.

This was not a date, he told himself. He was imagining things. They were just friends. Pete's attire served as a further reminder. He had on blue jeans and a lightweight black sweater. Very informal compared to what Corinne sported.

"Not too bad actually," Pete replied, finally, having cleared some unusual nervousness in his throat. "It's kind of cool being back on campus again. I don't know why I was so apprehensive. Now that I'm here, avoiding Todd and Brandi—together as an official couple—doesn't seem like that big a deal. I think I could handle it if I bumped into them again … No, I know I can handle it."

Corinne smiled proudly. That was the strong, self-assured man she knew.

They spent the remaining p.m. hours catching up and sharing laughs. Old-time reminiscences generated quite a number of chuckles, as did Pete's present adventures at *Jersey News Central*. Thanks to his hilarious boss, Vito, of course. They joked around constantly, which made the workday a lot of fun. In one instance he rushed into his supervisor's office with breaking news off the wire: the price of coffee was to triple in the next four to six weeks, and people all over the country had begun flocking to stores and emptying shelves. Everyone at *JNC* knew his very consciousness depended on the beverage—and Vito knew a gag when he choked on it. He let out a vigorous laugh.

"Yeah, right," he later said, "and so is my salary."

Pete could also talk to his boss like a friend, much the same way he could talk to Corinne, though no one could take her place.

She appreciated the sentiment and scooted closer to the foot of the bed. It was time to end this small talk and get down to business. She had to make her move. According to Pete's new policy, women had to pursue him from now on. So she changed the subject to dating, asking if any young ladies had caught his eye recently.

"Not really," he said, "but I'm not really looking, either."

Look my way then. Look right in front of you.

She gently lifted his chin and stared lovingly into his eyes.

"I'm here you know," she said softly. "I'm always here for you."

"Thanks, Corinne."

"I'm here as a friend … and more."

"More?"

The moment had arrived. The heart drums inside her chest told her so, as did the love song reaching its climax in the background.

"This is what I mean."

Corinne cupped the sides of his face into her smooth delicate hands. Her lips moistened as she tilted her head and leveled her mouth to that of the man she long adored. She then closed her eyes—and kissed him.

27

Usual time to hit Philly's bar scene was now, just after midnight. But Adam needed money for drinks. It was his turn, as Belinda paid for them last time. With Sweet Pete away until tomorrow, he could search his brother's room for loose change. No chance of the little prick coming home early. But Mom could, though. She was due back from her job in Trenton soon. Her shift just ended. He had to make this quick.

"Stay here," he ordered Belinda, sprawled like a jellyfish on his bed, "I'll be back."

She acknowledged in the form of a grunt. Still groggy from her nap, it took too much energy to utter a proper reply.

Adam, wearing nothing but gray cutoff sweatpants, closed his bedroom door and opened that of his younger brother a mere step away. Inside, he flicked on the light switch and looked around the room, wondering where Sweet Pete may have stashed a few extra bucks. Doubtless he had his wallet with him—and doubtless he kept it filled with *all* his cash. There had to be some around here, but where exactly?

He had to put back whatever he touched or moved. In this dork's room everything had a set place.

Nothing was found in the drawers, neither the desk nor dresser. His closet also turned up nothing—and the nightstand, zilch. The bed was Adam's last hope. Only a set of dumbbells lay on the rug underneath it. And he spotted no cash under the mattress.

He needed cash—and fast. The more minutes that passed, the closer to Woodlake Square his mother drove.

In a fit of temper he picked up Pete's pillow and thrashed it against the closet door. As it plopped to the floor an envelope slipped out of the case. His curiosity aroused, Adam knelt to retrieve it. The envelope was unsealed, he noted, but its flap had been tucked underneath the bottom portion. He fingered his way inside and pulled out three 20-dollar bills.

"Come to Daddy," he said, dropping the envelope as he rose.

The green in Adam's eyes camouflaged to that in his thieving hands. Sixty dollars … free for the taking.

Suddenly, someone keyed into the front door downstairs.

Janice was home, and Adam had to get out of here—now—before she could witness a suspicious exit from the room. There wasn't a second to spare. No time to put back the pillow or straighten the quilt. Screw it. There would be plenty of time to straighten up the room later, once he got home from Philly. Sweet Pete wasn't due home until tomorrow afternoon anyway.

Adam tiptoed out, closing the door behind him with only a whisper of a squeak. He escaped into his bedroom just as Janice made her way upstairs.

Inside, Belinda asked why he was standing with his ear to the door.

"Shut up!" he barked.

As soon as Janice's bedroom door closed, Adam turned to his girlfriend.

"Get dressed, we're going out."

Belinda's eyebrows arched in doubt.

"I thought you didn't have any money," she said.

Adam smiled in wicked smugness. He unfolded his hand, revealed the three 20s he had "found," and tossed them on her lap.

"We do now."

28

Ordinarily he would have been flattered, extremely flattered, by such a romantic gesture. But Corinne was his friend. Kissing like this was something friends just did not do—and were not supposed to do. It had to stop. He would only get hurt in the end. These encounters, in his case, always ended in heartache. Corinne knew this, too, so why was she doing this? More so, why was he doing this?

Pete pulled away. The look on his face displayed several emotions, but confusion stood out most of all. The fear of being hurt—and hurting Corinne, the best friend he ever had—came in second and third place, respectively.

"What's the matter?" she asked, despite the answers plastered on his face.

Not knowing what to say, Pete sprung off the bed. He approached the window and rested his sweaty hands on the cool sill. Four stories above ground, he gazed outside, hoping the right words would magically appear in the nighttime sky. Unfortunately, no teleprompter materialized. There was nothing to read. The sky, like his mind, was totally blank.

"Pete, look at me."

He tried but couldn't, not just yet.

Corinne sighed. Everything had been going so well. When she kissed him he did not resist. Not right away, that is. He kissed her back. He had to feel something, he just had to. But would he allow himself to feel it? She certainly hoped so. However, his silent stance conveyed no such intention.

Damn. Homecoming wasn't supposed to end like this. It was to be a special night. In a way it was. She finally made her move. And he reciprocated … initially.

What have I done?

Streams of panic began flooding her vessels. Could she have been wrong all this time? Did she read too much into Pete's correspondence these past few months? His texts and emails about how much he missed her, how he wished they could meet for meals inside the sunroom? Could she have misinterpreted his phone calls as well? After all, friends did this sort of thing all the time. Her heart, damn it, kept telling her otherwise, that the gestures meant something more.

Corinne's heartbeat accelerated as the panicky streams stormed into rapids, with tsunami-high waves. She couldn't bear to lose Pete's friendship over this. He was her best friend, and she, his. Or was she? After tonight who knew?

No. That must not happen.

It was up to her to clear the uneasy air between them. Then their friendship could return to normal—hopefully.

"I'm sorry," she said, most remorsefully. "I'm really s—"

Unable to finish, Corinne buried her face into her hands. The woman who was always so strong had lost her composure.

Pete turned away from the window and faced his weeping friend. He couldn't move any farther, despite his impulse to throw a comforting arm around her. This wouldn't have been a problem 30 minutes ago. But now things were different. Such a gesture could be misinterpreted. Their friendship—if he could still call it that—had changed. It had traveled a forbidden plane, one that dared cross its platonic boundaries.

At least she apologized. And he should as well. He could have ended the kiss before it even started. He was responsible for that much.

"I'm sorry, too, Corinne," he said, finally breaking his silence.

Her hands unfolded from her face. The salty seas in her Mediterranean blue eyes began to recede. Though upset over tonight's miscalculations, she was very much relieved to hear the words he just uttered. Perhaps their friendship could resume. There was only one way to find out for sure. She had to ask him pointblank.

"I don't want to lose you," she said. "Your friendship means the world to me. Can you ever forgive me, Pete?"

"There's nothing to forgive," he assured her. "Let's just forget it ever happened, okay?"

Corinne nodded meekly. Part of her wanted to do just that, but another—her heart—would not allow the memory to fade so quickly.

Pete figured as much. He searched his writer's mind for a few diversionary words.

"By the way," he said, having found some, "I noticed your hair had grown a bit ... looks good."

"Thanks."

How sweet. Not only did he notice her hair's new length, he was doing his best to ease her mind. Here he was trying to solve the problem that she herself created. Corinne admired him even more. His selflessness never ceased to amaze.

God, she loved him. The feeling may not be mutual, at least not now, but she was willing to wait. Kissing him was the first step ... in the right direction. Indeed, the gesture would give him something to think about.

But he was already thinking about it. In fact, he never stopped since her lips touched his. Pete did his best to restore some sense of normalcy to their friendship. However, a simple comment on her hair couldn't shake his all-around confusion—and discomfort. He had to get out of here. Everything was happening so quickly. He needed time to clear his head, to put tonight's events into proper perspective. It was impossible to do so here in this dimly lit room, the place where he and his best friend had just made out.

"Anyway," said Pete, collecting his belongings, "thanks for having me over."

"You're leaving?"

"I think it's for the best," he replied, and with an intense stare, added, "Don't you think?"

Corinne nodded reluctantly. As much as she wanted him to stay she realized he needed some space.

"Pete," she said in all seriousness, "things are okay between us, right?"

He smiled assuredly.

"Yes, of course they are," he said, masking his own doubts.

Corinne wasn't entirely convinced herself but conveyed no such feeling. A proud, closemouthed smile formed as she hopped off the bed.

"I'll walk you out to your car," she said.

"No, it's okay, I'll just say goodbye here."

An awkward pause loitered at the bedroom door. For the first time in their friendship neither Pete nor Corinne knew how to part company. A friendly hug could have additional meaning now, as could a peck on the cheek. And if they shook hands—something they never did—it would classify their status as something less than best friends.

Pete ignored their history of casual hugs and kisses and simply bid Corinne good night. She did the same.

"Drive safely," she added.

"Yeah, okay … Bye."

"Bye."

Corinne closed the door steadily, cherishing every last glimpse of the man she loved through the narrow crack.

"Damn."

The one-syllable word summed up the blizzard of emotions whirling inside her: confusion, hurt, embarrassment, even fear and loneliness. She had never felt so insecure. Why, she asked herself, was she sinking? She could always swim over life's challenges, but this latest one had thrust an impossible obstacle in her path. She had no control over it. The situation was in Pete's hands. He would make the decision whether to upgrade their friendship to something more intimate. He already knew how she felt, but not the other way around.

Or did she? It was possible, quite possible, that he didn't feel the same … and wouldn't in the future. She had to face that fact. Her feelings may never be returned.

Corinne collapsed backwards into bed. Tears began to bubble—again—as she gazed at the dull white ceiling. She had her chance and took it. But now, she wished she never had. Pete would still be here right now. Now he was gone.

And he may never come back.

29

Pete took his time driving home. There was no need to rush. The roads were practically his. Hardly anyone was about this late hour. Plus he needed time to reflect. His favorite radio program, *Under the Stars with Evangeline*, was long over by 2:30 a.m. Just as well anyway. Sometimes a little silence helped clear his mind. Considering what happened tonight, every tad would come in handy.

He had grown rather content with his post-graduation life, one with no dating relationships. His part-time job at the cinema filled in that social void on the weekends. And he was fine with this. Working two jobs and helping Mom maintain the house kept his activity plate chock full. He had no time for romance. Nor did he desire it, at least for the time being. Someday he may date again but not anytime soon. Not while the stench of the Brandi strikeout lingered in his nostrils. He wished he could talk with his best friend about all this, but his best friend was the problem. Or was it himself?

Not knowing the answer, Pete sighed in frustration. Obviously this dilemma wouldn't resolve itself anytime soon, surely by the time he got home tonight—this morning, that is. He had better grasp this fact. If not, then he would endure a restless romp of tossing and turning. Somehow, though, he knew a solution would present itself, one where he and Corinne could resume their platonic relationship. He had no idea when, but a solution would arrive. It was out there somewhere.

The notion settled Pete's mind, albeit temporarily, just as he ventured into Woodlake Square. Entering the Webb townhouse, he headed upstairs.

His shower could wait until tomorrow. It had been a grueling night. The toll on his emotions had drained his body as well.

What the …?

Pete suddenly found himself fully awake—in fury. The state of his room was definitely not how he had left it. The quilt on his bed had been flung back. Obviously to remove the pillow, he noticed, which lay on the floor by the closet. Next to it rested an envelope, an empty envelope. Sixty dollars gone!

That son of a…

Realizing he and Adam shared the same mother, Pete stopped himself before completing the thought. But he couldn't prevent the clouds of rage from steaming. His cool collectiveness dissipated in no time.

"Adam!!!"

He roared his older brother's name so ferociously he could swear the room just quaked. As he turned to exit, his hands and fingers clinched into fists. They throbbed in anticipation of the pain ahead. Though pounding Adam's door down would also bring a great deal of pleasure.

But he never made it out of his room.

"Peter!"

Janice, having woken, arrived at the threshold wearing a long turquoise robe. She demanded to know why her son yelled the way he did, and in the middle of the night.

"*This* is why."

Pete scooped up the empty envelope and hurled it onto his unmade bed.

"I had $60 in there," he said, "and Adam took it. He stole it."

Janice was silent. She didn't want to believe what she just heard. No, Peter had to be mistaken.

"How do you know for sure?"

"Oh, come on, Mom!"

"Don't raise your voice to me, young man."

Pete sighed. He knew he was out of line. But his mother was so blind when it came to Adam. She either didn't, or wouldn't, see him for what he truly was: a lazy, good-for-nothing, freeloading thief.

"I'm sorry," he said, having calmed down. "Just think about it, okay? Who else could have taken my money?"

There was no one else, and Janice knew it.

"It's not as if he never did this before," Pete added seriously. "Isn't that right, Mom?"

She did not answer. But saying nothing was as good as saying yes. Her son was correct. Adam had stolen from her.

"That's why you don't keep your purse downstairs in the closet anymore," Pete pointed out. "That's why it's in your room now, isn't it?"

A somber Janice nodded.

"This is your house, Mom. You shouldn't have key into your own bedroom."

"I know."

"Then why do you?"

She didn't want to get into this now. It was nearly 3 a.m. And her shift at the bar was exhausting. But her all-too-wise son wasn't about to drop the subject. After all, he'd just been violated. Janice knew just how he felt—more so, in fact. She was robbed by her own child, not a sibling. But that child and that sibling were the same person. One plus one equaled one in this equation.

Rae had advised—to put it mildly—that it was high time to kick Adam out of the house. It was one thing to lie around and do nothing, she told her, but quite another to steal from someone, especially family. Janice agreed wholeheartedly ... but couldn't bring herself to do it. A dagger of sympathy pierced her heart every time she thought about it. She wondered where he would go, how he would survive out there in the world. He had no special skills and a disgraceful job history. But that was his fault, his problem, not hers, Rae explained.

"Look, Peter," his mother said, "this happened a long time ago, okay? He hasn't taken anything from me since the spring. It was a one-time incident."

"A one-time incident?!" he said incredulously. "Well, not anymore it isn't."

"How I wish you and your brother could get along."

By getting along did she mean tolerating theft? Putting up with all his insults? They seemed to be the only words uttered out of his filthy mouth—in addition to his trademark profanity, of course.

"Oh, we'll get along just fine," Pete began, "as soon as I move out."

"What!"

"You don't really expect me to live with a thief, do you?"

She did actually, and Pete could see that in her eyes.

"You may be able to, Mom, but not me."

"Let me talk to him, okay?"

There was a time he could accept this so-called solution, but not much longer. She could talk to Adam until she turned purple, but nothing would soak into that rotting sponge he had for a heart. Too many holes, Pete realized, ones that spat out anything good or decent. How they could possibly be related—much less brothers—boggled his mind.

Nevertheless he didn't want to leave his mother, especially with Adam here. No telling what he could do next. Moreover, Pete enjoyed helping pay the bills. His mother's heavy burdens were finally lifting. About time, too. She had enough worrisome lines splintering the prettiness on her face. Slowing them down, preventing an all-out invasion, did his heart a lot of good.

Now if Adam could just call off *his* invasions.

His brother was hardly ever held accountable for his actions, and that sent a dangerous message, one he had no trouble heeding. His deviant behavior had worsened over the years, excused incessantly by their mother. "It's my fault because I was out working day and night," she would say. "I wasn't as good a parent as I should've been." She always blamed herself, it seemed, at least partially. She knew she wasn't directly responsible for how her son behaved. However, she could not shake the guilt … and Adam sure as hell knew it.

"Okay," said Pete, "have your talk with him. But I guarantee it won't do any good."

Deep down Janice felt the same but kept her doubts to herself. Although her silent, pensive stare spoke volumes.

"I said I would talk to him, okay?" she said finally. "Let me handle your brother. Don't say anything about this to him."

Pete agreed, reluctantly. He was willing to give her one more chance—just one. If this talk of hers failed, if Adam didn't change his ways, then he was out of here. He could not go on living like this. Nor should he have to. His brother was 27 years old for God's sake. This juvenile delinquency had to end … now.

Janice understood and bid her youngest son goodnight. She never even asked why he had come home so early. She probably forgot, Pete thought. Just as well anyway. Now he could crash into bed. That is, after he hopped into a nice hot shower.

He was no longer too tired for that.

30

Diving into the next issue's articles first thing Monday morning was just what he needed. They made the ideal distraction, albeit temporarily. This weekend's events haunted him all day yesterday. Uninvited migraines hammered their way inside his head and made themselves at home. The intimate encounter with Corinne, Adam's stealing, and his mother's inability to control it ... Pete honestly didn't know which was worse.

He got so involved in his work that he forgot what time it was. Not good, especially when Vito wanted to see him in his office at 10 o'clock—15 minutes ago. Shoot. Pete could kick himself for forgetting. There was no excuse for his lack of professionalism, none whatsoever. He rose immediately. The movie review he was currently editing had to wait. Exiting his cubicle, he zigzagged through a few short aisles and approached his supervisor's office.

A most amusing sight prevented him from knocking right away. He didn't want to spoil Vito's fun. Heavy metal music was jamming out of the desktop computer. Seated in front of it, with closed eyes, the managing editor of *Jersey News Central* strummed away on a belly-level air guitar. His head lobbed up and down, sideways, and every direction between—all the while sporting a suit and tie.

"Yeah, yeah, yeah," he screeched. "Oh, baby, yeah."

He lip-synched the rest of the words, whatever they were.

Pete chuckled at the one-man concert in front of him. He was also relieved. Apparently, Vito wasn't that bothered by his tardiness.

"Sorry I'm late," he said anyway.

His boss's brown eyes instantly flicked open. His head lurched forward to its standard position. And his guitar vanished back into the thin air.

"Hey, man," he said with a laugh, turning off the music. "What can I say, you caught me red handed."

"And red faced."

Vito laughed again, this time with more gusto. His voice sure did carry well, Pete thought.

"Have a seat, guy."

"Thanks."

"What I wanted to tell you is…"

Vito held his words until after he shut the door, which he did rapidly. Pete figured he must have had at least three cups of coffee by now. Maybe more, on second thought, considering that musical performance he walked in on.

"Dude," said Vito, back at his desk, shaking his head in amazement, "you're doing one hell of a good job."

"Thank you."

"And that's why I'm giving you a raise. How does $7,500 more a year sound?"

"Great. Thanks, Vito."

His reply was polite, humble, but also timid. It lacked zest. Not a trace of excitement, or even surprise, existed. Something wasn't right here.

"Okay, bud, what's going on?"

"Excuse me?"

"I just told you that you're getting a $7,500 raise, and you're as stiff as your gelled hair. What's up, man?"

"I'm sorry," said Pete. "It's not that I'm ungrateful. Believe me, I'm very grateful."

"The thought never even crossed my mind."

Quite true. Vito knew what kind of fellow he was since day one. He never doubted his genuine character, not for a moment, and certainly not now.

"Come on, talk to me," he persisted. "I've been around long enough to know when someone has some serious shit on his mind."

Pete sighed. He didn't want to bring his problems into the workplace. But he had, apparently. First he was late for the meeting. Now his personal frustrations were showing. His professionalism had taken quite a beating today—and it was still morning.

"I don't want to burden you."

"Hey, I offered to listen, didn't I?" said Vito. "Just spill it, man."

Pete could tell his boss was serious, that he meant what he said. At last, someone to talk to, someone to confide in. The collar of problems that kept choking him could finally loosen.

He unleashed all that plagued him: the long history of problems with his brother, and consequently, his mother—and also his love life, or lack thereof, including what happened with Corinne over the weekend.

"Dude, I had no idea you were going through any of this," said Vito, who had listened attentively, and most kindly. "Your brother's got issues, serious issues. It's pretty clear to me how jealous he is of you."

"Jealous?"

"Big time," Vito stressed. "That's why he's the way he is toward you. He's not angry at you; he's angry at himself. He sees in you the man he could have been."

Pete's stare sharpened when he heard this.

"Think about it, man. You have a college degree—and not just any degree, but one from Stepney Green. You studied really hard to earn it; he barely got out of high school. You're working a full-time career job, one that utilizes your talent; he can't even hold on to a basic part-time job. You're a success, and he isn't. And he knows it. And he resents you for it. It's that simple, man."

Pete sat silently as his brain absorbed these simple, but powerful, words.

"And your frustration will only get worse the longer you stay in that house," said Vito. "Let's face it: you're not the homeowner, you have no authority there, no control of the situation. Only your mother does. And if she won't take action, then nothing is going to change."

Yeah, you're probably right.

"Sounds like it may be time for you to move out on your own."

It was, but he had agreed to give his mother one last chance to clean up the Adam mess. She probably had her talk with him yesterday. His older brother had avoided him all day long. He wasn't man enough to admit any wrongdoing, but at least he stayed out of his way. For the first time in ages Pete enjoyed a pleasant Sunday at home, despite a migraine. It was an insult-free day. Adam said nothing to him. No immature wisecracks, no profanity or vulgarity, not a single solitary syllable. His silence was a real treat. Pete prayed the trend would continue. How sad to have a brother he hoped would never speak to him. But Adam knew only one tone, that which was indecent and uncivilized.

Regarding his string of failed romances, Vito suggested something totally unexpected.

"Write about them," he said matter-of-factly. "After all, your dream is to become a novelist someday, right?"

"Yes."

"So why not start now? No time like the present, as the saying goes. It's great therapy, too. The good thing is no people or walls get punched, only computer keys."

This made Pete smile. And he needed something to cheer him.

"I'm serious, dude," Vito continued. "Write a book about it all. I mean, a lot of fiction out there is based on real life, real events that have happened to real people."

"Isn't that libelous?"

"Not when you change around the names, places and events … even genders. Believe me, man, writers, including famous ones, do this shit all the time."

Pete was intrigued. He had written about his life's events in the form of poetry, as with *Out of Nowhere*, but never considered a novel. Not about his dating relationships. He always imagined writing a story about something else, something far more exciting. But it could be exciting if he took what Vito said into consideration. Yes, a number of changes here and there, and he could have himself one handsome piece of literature.

The juices of creativity began to stir. His heart drummed in exhilaration. Ideas pumped into his mind faster than he could breathe… Indeed he could write about the women in his life, the ones who had shattered his heart so ruthlessly. Not so much Mary Ann, his high school sweetheart, but definitely Dana and Liz—and especially Brandi. She had hurt him most of all. He never forgot that "standards" comment. It was the cruelest, most callous thing anyone ever said about him. She was so damned twofaced.

Vito was right. Writing about this would be very therapeutic. And it would make great reading material.

He could hardly wait to get started. And with his laptop, he could begin anytime.

"Thanks," Pete said to his boss. "Thanks a lot. You've helped me more than you know."

Vito winked.

"You're welcome, bud."

Still, one question remained: what to do about Corinne. No way could he write about what happened with her. She did not hurt him. She may have confused him, but she did not hurt him. In fact, he was the one who probably hurt her.

"Can I ask one more thing?"

"Sure, man."

"What about Corinne? How should I handle her now?"

"The same way you've always handled her," his boss—and friend—advised. "Don't treat her any differently. Be her friend like you always have been. There's no need to bring up the make-out session or whatever you want to call it—after all, you already told her things were cool between you two before you went home. It's that simple, my man. Things should return to normal in no time."

Pete certainly hoped so … and that this was the solution to his dilemma.

31

Vito Caparelli's advice worked miracles. Words of wisdom, they were, divine wisdom. Three months had passed, and there was no mention, not one remark, about homecoming night. It was as if nothing ever happened. Pete had decided to text Corinne the day he talked to his boss. He kept his message casual, just like always. She had texted back, keeping the same tone. She did the same with her phone calls, as did Pete. Their friendship seemed to pick up right where it left off: before that bewildering night.

Corinne was most relieved. She still had her good ole best friend on campus. He had come back into her life. In fact, he never left. She hadn't seen him since October but knew she would sometime, eventually. Could she suppress her feelings then? How well? Could she suppress them at all? She would have to, somehow, despite loving him with all her heart. It was the only way to maintain the friendship, to keep the man she adored in her life. One day, though, he would fall into her loving arms. This she truly believed. And she was willing to wait, however long it took. She no longer regretted planting that kiss on him. No more second thoughts. It *was* the right thing to do. It *was* the right time. Despite not talking about it, the thought was there. It existed. And in Pete's mind as well. Yes, he had to think about it on occasion. He just had to. There was still hope.

Pete had indeed thought about the kiss he and his best friend shared—and it bothered him. Vito was the only person he told. Thank goodness, too. No one back home knew, and that was how he wanted it. Plus Vito's suggestion worked perfectly. Corinne was his best friend again, just like always. What a relief to put homecoming night behind them.

In fact, he nearly blocked it out completely. His novel consumed virtually all his thoughts nowadays. Pete typed away on his laptop computer, which he loved to do, every chance he got. Any extra minutes in the morning before heading to work, after dinner, after his shower, any free time at all he could possibly muster. He was having so much fun, he never even thought about his nightmare of a love life. In the context of the present day, that is. For this novel it was essential to open the Stepney Green diary, something he'd vowed never to do. But as Vito predicted, writing about what happened with Dana, Liz and Brandi had become very therapeutic. His heart was now totally ache-free. The last shreds of pain had escaped out through his fingertips and onto the computer screen. To Pete's surprise it actually felt good to exhume these buried memories. Releasing his past hurt in such a creative manner was nothing short of brilliant. Kudos to Vito!

Dana had become Donna in his story and Liz, Lisa. Bethany replaced Brandi. Substituting their names was not a problem. The title, on the other hand, was. Pete had no idea what to call his work. Somehow, though, he knew the perfect title would surface. It was definitely out there.

Janice wished her youngest son were, too. Out of his room, that is. She had grown a little concerned. Her 24-year-old son was spending way too much time on his computer. Secluding himself in his room, he shunned reality's events as they passed outside. He hardly ever went out anymore. And when he did, it was to go to work. That seemed to be his entire life now: out to work and back home to write. Of course, it was January, arguably the coldest month of the year.

Pete couldn't have cared less about the wintry weather. In fact, he rather enjoyed his hermit lifestyle. The best thing about it was Adam had stayed out of his face—and out of his room. With no loose cash inside his pillowcase he had no reason to invade his territory.

Or did he?

Adam had grown increasingly curious. Just what was the little prick doing in there? What was he writing about? Whatever it was, it was important to him. So was that laptop of his, that expensive laptop. Sweet Pete must have paid a fortune for it. He sure had a lot of dough. And there was only one way to get hold of that dough. Hocking the laptop at the pawnshop should give him a cool grand at least. Man, he could party off that for a while. And stick it to Sweet Pete at the same time.

Adam chose Friday, the last in January, as the day of the dirty deed. Perfect. Just in time for the weekend—when the dork wrote most. Yeah, that would really piss him off. And it had been a while since he last did that, since October.

He had kept a low profile long enough.

32

Adam got out of bed at 11 a.m. The house was empty this morning. He didn't want Belinda anywhere near the place today. With her not around she could avoid the finger of blame. That was something he wanted aimed directly at himself.

Just wait until he gets home from work!

Yeah, Adam thought, smiling as only a conniving scoundrel could. Sweet Pete was in for quite a surprise. No more precious laptop. What would the poor baby do now, cry to Mommy? Like that would do any good.

He slipped on a pair of light-blue, almost gray, jeans. Several holes ran up and down each leg, front and back. A similarly odd pattern dotted his cotton black shirt. Around his forehead, above his sea-green eyes, he wrapped a black bandana. Matching wristbands were put on next, and last.

Okay, time to get to work.

Now this was the kind of job he loved.

Adam entered his brother's room to hunt for the laptop. He had plenty of time to find it. His mother wouldn't be home for at least another four hours, and Sweet Pete a couple more after that. He found it within a few minutes. It rested in the closet, on a shelf, wrapped inside a couple of folded blankets. Hidden well, but not well enough.

He placed it on the tiny wooden desk in the corner, sat down, flipped up the monitor, and turned on the power. After a minute or so the screen lit up. Luckily there was no password to enter. Two columns of icons appeared on the left side. Adam moved the cursor to the icon marked

"My Documents" and double-clicked it. He knew just how to navigate computers, one of the few things he learned—and enjoyed—in high school.

Six Word files emerged, each labeled according to chapter. But it was way too quiet in here to read. He needed music, his music, loud enough to drown out the room's silence. Sweet Pete's mini-stereo rested on the adjacent dresser. Adam reached over and turned it on.

"Man, what a dork."

His little brother had set the station to one that played easy-listening favorites—love songs, ballads and instrumentals. And the volume was at a considerate low. Not anymore, though. Adam turned it up, way up, and also changed the station. Only hard rock would do. Now he could read.

And did he ever read.

Two hours later his eyes had glued to the screen. He no longer heard the blaring music, only character voices and other sounds created in his imagination. His mind had traveled to another dimension, a literary world, and visited a whole lot longer than expected.

Shit's not bad.

As much as he hated to admit it he really liked these chapters. There was something unique about Sweet Pete's writing as well as his story. And that was exactly what it was, *his* story. Obviously the main character who longed for a girlfriend, Parker West, was Sweet Pete himself.

"Too bad neither will live happily ever after."

Adam's wicked smile returned. A sinister chuckle followed as he dumped the Word files into the recycle bin one by one. Their permanent deletion was just about complete.

"Now for the grand finale," he proudly announced, "then it's off to pawn this baby."

He edged the cursor ever closer to the Empty Recycle Bin option. But before he could click, a hand grabbed his wrist from behind and whisked it away. Another hand shut off the music.

"Don't even think about it."

Pete's stern, eerily monotone voice emitted through a wall of clinched teeth. His dark-brown eyes had turned red as lava, a reflection of the sheer rage erupting within. Never in his life had he felt so angry, so violated. Not only did Adam invade his privacy—again—he was going to hock his laptop computer. Pete worked long and hard to pay for it, a foreign concept to someone like his brother. That lazy, good-for-nothing, freeloading thief had to steal to get what he wanted.

And why on earth did he want to erase the chapters of his novel? What reason could there possibly be to do something like that? Did he resent him that much? He must, Pete realized. There was no other explanation.

Even if he had successfully deleted the files, at least there were backups. Pete thanked his lucky stars for storing his work on two USB flash drives, one of which stayed with him at all times. Still, there was no excuse for his brother's behavior, none whatsoever. Adam's jealousy was out of control now. Someone had to put him in his place—and not their mother. She failed for the last time. It was up to Pete now. And he would sugarcoat nothing. Reality was going to hit Adam hard. This was it, the last straw.

"I always knew I'd catch you one day."

Damn, the little prick came home early. And with the loud music I never even heard him come in. But he did, and he probably heard everything I said. Shit, there goes all the dough I was going to get for this laptop.

And just look at him staring at me like that. Who does he think he is, our father or something? Well, he isn't. He's a nobody, and he'll always be a nobody. He may think he's a big shit—the Stepney Green graduate, the whatever-he-is at Jersey News Central—but he's a nobody. Not in Mom's eyes, of course. She's always so proud of him. I bet Sweet Pete's proud right now, too, now that he caught me in his room—a place that sees no action by the way. No surprise there. I mean, why would any girl go for a dork like him anyway? It's about time I spat this little fact in his face...and more.

Hmm, maybe his coming home early wasn't such a bad thing after all.

Adam rose off the desk chair, decorating his face in overt smugness on the way. He was all too glad to meet his younger brother's irate gaze—and launch the first missile in this war of words.

"You are such a *dork*."

This remark infuriated Pete even more, if that were possible. He'd heard that word spew out of Adam's mouth a million times. Why was it different this time? Maybe because it was accompanied by such a self-satisfied, unapologetic grin. Pete wanted to smack it off right now with a first-class punch. Man, it would feel really good. But he resisted. He kept a lid on his boiling temper—barely. Not quite time to take it off, not just yet, but almost.

"That's your answer for everything, isn't it, Adam? Calling me names."

"Damn right."

"Well, you're not getting away with stealing from me this time. You almost did though, didn't you? Didn't expect me to knock off work early today, did you, *bro?*"

Ooh, a little sarcasm in that last word. Adam liked the sound of it. It meant he was getting to him. He couldn't be more delighted.

"Your stealing ends right here, right now," Pete stated firmly.

"Now I'm really shaking," his undeterred brother replied, humoring only himself. "What's big man on campus going to do? Tell Mommy?"

"I can take care of myself."

"Ha!"

That would be the day when Sweet Pete didn't run and tell Mommy how mean his big brother was. In fact, he told her everything. She was the only woman in his life. What a momma's boy. He was always her favorite. He could do no wrong in her eyes. Not one damn thing. He was her darling little angel ... and always would be.

I hate him.

Adam's smug, yet calm, demeanor crumbled. Rage had seized control. Now, his were the eyes that broiled in volcanic red. A far cry from their soothing sea green just seconds ago.

"You know what you are, Sweet Pete?" said Adam, his face mere millimeters away. "You're a *piece of shit.*"

Pete did not move a hair. He maintained his composure on purpose. By not lashing out he knew his brother would only grow more irritated.

So he responded with a nonchalant, "Haven't heard that one before."

"You *are* a piece of shit," Adam reiterated, in a louder voice. "Nobody likes you—nobody!"

"Well, considering your acquaintances, I'll take that as a compliment."

"You know what else? You're going to be a lonely old man. When you come home from work, you'll come home to nothing but your dogs. And you can screw yourself every night ... all night long."

Nice try, but it wouldn't work. Pete wasn't the least bit rattled by these asinine predictions. He expected this kind of talk from Adam. It reminded him of the confrontations he'd had with disorderly students back at the college. RA rounds were never dull on those nights. He couldn't retaliate then, but he sure could now. And he would love every minute of it.

"Well," Pete began, "I'd much rather screw myself every night than a hideous, disgusting fat pig like Belinda Price."

"What did you just call her?"

"You heard me—she's a pig! And the only thing on the planet that would go out with a piece-of-trash loser like you."

Adam backed away, stunned by what he just heard. His brother had never been this bold. And, like it or not, the little prick was right. Belinda was the only girl who would go out with him. But he was not about to give Sweet Pete the satisfaction of knowing.

"What's the matter, Adam?" his little brother said, pleased by the silent retort. "Does the truth hurt that much?"

"Oh, you want to talk about the truth, well try this: All you have is Mom, and when she dies you're going to be all alone in this world."

"Whatever."

"Lonely old man! Lonely old man!! Lonely old man!!!"

"Oh, I may be alone," Pete retorted, "but I'll never be lonely."

Hey, that's it! That's the title of my novel: But I'll Never Be Lonely. It's perfect! And I have my infantile big brother to thank. Who would've thought? I knew the title was out there somewhere, but I never dreamed it would surface like this. Man, things sure do happen for a reason.

"Oh, yes, you will, dork," said Adam, hardly convinced. "Just what will you do when Mom isn't around to tell you how proud she is of you? No more, 'Oh, Peter, you're such a good young man, such a hard worker.' 'I'm so proud of you, son.'"

Adam glared directly into his brother's eyes as he finished with, "I … hate … you."

"You don't hate me," said a much calmer Pete. "You hate yourself."

He told his brother exactly what Vito explained to him back in October. Adam hated himself for not becoming the man he could have been—the accomplished, hardworking young man he saw in his little brother.

"And you're downright jealous, too."

"Jealous? Yeah, right."

Adam rolled his eyes in disbelief, laughing off the psychobabble. But deep down he knew the analysis was right on target. He was jealous, all right, not only of Sweet Pete's college degree and high-paying job but of his special bond with their mother.

Uncomfortable, he darted for the door.

"You are, Adam," Pete said. "But you really shouldn't be. You should be happy for me instead."

"Ha!" he yelled back.

"You could've studied hard, went to college, and found a good job just like I did. But you didn't. You chose not to. That's fine, college isn't for everyone. But you could at least go out there and get a job, earn some money, and help out Mom. Do you realize all she's done for you, for us? When we were growing up she gave us everything we needed. She went without things for herself all the time. She's sacrificed so much. Why do you have to steal from her? Or me?"

"Lonely old man! Lonely old man!! Lonely old man!!!"

"Just be good to her, Adam. Treat Mom with respect. She deserves that much. And a 'thank you' every once in a while wouldn't hurt either. Please be good to our mother. That's all I ask."

"Piece of shit! Piece of shit!! Piece of shit!!!"

"No, *you're* the piece of shit!!!"

Adam's jaw hung in astonishment. He could not believe his ears. Was that Sweet Pete just now? Did he actually yell and curse?

Damn right he did. And he didn't care, either. He simply could take no more. Mr. Nice Guy was gone. And the saintly calm went with him. The lid on his boiling temper, secured just a moment ago, had exploded. Adam's cussword was just one too many. So to hell with remaining cool and collected! It never did any good in the past, did it? It didn't make his brother change his childish ways, his defiant behavior. A different approach was needed to end this war of words once and for all. It really was okay, just this once, to stoop to Adam's level. High time *his* ears got scorched by that foul three-word phrase.

"Got your attention, did I?"

Adam, still stunned, just stood there.

"Good," Pete continued, "because the only one who's going to be a lonely old man is you, Adam. Want to know why? I'll tell you why. It's because you treat people like dirt, especially your own family. And mark my words, one of these days you're going to push Mom too far

... just like you pushed me too far."

After a lengthy pause Pete concluded: "You're no brother to me, Adam. You're nothing but a liar and a thief. And there's nothing, *nothing* a lowlife like you can say or do that will ever make me feel bad about myself—ever. You lost, Adam. You failed to break me...and you always will."

"Finished?"

"I will be after this: *get...out.*"

A defeated Adam did just that—but not quietly. As he stormed out of the bedroom and into his own, he slammed both doors, nearly unhinging them.

Pete took a deep breath, dashed to his closet, took out a suitcase, and plopped it on his bed. It was time to pack up and leave. It was something he had to do. He could no longer put up with Adam's thievery or verbal abuse. He had had enough. Not even his mother could talk him out of it, not this time. He wished he could stay to help her with the bills, but he could not live here any longer. She was on her own now. It was up to her to deal with his loser of a brother. He had washed his hands of him ... for the last time. Goodbye and good riddance.

And goodbye, Woodlake Square, too.

33

Yelling and screaming like that, trying to steal the laptop… What was Adam thinking? Why did he make Peter leave home? Janice asked herself these questions all week—and now, on a crisp Saturday afternoon, at her kitchen table with Rae. Pete's mother had no answers. But his "aunt" sure as hell did.

"Honey," she said, after a long sip of coffee, "if I had a brother who said and did all those things to me, I'd pack up and leave, too. Wouldn't you?"

Janice ignored the two-word question at the tail end, saying she only wished things could be different.

A sympathetic Rae placed a consoling hand on that of her friend. The gesture said "I know" all by itself. Nevertheless, things would not change. Her sons were always at odds, Rae explained, and probably always would be. They were just two extremely different people.

Janice quite agreed.

"I just wish my boys could at least talk to each other," she said melancholically. "Not that they talked a lot anyway."

"And we both know why, don't we?"

Janice nodded. Deep down she knew Peter's leaving was for the best. He didn't deserve such horrid treatment. Plus he deserved better than a life in Woodlake Square. She was the only reason he stayed as long as he did. To help her out, bless his heart. With the bills, cleaning the house, laundry, taking out the garbage, anything at all. But he deserved better, so much better.

He moved out Wednesday, just five days after the showdown with

Adam. It didn't take him long to find an apartment. He even took off work to sign the lease and move in. Not only did he want to move out right away, he needed to. Though it broke her heart to see him go, Janice was happy for him. Ewing, north of Trenton, was a much nicer place to live than Woodlake Square to the south. His new home was small, but it was his. He no longer had to deal with Adam's stealing or insults. In fact, he didn't have to deal with him at all.

But she still did.

"Oh my, look at the time," Janice said, noting it was 2 p.m. "I should really try and rest a little bit before heading out to work tonight."

"Will you be okay, honey?"

Janice nodded, as confidently as she could.

"I'm here if you need me, okay?"

"Thanks, Rae."

And with a smile Janice picked up the two coffee mugs and dumped them into the sink's dishpan, along with the rest of the dishes. She reached across the sink to turn on the water but stopped suddenly.

"No, honey, let me do that," said Rae, approaching from behind. "You go on upstairs and get some rest, okay? Heaven knows you need it after all you've been through this week."

"Are you sure? I can't leave you with all these—"

"Yes, you can. Now go on upstairs."

Janice smiled.

"Thank you," she said softly, truly grateful.

"You are very welcome," said Rae. "I'll talk to you tomorrow, okay?"

"Okay."

As Janice headed up to bed for a rest, Rae slipped on the yellow rubber gloves next to the sink and got to work. Turning on the hot water, she scrubbed and rinsed the dishes clean. After a good 15 minutes she finally finished.

As soon as she placed the last plate in the dishrack, Belinda entered the cozy aqua kitchen. She had just woken up for the day and wanted something to eat. She wore only a bulky navy sweatshirt that stretched over her panties—barely. Despite her own dubious appearance, the sight of Rae Jacobson was highly amusing. She was, after all, Woodlake Square's very own gossipy glamour gal. And here she was all dressed up in a flashy yellow outfit with matching plastic earrings. Off-the-rack clothes she believed looked expensive.

"Would you look at this?" Belinda said with a snort. "The busybody of Woodlake Square—Mrs. Showoff herself—is in here washing dirty dishes. Well, I'll be a son of a bitch."

A fire sparked in Rae's hazel eyes as she turned to the contemptible 27-year-old misfit.

"No," she corrected her, "just a bitch."

Belinda scowled. She could not stand this interfering woman.

"Why are you always here?" she asked the neighborhood gossip. "You have a family of your own, so why don't you bother them for a change? Don't you have anything better else to do than come over here and make trouble for my Adam? Is your life that dull?"

"That's funny," answered Rae, removing the dishwashing gloves, "I was about to ask you the very same things."

Belinda's bleached frizzy hair spiked in fury. Her lips stretched into a wide circle of outrage.

Rae wasn't the least bit affected. In fact, she rather enjoyed throwing these assertions back in her face. After all, Belinda herself was the troublemaker.

"The one who causes problems around here is you, Belinda Price."

"*Excuse me?*"

"You heard me," Rae said firmly. "You don't help matters at all, not by your constant defense of Adam's actions. All I do is try and be there for Janice. I try and help her out the best way I can."

"Oh, yeah, right, of course," said Belinda, swinging her rippling hips in disbelief, "like bringing her oldest son down all the time, making all these comparisons between him and that goodie-goodie Pete."

"I don't do that," said Rae. "You do."

Belinda rolled her eyes.

"I only tell her the truth," Rae continued. "I tell it like it is. I've always done that. That's just the way I am. Sure, there are differences between Adam and Pete. Anybody who's ever met them can see that. But I don't stress these differences day in and day out like you do. I don't keep drilling them into Adam's head. No wonder he's the way he is."

"What*ever*."

"You keep making these comparisons because you enjoy making trouble. And you do this every chance you get, don't you, Belinda? You know that when you do this you're causing friction and resentment—not only between Adam and his brother but with Janice, too."

"Pete is her favorite. She loves him more. *Everyone* knows that."

"That's not true, not at all. Janice loves both her sons equally. I've known this family a hell of a lot longer than you have, missy."

"Oh, I'm sure you have," said Belinda, about to burst into obnoxious laughter, "and every other family in the Square, too. *Everyone* knows how much you love poking your nose in their business."

Rae, staying focused, ignored the snide remark and got to the point.

"Adam takes terrible advantage of his mother, and you damn well know it," she said. "In fact, you encourage it. You egg on his bad behavior. And you enjoy it, you actually enjoy it. Just what kind of girlfriend are you?"

Belinda, highly amused, answered in the form of a smirk.

"I know what kind," said Rae, "the cheap and tacky type."

"Oh, I'm cheap and tacky, huh? That's rich coming from you. Have you looked in a mirror lately? Only a cheap and tacky woman would wear cheap and tacky clothes like that."

Rae's patience had reached its peak.

"You know something?" she said. "Adam started going downhill some time ago, but he took one hell of a tumble after he met you."

Belinda lunged in to slap the gossipy know-it-all, but Rae grabbed the hand before it reached her face. She squeezed it hard, to the point where it produced tears in the 27-year-old's eyes.

"Let go of me."

But Rae held on to it. She even stepped closer. She would make damn sure Belinda heard what was coming to her.

"And *everyone* knows why you defend and patronize him so much," Rae began, "because he's the only good-looking man that ever gave you the time of day."

"Shut up!"

"No! I have one more thing to say. You better start treating Janice with some respect around here. This is *her* house not yours. Stop making trouble for her. Stop deepening the rift between her and her son. Stop pitting them against each other. You had better remember this, or you'll have me to deal with all over again. Got it?"

Belinda said nothing, but the fearful look on her face said she understood the warning completely.

And with that, Rae freed the captive hand inside her fist. But she remained leery, and rightfully so. Belinda's silent acknowledgment was as good as her word—and that wasn't saying much.

Besides, to understand a warning was one thing. To heed it was quite another.

34

Pete had finished all his unpacking Wednesday evening, just after moving in. He hardly had anything to unpack. He insisted his mother keep the furniture inside his room. Getting what he needed for his new place was his responsibility, he had said. So Pete's room back in Woodlake Square pretty much stayed as it was. His twin-sized bed, dresser, nightstand, even the tiny rickety desk remained unmoved. But he did take all his personal possessions, things he had bought with his own money: the 12" flat-screen TV in his room, mini-stereo, books, photo albums, the dumbbells under the bed, clothes, toiletries—and most importantly, his laptop.

His apartment was the smallest model in the complex. He had a living room, bathroom and kitchen, but no dining room. He ate at the breakfast bar instead. But he would do more than just eat there. It would serve as his desk, where he could go online, check emails, pay the bills—and of course, work on his novel.

In front of the breakfast bar he placed two chairs, each with elongated legs. He had bought these earlier today. They were the only furniture he could fit inside his car. His bedroom set would be delivered next weekend. Pete didn't mind sleeping on the carpeted floor for another seven nights. Nor did he mind taking out some clothes from the suitcase. Living here, alone, was paradise compared to living with Adam. He was no brother. He meant absolutely nothing to him. In fact, he was nothing.

He couldn't tell his mother this. It would break her heart even more. He wondered how she was coping, all alone with that conniving thief.

Blind Expectations

And would Adam take out his frustrations on her now that he was gone? He could not worry about it. This was something Mom would have to handle. At least Aunt Rae was there. She could always turn to her if she needed help.

Pete peered out the living room window. He loved being on the top floor, three stories high. The view was much more appealing than the littered alleyway outside his old bedroom, even in the numbing cold of winter. Leafless oak trees of all shapes and sizes scattered among the grounds, on both the parking-lot islands and around the apartment homes. So did green piney bushes. And when springtime rolled into New Jersey, the budding oak trees—along with the green grass and fragrant blossoming flowers—would produce a beautiful storybook scene. He could witness it all, outside, from atop his balcony.

Pete also liked living in Ewing because he was a little closer to work, though he had to travel a few extra minutes for his part-time job at the cinema. His next shift there started in an hour. He would have to leave shortly. Time to shave, shower, and slip on his uniform. And after work he could come home and work on his novel. All night long if he wanted.

And so he did. In fact, he spent every second of free time at his breakfast bar typing away on his laptop, day and night.

For the next three to four months.

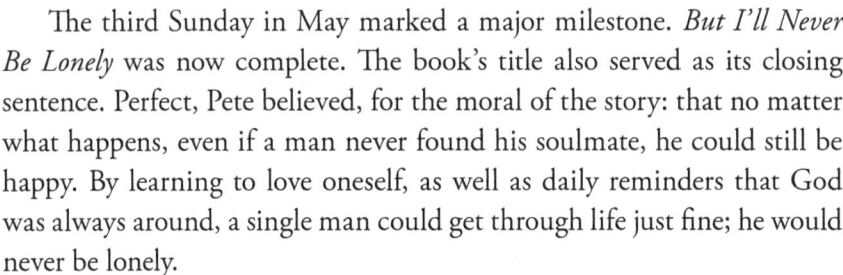

The third Sunday in May marked a major milestone. *But I'll Never Be Lonely* was now complete. The book's title also served as its closing sentence. Perfect, Pete believed, for the moral of the story: that no matter what happens, even if a man never found his soulmate, he could still be happy. By learning to love oneself, as well as daily reminders that God was always around, a single man could get through life just fine; he would never be lonely.

Pete wrote in the first person for his main character, Parker West, and in third person for everybody else. He loved it; he just loved the whole thing. Writing a novel was something he always wanted to do. And getting it published would be a dream come true. Deep down he knew this wasn't likely to happen given the difficult "big break" for new writers. But as he always told himself, you never know unless you try.

He had picked up a writer's guide at the bookstore Friday after work. He decided to buy it instead of checking it out from the library. There would be plenty of useful information inside, information he could retain for future use.

Now, flipping through it outside on his balcony, he knew he'd made the right decision. With a list of literary agents, query-letter tips, and information on manuscript presentation, the book was encyclopedic. A wealth of publishing knowledge lay within his fingertips. And it was his to keep.

Pete took a moment to admire the springtime view, which had changed drastically from when he moved in this winter. As he predicted, the freshness of the season had created a most picturesque scene. Nature had come to life. Green was everywhere, on the grass below to the oak-tree leaves above. A rainbow of blossoming flowers ringed around some of the trees and bushes. The kaleidoscopic colors were especially radiant today underneath the clear blue sky. No moisture inhabited the air. It was a day for open windows, to let in the refreshing mild breeze.

Pete couldn't help but think of his graduation day last year.

Last year? Where did the time go? It sure did whiz by. But what a year it had been. So much had happened: landing a great job at *Jersey News Central*, cutting ties with Todd and Adam, moving into an apartment, and writing a novel. Indeed, it was quite a list.

He deliberately blocked out the make-out session with Corinne. Still, he couldn't help but think of his best friend. Her graduation was this coming Saturday, less than a week away. She had invited him to the ceremony, and he could not refuse. After all, she attended his last year. He felt obligated to return the favor. Besides, their friendship was back to normal. There was nothing to worry about now.

In fact, he planned to call her shortly to share the good news regarding his novel. And who knew what could happen down the road? He could have even better news to spread then. If his work got accepted by an agent or publisher, that is.

Pete went indoors, sliding the glass door behind him. He dropped the writer's guide on the breakfast bar and picked up his mobile phone. He then dialed Corinne's number.

"Hi, Pete!"

She sounded really pleased to hear from him.

"How are you?" she said, very upbeat.

"Great, thanks. And you?"

Corinne felt the same, more so in fact. She was really excited about graduation next weekend—and about seeing Pete, though she kept this to herself.

"Guess what," he said, "I finished my novel today."

"You did? Oh, Pete, that's awesome."

"Thanks."

"Can I read it? Can you email a PDF file to me?"

Pete was surprised. This was her Senior Week. Surely she would travel someplace off campus to celebrate. Corinne was going to but decided to just chill out with her friend Alistair, who also wanted to relax this week. Pete recalled the not-so-common name. Alistair Brundidge was an exchange student from London and was to graduate next weekend as well. The 22-year-old Englishman wanted to study in America during his senior year, Corinne had explained, and catch a few sites at the same time.

Alistair thoroughly enjoyed his ventures into New York City. The fast pace reminded him of his native London, though the British capital seemed to sleep at night, unlike America's largest city. He loved the idea of being able to go out at 3 in the morning if he wanted. Everything was open: dance clubs, bars, cinemas, billiards halls, restaurants, even his gym. So were some supermarkets and department stores. He could do practically anything at any hour, day or night. There were always people out and about, and he could see himself among them.

His student visa allowed for six months of employment in the United States after graduation, from June to December. Alistair wanted to work in New York, as did Corinne, who had just landed a job there as a social worker. She would begin in three weeks.

"You are going to come and visit me in the City, right?"

Pete smiled.

"Yes, of course I will," he said.

"You better ... and you better send a copy of your novel, too. I can't wait to read it."

"Thanks, Corinne."

It meant a lot that she wanted to read his work, especially during Senior Week. She could be doing something far more thrilling to celebrate her graduation. But if this was what she wanted to do, then who was he to question it? Besides, there was no better place to read than the grounds of Stepney Green College. There, lying on a blanket, underneath the towering shady pines ... so relaxing, so peaceful. Better than the beach.

Pete explained he still had much to do. Time to put his editing skills to use yet again! The query letter he would send to literary agents must not contain any errors. Precision was just as important as concision. And sometimes he had to include a synopsis, a summary of the novel that sort of read like a book jacket. Written in the present tense, these brief descriptive paragraphs conveyed the novel's excitement. A well-written synopsis made agents want to explore the book. Pete hoped that his would entice them as well. It had to be good, damn good.

Submitting these query letters would also be expensive. Ones via snail mail, that is. Not only did he have to pay for their postage, he had to include self-addressed stamped envelopes. He would send no more than 50 query letters a month. Completing this task required 100 envelopes and an entire roll of stamps, which was quite costly. But he would do it. He would manage somehow.

"Well, I better get cracking," he said.

"After you email your novel, okay?"

Pete smiled.

"You got it."

"I'm sure it's going to rock," she said enthusiastically.

"I hope so."

"It will, Pete. I know it will rock. Trust me on this."

"It's nice to know I have such a devoted fan."

If you only knew just how devoted I am.

"Well," said Corinne, "good luck on your query letters."

"Thanks."

"See you this weekend."

"Looking forward to it."

So am I.

Pete said goodbye, ended the phone call, and returned to the breakfast bar, where his laptop lay. After emailing a PDF file of his novel to Corinne, he opened a new Word file to construct his query letter, complete with synopsis. It took a little more than an hour to get it just right. At least it was to him.

Next came preparing the envelopes, ones to be posted and returned. Pete flipped through the pages of his writer's book and noted which agencies may accept his novel. He had to be careful. Some were open to manuscript length; others were not. Some only considered specific genres. And a few may be fraudulent.

But he had to take a chance.

35

Corinne's graduation day was as beautiful as Pete's a year ago. Once again no humidity lingered in the mountain air above Stepney Green. The sky's serene blue arched into the heavens. Clouds were absent. And a pleasant breeze landed gently on spectator faces, including Pete's. From the top row of the stadium bleachers he watched proudly as his best friend collected her B.A. in social work. Several people stood and applauded toward the bottom. Pete figured they were her family, her parents and three younger sisters. It would be nice to finally meet them.

"Alistair Brundidge," the announcer said suddenly.

Thunderous applause and cheers ensued, much to Pete's surprise. A tall well-built man rose from his seat. As he scuttled across the platform to shake hands with the college president and take his degree, his profile revealed very sharp features: a strong jawline and chin, full lips, and a perfectly curved nose. Pete also noticed the man had dark curly hair. Draping out of his graduation cap, its length was longer than normal but didn't quite reach his shoulders.

Hmm, so this is Alistair.

The reason behind the ovation was revealed. He looked more like a Greek god than a common Englishman. The majority of cheers had come from his adoring female fans, including Corinne.

After the college president bid final congratulations to the graduates, a swarm of caps fluttered into the sky. Family and friends left the bleachers to greet their accomplished loved ones. But Pete stayed behind for a moment. He watched curiously as Alistair ran to Corinne, took her into his muscular

Blind Expectations

arms, and lifted her euphorically. Based on her ecstatic smile she must have enjoyed the gesture.

Pete also stayed behind because of another tall man in the distance: Todd Galloway. He hadn't seen the filthy-rich hotel heir since last summer's encounter in Woodlake Square. Still, it was too soon. He had barely clapped when Todd waltzed across the platform to collect his degree, unlike Brandi, the Queen of Standards. She had no idea of the peasant seated three rows behind her, and that was fine by him.

Now, on the field below, she jumped into Todd's lean and lofty arms, witnessed by his family and media photographers. Pete tried not to gag. This was no easy task, especially when she smothered him in kisses. Gross.

Pete turned away from the disgusting sight and concentrated on the reason he was here: to see Corinne. She was the one who invited him, and he should focus on her. It was time to spread some warm congratulations and meet her family, even Alistair.

As he rose from the bleachers, Pete tucked in his shirt, straightened his tie, and picked up the gift bag. Stepping down into the field, he headed to where the Aldrich family had assembled. Corinne's back was toward him.

"Hey, you," Pete said with a proud smile. "Congratulations."

Corinne swirled around and lit up like the sun above her.

"Hi, Pete!"

She wrapped loving arms around him and cherished the moment. This was the first time she had seen him, the man she adored, since homecoming night seven months ago. He was still cute as could be.

Pete hugged her back. It was okay to do so now. It was a simple friendly gesture. Besides, the Aldrich family was here—and of course Alistair and what appeared to be his parents. They must have jetted over from Britain, Pete concluded, to witness their son's magical day.

Corinne introduced her best friend on campus to her parents and three younger sisters: Debra, 17; Natalie, 14; and 12-year-old Hope. She then introduced him to the Brundidge family.

"Hello, mate, it's nice to finally meet you," said Alistair, shaking Pete's hand firmly. "I must say, I've heard a lot about you."

"Thank you … same here."

A tinge of skepticism resonated in his voice. Pete figured it was some sort of instinct, that of a protective big brother. Alistair seemed like a nice guy, but he was still a stranger. Not to Corinne, of course. She seemed quite comfortable around him.

"I understand you've written quite a novel," said Alistair, his British accent perfectly polished. "Corinne told me all about your writing project on the side. In fact, she hardly unglued her eyes from it all week."

Pete turned to his best friend. His arched eyebrows conveyed a surprised, "Really?"

Corinne nodded.

"It's true," she said. "It was excellent, it really was. I liked it a lot."

"So it rocked?"

"Yes," she answered with an amused smile, "it definitely rocked."

"Thanks, that means a lot to me," said Pete. "Oh, by the way, this is for you."

He handed over the gift bag, which contained a tiny box. When Corinne opened it she found a 24-karat-gold necklace with a charm in the shape of the letter C. She knew it was expensive, that it had cost him plenty.

"Oh, Pete, this is just beautiful," she gushed. "I love it. Thank you so much."

She kissed him, very quickly, on the lips. It was almost instinctive.

Oh no.

The last time she did this she nearly lost her best friend for good. She couldn't go through that again.

"Can you help me put it on?" she asked him, desperate for a distraction.

"Sure, no problem," Pete replied, seemingly unbothered.

As he secured the necklace around her neck, he caught a glimpse of Corinne's parents and sisters exchanging curious glances. He knew what they were thinking: that the two of them could be more than just friends. Alistair probably wondered the same thing.

A relieved Corinne turned back around.

"So why don't you join us for lunch?" she asked.

Part of him wanted to, but another didn't. Corinne was with her family, and Alistair with his. Pete, alone, would feel like a third wheel if he joined them, something that was out of place and did not belong. He felt it best to leave now.

"Thanks anyway," he said, "but I should head home. I have some things to do before work tomorrow."

Corinne masked her disappointment with a tough, wide-lined smile.

"Okay, I understand," she said, after a moment. "But I'm going to hold you to that promise you made me, to come and visit me in New York."

"Oh, I'm sure you will," Pete said with a chuckle.

"Thanks again for coming," said Corinne, who then embraced the man she loved. "It meant so much to have you here."

"I wouldn't miss it for the world."

Pete broke away from the rather tight squeeze and excused himself.

"It was a pleasure to meet you all," he said.

He then headed back toward his rusty white compact car in the student parking lot. The familiar sight rushed in lots of memories, ones he would like to forget, namely last year's movie date with the lowly Miss Sparks. At the same time it was these memories that fueled the creation of his novel. For this he was grateful. Indeed there was a reason behind the Brandi disaster.

As he hopped inside, Pete decided then and there to buy a new car. It was time. Besides, summer was just around the corner. He didn't want to endure another season of driving in the scorching heat. He needed a car with air conditioning. He owed it to himself.

And he deserved some happiness in the romance department as well. It was time to start dating again ... if he could find someone who wanted to go out with him.

36

Five days after Corinne's graduation, on a sunny Thursday morning, Pete entered his supervisor's office with good news: an agent had requested a copy of his novel. It took less than two weeks to generate a positive response. A few of the remaining 50 weren't so positive. The majority of literary agents had too many clients at the moment. Others simply stated they weren't interested but wished him well. More than 25 query letters were still unaccounted for. Pete had no idea if he would ever hear from them. Still, it was early days. At least he had one interested agent.

"Dude, that's awesome," said Vito, truly happy for him. "As I keep telling you, you're one of the good ones, man."

"Thanks," said Pete, "but it's far from a done deal. She still has to read it and decide if it's worth publishing."

Her name was Margaret Goldberg. She had been a literary agent for 20 years. Her office was in Brooklyn, New York. Pete didn't want to get his hopes up, but he hoped Ms. Goldberg would like *But I'll Never Be Lonely*—and take a chance on it.

"Well, if she doesn't want to represent you, then there's something wrong with the babe," Vito said. "I read your whole book in a weekend, man, a weekend! I couldn't put it down, I enjoyed it that much. Needless to say, Carla wasn't too happy with me … until she started reading it herself."

"Your wife likes it, too?"

"She sure as hell does."

Carla could be quite critical at times, Vito explained. For her to like a book it had to be pretty damn good. She said she could truly sympathize with the main character. The way those women treated Parker made her want to reach into the book and smack them.

"Your book's different, dude," Vito continued. "That's what we like about it. Usually it's the guy dumping all these chicks, not the other way around."

So true.

"You did a great job fictionalizing what happened to you," his boss complimented. "Your writing rocked, my friend, it really did."

Rocked? Man, does that sound familiar.

"Thanks, Vito. I appreciate that."

"And I'm sure this babe in Brooklyn will feel the same."

"I hope so."

Vito winked.

"I got my fingers crossed for you, bud. Carla and I both do."

"Yes, we sure do."

The two men turned to find Mrs. Caparelli standing in the threshold. The 32-year-old woman was well-dressed, slim, petite, and had kinky brown hair. Pete learned fast not to be fooled by her small frame. Her powerhouse of a voice easily outweighed that of her husband. And he thought Vito's voice carried well…

"Thanks, Carla," Pete said with a grateful smile. "It's nice to see you again."

"Gosh, you're such a cutie. Why no girl has snapped you up I'll never know."

Pete blushed, while Vito cleared his throat.

"Yes, dear?" Carla said, flashing a playful smile to her husband.

"You sure have a way with the gentlemen," he answered, shaking his head in amusement. "Yet you picked me. I'm so special."

"Well, there's only one candy bear for me, and that's you."

"Why thank you, sugarloaf."

Candy bear? Sugarloaf? Too funny!

Carla approached her husband's desk.

"Here, dear," she said, handing over a work folder, "you left this in the kitchen."

Vito's brown eyes electrified.

"I was looking all morning for that!" he said, standing up and taking his wife into his arms. "You're such a babe. I knew there was a reason I married you."

"And all this time I thought it was my being a tall Swedish blonde with big tits."

"Well, that too."

After a brief kiss they looked at Pete, who was trying not to laugh. He found their exchanges highly amusing—and admirable. They had such a strong relationship. They knew each other so well and joked around all the time. Deep down, he longed for a similar relationship. But given his abysmal track record the odds were stacked against him—harshly.

"So what are you two doing for lunch?" Carla asked.

"Haven't even thought about it," said her husband.

"Well, we're going out."

"Yes, dear."

"Pete?"

"I think I'll pass," he said, again feeling like a third wheel. "But thanks for the invitation."

"Well, we're taking you out to dinner when this agent accepts your novel," Carla said firmly, "and that's final."

Pete chuckled.

"Don't bother arguing with her, dude," said Vito. "You should see the scars I have from trying."

"Thanks for the warning."

"Good, it's settled then," a pleased Carla announced.

Pete reiterated that there was a genuine possibility Margaret Goldberg may not even like his work. This was not a time to celebrate, he told the Caparellis. Nevertheless he agreed. If—and it was a big if—Ms. Goldberg agreed to take on *But I'll Never Be Lonely*. Only then would he celebrate.

Three weeks later dinner with the Caparellis was on.

37

A deal was a deal. Pete had agreed to join Vito and Carla for a meal out on the town. They lived in Princeton, to the east of Ewing and northeast of Trenton. They invited their special guest to join them at their favorite Italian restaurant, Godfather Italiano, at 7 p.m. It was the second Saturday night in June, which was rather humid.

The climate was the farthest thing on Pete's mind. Just yesterday he received a contract in the mail from literary agent Margaret Goldberg. The day before that, she called him at the office. He would never forget that magical moment—or the sound of Margaret's raspy, heavy Brooklyn accent. She must have smoked a lot of cigarettes to have a scratchy voice like that. Somehow, in the midst of those inflamed vocal cords, a maternal sweetness dwelled. From talking to her, Pete could tell she was a very charming lady.

"Hello, Peter Michael Webb, this is Margaret Goldberg calling."

"Oh, hello, how are you?"

"Fine, sweetheart, hope you are, too. I'm just calling because…" After a cough Margaret continued. "Sorry about that, sweetheart. Anyway, I just have to say you had me in *tears* here. I fell in love with your novel. The way Parker West rose above all that heartache and being thankful for it because it made him a stronger person… Oh, sweetheart, it was just wonderful. I loved the whole thing."

Wow, this is awesome.

"Thank you," said Pete. "Thank you very much."

"You're welcome, sweetheart, you're so welcome." Margaret coughed again. "Excuse me. Well, I just wanted to let you know I'm sending you a contract if you're interested, okay?"

Wow! A contract!

"Okay," Pete replied, fighting to keep his excitement under control, "thank you so much."

"Thank *you*, sweetheart. Bye now."

"Bye."

His heart raced as he came to terms with what just happened. A contract, an actual contract from a literary agent, had been offered. When he dashed into Vito's office to share the news, his boss grinned, shook his head in wonder, and uttered his classic line, "You're one of the good ones, man."

Now he was off to celebrate—in his new air-conditioned car, a blue sedan. Driving in the humidity never felt so comfortable. Princeton was a half-hour drive from Ewing, and Pete enjoyed every minute of it. He also liked having a night off from the cinema, though tomorrow he would have to work a full eight-hour shift.

Godfather Italiano was crowded. Understandable, though, given that it was a Saturday evening. Soothing Italian music serenaded the dining area. A mural covered the elongated far wall. The artwork was extraordinary. Pete felt like he was actually in Italy. Romanesque buildings had been painted throughout, interspersed with the peninsula's magnificent countryside and coastline. Dozens of tables lay in front of the mural, one of which the Caparellis occupied. They were sitting in the corner, near a large flag of Italy hoisted on a pole.

Pete walked on the plush red carpet toward his friends.

"Hey, guys," he said with a bright cheery smile. "This place is so cool. Thanks for the invite."

"You're welcome, bud," said Vito.

"The bill is in the mail," said his wife, looking serious but joking mercilessly.

Pete smiled and took his seat. It was a table for four, though a party of three would be served. It was times like this that really made him feel like a third wheel. But he was happy to be here among friends—and happy to celebrate. Even though a publisher hadn't accepted his novel, landing an agent was a major accomplishment.

Corinne was so happy for him. Had she been asked, she would have hopped on the first train into New Jersey to join him and his friends. But this was her first weekend living in the City. Pete thought she should stay in the area and enjoy the nightlife Manhattan had to offer. He didn't want to spoil her weekend out. Corinne had urged him to celebrate his big achievement this weekend, if not with her in New York then with some other friends.

So he did.

"This is really nice of you guys," Pete said. "You didn't have to do this you know."

"Well, we wanted to," said Carla. "And if you thank us again I'm going to rip out that perfectly combed hair of yours."

"Yes, ma'am," Pete said, saluting.

"She's serious, dude," said Vito, patting his balding head. "Look what she did to mine."

"Stop it, you."

Seconds later the waitress arrived. She was Vito's favorite. And Carla's as well, though for her courteous service not the gym-trim figure she sported.

"Well, hello there, Mr. and Mrs. Caparelli," the young brunette waitress said, smiling warmly. "Welcome back to Godfather Italiano. Once again it'll be my pleasure to serve you tonight."

She then looked at Pete and continued with, "Welcome, sir, I'm Ginny."

"Hi."

She gazed at him for a moment, especially into his dark-brown eyes, which were quite alluring. What a cute guy. She then checked out his left hand, which was ring-free.

"Are you all ready to order now or do you need another few minutes?"

"No, we're ready," said Vito. "I'll have the Ginny special. Uh, I mean, the linguini special."

Carla shot her husband a slightly miffed glance then placed her order of chicken parmesan.

"I'll have the same, thanks," said Pete.

Ginny smiled a bit more radiantly.

"I hope you enjoy it, sir," she said. "It's one of our specialties ... and my favorite."

"I'm sure I will."

Ginny, infatuated, paused once again. For some reason she found herself in awe of this single good-looking man. But she was working. She had to land back on earth and regain her senses.

"All right," she said to her table of three, "I'll be back with your meals as soon as I can."

As their waitress left, Carla rose from the table. She wanted to freshen up a bit in the ladies room and call the sitter to check on the kids.

"Okay, honey graham," Vito said to his wife.

"Love me," she said.

"Love me, too."

Pete shook his head and chuckled. He got the biggest kick out of their jokey, lovey-dovey dialogue.

As soon as Carla was out of hearing range, Vito dropped his hand on his pal's shoulder.

"Dude," he said, "is Ginny a babe or what?"

"Sure, she's very pretty."

And she was. She had enchanting brown eyes—and hair, which shimmered as it cascaded down her back. She had an attractive face as well, despite the awkward indention on the upper part of her nose. Only when she stood at a profile was it noticeable.

"Why don't you ask her out?" Vito urged. "She's 25, only a year older than you."

"I don't think so."

"Why? She was so flirting with you, man."

Pete was stunned.

"She was?"

"Dude, didn't you see the way she smiled at you? She doesn't smile like that to me."

"That's because you're married."

Amused, Vito shook his head.

"Listen, man," he said, "she smiled like that because she likes you. She thinks you're a cute guy, I can tell. I'm going to tell you something else, too.

You know what my wife said to me when she first met you?" Vito leaned into his ear to finish discreetly. "She said that if she weren't married she'd screw your brains out."

"I see," said Pete, who then chugged down a full glass of ice water.

"So go ahead and ask out this Ginny chick, okay? Just go for it, man. She's a babe, and you're a great catch. You two could have a lot of fun together."

"Yeah, maybe I will. Thanks, Vito."

He really had nothing to lose. So what if Ginny said no? At least he could say he tried.

Pete was willing to make an exception, just this once, to his women-had-to-pursue-him-from-now-on rule. But was it really an exception? After all, she sort of made the first move. Her radiant smile and special attentiveness proved this. So what the heck? As Vito said, just go for it.

And he did, after dinner, at the door on the way out.

"Good night," Ginny said sweetly.

Pete told the Caparellis he would meet them outside in a moment. Summoning his courage, he handed the pretty waitress his business card. The back contained his personal cellphone number, which he had handwritten.

"I'd like to take you out to lunch sometime if you're interested," he said. "If not, that's cool, I understand. Just thought I'd—"

"How about tomorrow?" she suggested.

Tomorrow? Absolutely!

"Sure," said Pete, "tomorrow sounds fine."

"How 'bout I call you around 10-10:30?"

"Great ... well, good night."

"Night, Pete," she said, her brown eyes sparkling.

As he exited into the humid summer air his hand smacked against his forehead. Shoot! He forgot all about his eight-hour shift at the movie theater tomorrow. But a childlike grin soon emerged, having thought of the perfect, and simple, solution: just call in sick. How ironic to do this when he was feeling so well.

And he had waited a long, long time to feel like this again.

38

Falling asleep last night took a while. Pete kept thinking about what transpired last night at the Italian restaurant in Princeton. Ginny was a very pretty girl—sans the nose—and she wanted to see him today. He wondered why. What was it that made her want to go out with him? Pete also thought about fate's role in this setup. If he had reneged on his deal to dine with Vito and Carla, then none of this would be happening right now. He and Ginny never would have met.

More than a year had passed since he had been involved with anyone. Thanks to writing his novel mostly. But now that it was completed he could focus on revving up his love life. With his upcoming lunch date he felt he was off to a good start.

A new start was more like it. Things would be different this time. No more crossing the border into the land of love until much later. The first couple of dates—that is, if more occurred after this one—would no longer push him that far. There had to be many, and it would be up to the woman to give clear signals. Or just tell him pointblank that she wanted to date him exclusively.

This woman may, or may not, be Ginny. But it would be fun to find out.

Pete's phone rang five minutes before 10:30. It had to be her, he thought. She said she would call during this time.

And she did.

"Hello?"

"Hi, Pete," she said with a touch of flirtatiousness. "It's Ginny."

"Well, hello there."

"How are you doing?"

"Fine, thanks," he said. "And you?"

Ginny was all right, just not hungry. She asked if they could skip lunch and catch a movie instead.

A movie? Already? This girl barely knew him. And she wanted to go to the movies so soon? Why not, Pete thought, remembering what Vito had said last night. Really, what the heck? What did he have to lose? In fact, by going to the movies he would actually gain something: time. They could be together longer this way. Lunch would be over in an hour. A film, on the other hand, lasted longer.

"There's this new romantic comedy I'd like to see," said Ginny. "Is that okay?"

A romantic comedy? Not one of those, anything but that. He had vowed to steer clear of movies like these, ones that invoked a false illusion of what love was supposed to be. But he was different then, naïve and gullible. A new Pete existed now. He was stronger, smarter. He knew how to avoid that silver-screen trap. He knew the difference between fluff and love. Though, admittedly, he had yet to experience—truly experience—the latter.

"Sure, we can see it," Pete said confidently. "I'm cool with that."

And he was ... now.

Ginny lived in a modest one-bedroom apartment on the second floor of her building. The complex, in Princeton's northwestern outskirts, was relatively new. As Pete entered her building, he noted the somewhat-fresh scent of the paint and carpet.

He walked upstairs to the second floor, turned right, and headed toward her apartment, several footsteps away on the left. He approached her door at 1 p.m., the exact time he was to pick her up. He could not have planned his arrival any better.

Ginny opened the door seconds after Pete's knock. She smiled at him cheerfully and gave him a quick, but affectionate, hug. Her date smiled in return. Though flattered by the warm reception, he made sure not to read too much into it. She was simply being friendly, he told himself. There was nothing more to it than that.

Not yet at least.

"Wow, this is a nice place," Pete said as he glanced around.

Ginny's one-bedroom apartment differed than his. It was more open, which conveyed a spacious appearance. He could see virtually everything from the foyer. A small kitchen, tastefully decorated in black and white, sat to the right. It overlooked a large dining area that connected to an even larger living room. Two rectangular windows on the far wall emitted lots of light.

"Glad you like it," said Ginny. "It's not much, but it's mine."

"That's exactly how I feel about my place."

"Would you like a tour?"

"Sure," said Pete, though there was really not much left to see.

Ginny led him down a tiny corridor to his left, which led to the bathroom. It was decorated in several pastel colors—lots of light pinks, blues, greens and yellows. Pete thought it rather girlie. Of course, a female tenant lived here.

And what a tenant she was … in those tight blue jeans. Pete couldn't help but notice how they outlined that perfect ass of hers.

Another bathroom door, to the right, led to another tiny corridor. A walk-in closet sat to the left, laundry facilities to the right, and an airy bedroom ahead. One last door connected the bedroom to the living room, creating a square-like floor plan.

"Have a seat," she said, gesturing toward the maroon sofa. "Can I get you anything, something to drink?"

"No, thanks, I'm fine," said Pete. "Besides, you're home now. No need to serve any customers here."

Ginny smiled and sat on the loveseat beside the sofa.

"So how do you know the Caparellis?" she asked.

"Vito's my supervisor at *Jersey News Central*. He's awesome to work with."

"I bet he's a lot of fun."

"He sure is. Never a dull moment with Vito around, that's for sure."

Ginny chuckled.

"So do you waitress full time?" Pete asked.

"No, only part time," she said. "I actually work full time in my college's human resources office."

She went on to explain that by working there she could also earn a tuition-free master's degree. Her date thought it an excellent opportunity, as did Ginny. She attended two evening classes a semester. Other evenings she spent earning extra money at Godfather Italiano … and meeting new people.

"I have a part-time job, too," said Pete, "at a movie theater. Pretty ironic, isn't it, considering our plans for the day."

Ginny agreed. Little did she know her date had called in sick earlier … so that he could go to the movies.

"I wish we could've gone to a later show instead," she said, "but I have a wedding shower to go to this evening."

"Not a problem."

Ginny smiled, amazed by his easygoing nature. She also liked the outfit he wore: off-white pants with a royal-blue button-down shirt overtop. His short brown hair, combed and gelled to perfection, appealed as well. And that smile of his.

She also liked his new blue sedan parked outside, which they now approached.

"Wow, you have a really great car," she said.

Now I do.

"Thanks."

The gentleman he was, Pete opened the door for her and closed it after she got inside. They then headed to a popular cinema in the heart of Princeton. The parking lot was full. Somehow, though, they managed to find an empty space.

The 2 o'clock show had no available tickets. Neither did the one after it, at 4:45. Ginny apologized, adding she should have gone online to check the seating before they left. There was no need to be sorry, of course. An alternative plan quickly swooshed to the surface.

"So is there another theater around?" Pete said. "Maybe we can see it there."

There was, Ginny told him, but on the northeastern fringes. This was not a problem for Pete.

"Want to check it out there?"

Impressed by her date's resourcefulness, she answered with a smile. It was just the signal he needed to head out to Princeton's outer edge.

And to know that the date was going really well.

◆●◆

This other cinema wasn't nearly as crowded, which Pete found surprising as it was inside a mall. Maybe the weather had something to do with it. The blue sky had changed to gray and was growing blacker by the minute. People probably didn't want to venture out into an impending storm unless they had to, Pete concluded.

Before heading inside to purchase the tickets he glanced around a moment, spotting a manmade lake to the side. A boardwalk encircled it. Perfect for a relaxing stroll. But there may not be enough time for one, either before the movie or looming downpour.

There was only one way to find out.

Inside the mall, they headed toward the cinema. The next show started at 3:30, in a little more than an hour.

Ginny cut in as Pete took out his credit card.

"I can treat," she said. "After all, this was my idea."

"Not a problem. I got it, really." He then added an interesting little something. "You pay next time, how's that?"

Ginny smiled. Obviously this meant he wanted to see her again.

"Sure, okay," she said, softly and sweetly.

"Cool … Well, we've got some time before the movie. How about we take a walk around the lake outside?"

"Sounds good."

Pete was amazed. Ginny seemed pretty easygoing, much like he was. She had agreed to all his ideas so far. And he didn't second-guess himself. No more nagging questions bouncing off the walls in his brain. No more: Was she enjoying herself? Was he showing her a good time? What if he did or said something inappropriate? No more of that—not with the new, relaxed, carefree, and stronger Peter Michael Webb. He was at the helm now. He was in control. Though he wanted Ginny to have a fun time, he wasn't bending over backwards trying to impress her. He was simply being himself. And he liked this person. Ginny may like him, too. Then again she may not. And that was totally okay. It didn't matter either way.

Outside, the sky had darkened even more. Rain was definitely on its way. Nevertheless, Pete and his date headed toward the lake's boardwalk.

"I didn't bring an umbrella," he warned.

"That's okay," said Ginny, "neither did I."

The pair smiled at each other and began their trek on the boardwalk. Neither knew if the threatening sky would unleash its wrath upon them. Nor did they seem to care.

Ginny, which she revealed was a nickname for Ginger, described her family. Her parents, the Leeds, adopted her at infancy, she explained, as well as her younger brother John-Paul. She was very close to them, though her parents were quite strict. They had tried to have their own biological children but couldn't conceive. Still, they treated John-Paul and her like they were their own flesh and blood. Their love for them was unconditional. As a result, Ginny never felt out of place in the family. Nor did she have a desire to locate her biological mother and father. To her, the people who adopted her were her parents. And the blond-haired, blue-eyed John-Paul was her brother.

"Who knows," she said, strolling alongside her handsome date, "maybe you can meet them sometime."

"Sure," Pete said, "sounds like fun."

"I know my brother and sister-in-law like to play cards and other games at home," she said, adding that as a young married couple they didn't have a lot of money to go out. "Maybe we can hang out with them sometime."

"Sounds like a plan."

Ginny smiled.

"So," she said, "what about your family?"

He knew this was coming—and didn't beat around the bush like he did with Brandi last year in the park.

"I don't have many relatives," said Pete. "I'm close to my mother but not my brother. We're estranged actually."

"I'm sorry."

"Don't be."

And that was that. Ginny didn't press him for details. Maybe she would at a later time, but for now she changed the subject ... to careers and ambitions. Working in a human resources office was quite enjoyable for her, she said. She could really advance once she earned her M.B.A.

Pete was perfectly content at *Jersey News Central*, at least for now. Of course, his dream was to become a novelist. With an agent ready to knock down publisher doors, the dream drifted ever closer into the realm of reality.

"Wow," said an amazed Ginny, "you actually have an agent? That is so cool."

"Thanks," he said. "By the way that's why I was at Godfather Italiano with the Caparellis last night: to celebrate my landing an agent."

"You mean it wasn't because of me?" Ginny joked, placing her hand over a shattered heart.

With a smile Pete glimpsed over to the pretty brunette by his side, one with an excellent sense of humor. For a moment he felt an urge to throw his arm around her. But he resisted. Besides, they were nearing the end of their boardwalk lakeside tour. And just in time. It was 3:10 p.m. The movie would begin in 20 minutes, unlike the unpredictable thunderstorm hovering overhead.

"This walk was fun," said Pete, holding open the mall door. "I enjoyed it."

Ginny agreed, confirmed by her impressive smile.

Inside the cinema, the pair made their way up to the top row. As soon as they sat down, their heads lurched up toward the ceiling.

"What's that noise?" Ginny asked, disturbed by the violent shuddering.

"That's the rain we just avoided," Pete told her.

"Are you serious?"

Indeed he was. The bullets trying to blast through the roof of the theater were actually fierce raindrops. Their raid soon halted—right when the movie started. Pete was stunned at his impeccable timing. First his arrival at Ginny's then their rain-free walk around the lake, and now, watching a movie in peace.

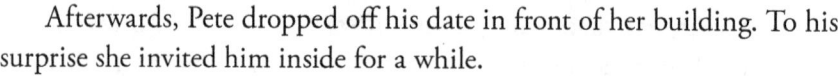

Afterwards, Pete dropped off his date in front of her building. To his surprise she invited him inside for a while.

"That is, if you have the time," she added.

"Sure, why not?"

They sat next to one another on her maroon sofa in the living room. Ginny had this seductive twinkle in her eye. Pete could tell she wanted some affection, whether it a hug, kiss, or more. But he held back. He wanted to be sure of her intentions. Was she just another pretty face that wanted to use him for a pleasurable afternoon? It was too soon to tell. He needed more time to be certain.

"So what are you doing next weekend?" Ginny asked.

"I'm actually heading into New York to visit a friend of mine."

This was true.

Pete had accepted Corinne's invitation to get together. He had emailed his confirmation late last night—but did not disclose news of today's date with Ginny.

"How about we get together the weekend after that?" he offered. "Is that cool?"

"Sure," she said, disappointed but understanding.

Pete squeezed her hand.

"I'm serious, Ginny," he said. "I'm not trying to blow you off here. I'll give you a call when I get back, and we'll make plans then."

"How about you call me before, then, and after?"

"You got it," her date replied, with a flattered smile.

The pair rose hand in hand from the sofa and made their way to the front door. There, they gazed into each other's dark-brown eyes.

"I had a great time today," said Ginny.

"I did, too."

"If I didn't have this wedding shower later, I'd ask you to stay longer."

"Not a problem."

And with that, Ginny drew his lips to hers, kissing him gently but firmly—and for quite a while. That was some kiss goodbye, Pete thought afterwards. And he sensed there would be more to come.

39

New York City never ceased to amaze. Its liveliness stretched as far as the naked eye would allow. People covered the sidewalks like ants on a picnic basket. So did all the vehicles atop the streets. It was quite a view outside Penn Station's 7th Avenue exit, where Pete had emerged. His Saturday-afternoon train from Trenton was quite pleasant.

As was the taxi drive to Corinne's apartment. It took longer than expected to reach her building in the Upper West Side, but Pete didn't mind, not in the slightest. He loved the surrounding energy, the vivacity of this magnificent city ... and all the buildings.

Corinne's was no exception. With an overnight bag over his shoulder Pete approached the classy beige condominium complex. Corinne was wise to purchase her two-bedroom unit here, he thought. She had invested the money from her trust fund wisely. A social worker's salary did not pay nearly enough to live in a place like this. However, with no rent or mortgage, it could easily take care of the other monthly bills and expenses.

Pete rode the elevator to the ninth floor, where his best friend resided. Plush carpet blanketed the hallway, much like that in a posh hotel. He then knocked on Corinne's cream-colored door with fancy teal trim. When it opened, his best friend appeared with the brightest of smiles.

"Hi, Pete!" she said with a warm embrace. "I'm so happy you're here. Welcome to my home. And welcome to New York!"

"Thanks, Corinne."

She ushered him inside her grandiose condo and showed him around. Pete was in awe of the décor. Fancy woodwork bordered the high ceilings as well as the columns in the corners. A beautiful hardwood floor lay at his feet, covered partially by an ornate Oriental carpet. Three enormous windows centered themselves on the main wall, bounded by velvety teal curtains, the same color as the trim on the front door.

"Wow," said Pete, "this place is incredible."

"Thank you," said Corinne, who then escorted her guest to the spare bedroom. "This is where you'll be sleeping tonight. Hope it meets your… standards."

Pete dropped his overnight bag in feigned over-the-top histrionics.

"Well, you know I have some really, really high standards," he joked, "and this room will just never meet my standards."

The two best friends shared a hearty laugh and adjourned back to the living room.

"So," said Corinne, lounging on the cream-colored sofa. "How are things with you? What's new?"

Pete, relaxing on the recliner, almost fell asleep. But his eyes darted open to answer his friend's question.

"Same ole, same ole," he said.

"Oh, don't give me that, Mr. Soon-to-be-Published Novelist."

"If only that were true…"

"In a matter of time, it will be," said Corinne. "Trust me on this, Pete. Your book's really good. If it weren't, that agent would never have signed you on."

"Thanks for the vote of confidence."

He then yawned, which Corinne noticed.

"Would you like to lie down for a while?" she asked. "You seem pretty tired."

"I am, but—"

"But nothing," she interrupted, albeit with good intentions. "Go and have a rest, and we'll go out to dinner afterwards."

"But—"

"No buts. Now go."

Pete smiled and shook his head in defeat.

"No use arguing with you," he said on his way to bed, "just like the good ole college days."

"Some things never change."

Pete wondered if this included sharing what went on with his love life. He could always disclose this information in the past—before their more-than-friendly kisses last year. But was it okay to do so now? Could he share the Ginny news?

He would soon find out ... but not the way he would have liked.

40

They arrived at The Piccadilly, a British pub, at 7:30. It was a short four-block walk from Corinne's place. She was dressed rather sharply, in off-white pants and a blue silky blouse, just about the same color as her eyes. Pete wore casual tan pants, a white polo shirt, and brown shoes. Corinne thought he looked quite attractive. Then again she always thought that no matter what he had on.

The petite British hostess escorted them to a corner booth, adjacent to the restroom corridor, and handed them menus.

"Right, someone will be with you shortly to take your order."

"Okay, thanks," said Corinne, whose cellphone rang. "Excuse me for just a moment, Pete."

"Sure."

"Hello? ... Hi Alistair, are you upstairs?"

Alistair. Gee, what a coincidence. Pete knew he would run into him eventually. It was a case of sooner rather than later when Corinne led him here, his workplace. She had explained his whole setup. Alistair could work at the pub and live upstairs rent-free. The tips he earned waiting tables were his to keep. Not a bad arrangement, though it would end when his six-month visa expired in December. He could find other employment in the meantime, a company that would sponsor him, but he longed to return to his native England.

Pete knew of another reason Alistair chose to live and work at The Piccadilly, here in New York City's Upper West Side: to be close to Corinne.

"Well, we're here getting ready to order our dinner," she said to her British friend. "Sure, you can join us."

Oh goodie.

"See you soon. Bye."

Corinne hung up and apologized to Pete, hoping he didn't mind if Alistair joined them.

"No," he said, fibbing a bit, "not at all."

But he did mind in a way—and wished he knew why. Alistair Brundidge could not have been nicer when they met at Corinne's graduation. Nevertheless, something about this suave Englishman bothered him. Something had gnawed in his gut … but what?

"Well, I know what I want," said Corinne, closing the menu, "bangers and mash."

"What's that?"

"It's—"

"A lovely choice, gorgeous," said Alistair, arriving at the booth. "I fancy that myself tonight."

He planted a rather long kiss on Corinne's cheek—on purpose, Pete thought—before sitting down next to her. He then stretched his hand across the table.

"Hello, Pete," he said. "Nice to see you again, mate."

"And you."

"Corinne tells me you've landed an agent for your novel. Congratulations. That's fantastic news."

"Thank you."

"I can see it now," the dashing Alistair continued, "women jumping over each other in these massive queues at your book signings."

"A nice thought," said Pete. "We'll just have to wait and see."

"I'm sure they're jumping right now vying for your affection."

"If only they were…"

"Oh, come on, there's got to be at least one lucky girl."

Corinne interrupted with an annoyed, "Alistair…"

She thought it intrusive to ask her best friend these personal questions. After all, his love life was off limits to practically everyone, including Alistair Brundidge.

"No, Corinne, it's okay."

I'll show that magazine model pinup.

Pete felt now was the perfect time to share his Ginny news.

"I actually went out on a date last weekend," he said, shocking his longtime friend.

You did?

Corinne's eyes had widened so much they could have popped out onto the table.

Alistair was secretly delighted.

Just as I thought, Pete never told her.

"So, mate, tell us about this lovely bird. What's she like? I bet she's quite pretty."

"Yes, she is," Pete confirmed. "We had a really nice time at the movies, and we plan to—"

He stopped suddenly, having read the hurt across Corinne's face. She couldn't hide it no matter how hard she may have tried. Shoot. The last thing in the world he wanted to do was hurt her. But now he had. He should have told her all about it last week. Too late now. Thanks to Alistair, of course. Pete could kick himself for falling into his trap.

He heaved a silent sigh of relief when the waitress arrived. She came at a good time. It was just the distraction he—and Corinne— needed.

"Hello, everyone, I'm Sue."

She spoke with a working-class East London accent.

"Yes, I know," Alistair said to his coworker, raising his eyebrows in playful flirtation.

"Hello there, handsome, what can I get you tonight?"

"The lovely and charming Corinne and I will each have bangers and mash, thank you."

"Right," said Sue, who then turned to Pete. "What about you, love?"

"What exactly is bangers and mash?"

The waitress explained it was a British everyday name for sausages served alongside mash potato, with gravy poured over both. The meal also included peas. That sounded good, but Pete ordered fish and chips instead, with mushy peas.

He rose from the table as Sue left, explaining he had to use the men's room. Alistair pointed to the corridor behind him.

"The gents is right down here, mate," he said.

Pete thanked him, though he already knew where it was. But he didn't use the bathroom. Instead, he leaned against the corridor's stony wall to eavesdrop on the conversation Corinne and the debonair Brit were likely to have—about him.

"Are you all right?" Alistair asked softly.

Corinne said she was fine, though unconvincingly.

"No, you're not, not at all."

She turned to him with glassy eyes. Alistair took his cue and offered his shoulder. Corinne certainly needed to lean on one.

Pete glimpsed at the sight then turned away quickly.

Is she that upset I didn't tell her about Ginny?

"You see where you stand with him now, don't you?" said Alistair. "He's made it perfectly clear that he's not interested in you romantically."

Corinne sniffled.

"Yes, I suppose you're right," she said.

"Now you can finally move on with your life, which is a good thing."

He lifted her head from his shoulder to gaze into those beautiful blue eyes of hers.

"Corinne," he said tenderly, "I care about you so much. I've fancied you the moment I met you."

"I bet you say that to all the girls."

Alistair shook his head.

"No, I don't," he said. "Really, I don't."

"You must get dozens of phone numbers from girls who come in here."

"I do, but I never ring any of them." Alistair strummed Corinne's face with his finger as he continued. "You're the only woman I want to talk to … and be with. I know I've told you this before, but now you can finally give us a chance. What do you say?"

Pete was right to trust his instincts and stick to the corridor wall like a fly. Corinne was indeed that upset about his date with Ginny—and more so. Apparently she had very strong feelings for him. And she had harbored them for quite some time, since last year's homecoming … if not longer. For months, maybe even a year, she kept hoping he would return these feelings. That was something he couldn't do. He loved her but was not *in love* with her. She was the best friend he ever had. He could not risk hurting her. But he already did.

Alistair was all too ready to pick up the pieces of her broken heart. He probably planned this whole thing, Pete concluded, to open her weak spot and exploit it for his own personal gain. Before he could do this he had to damage the rock-solid bond she shared with her best friend. Breaking the Ginny news did the trick. Pete's friendship with Corinne once again contained crusty edges, just like after homecoming back in October. Alistair Brundidge had accomplished his mission. The bastard. Still, there was one good thing to come out of all this: he now knew why the Briton made him so uncomfortable.

Pete glanced around the corner and spied Alistair stroking Corinne's hair. She hadn't answered his question about giving him a chance. She was just too confused at the moment. But she would be thinking about it, long and hard.

And Pete would have to be there for her. He would be her friend, her best friend, just like always.

He had to pretend he never overheard this revealing conversation. Somehow.

41

Onboard the Trenton-bound train early Sunday afternoon, Pete gazed out the window and reflected on Corinne's stunning admission—though not to him, of course. He wondered if their friendship could continue as it was. A chunk of its honesty had been severed. Faking behavior just wasn't appropriate. Best friends should never do this sort of thing. But what choice did he have?

Pete had acted like he normally did around Corinne for the remainder of the visit. Given what he overheard at The Piccadilly last night, it wasn't easy. But he managed. One thing was certain, though. He could not disclose any new details about Ginny. His dating status was a sore subject for Corinne, one that would undoubtedly puncture more holes into her heart. Pete would do whatever necessary to prevent that from happening. He hoped the physical distance between them, though not drastic, would help.

Ginny also swirled in the rapids of thought. She had texted him immediately after last Sunday's date, much to his surprise. She wrote how much she enjoyed their time together, especially the walk. Pete wrote the same when he answered back. Ginny kept the texts coming, every day, with amorous Xs and Os adorned below her name. She even called him Saturday before his train to New York.

"I thought I was supposed to call you," Pete had said.

"You were," she replied, "but I couldn't wait that long. Hope you don't mind. I just wanted to hear your voice again."

Whoa, how cool was that? She sure knew how to flatter a guy.

And she flattered him some more… Pete received another text when he got home. He loved Ginny's most recent message:

I couldn't bear another weekend going by without seeing you.

Again, how cool was that?

He was grateful for the distraction, to get his mind off Corinne for a while. And what a distraction it was! Vito was right on: Ginny *was* a babe. Pete could now concentrate on this pretty young thing instead … and any relationship that may follow.

After a week of phone calls and mushy text messages, Pete drove to Ginny's place in Princeton Friday night. She had invited him over to watch a movie. Two movie dates in a row, but this time in her apartment. He told her to expect him by 8 o'clock. But he arrived 10 minutes late. With good reason, as Ginny would happily discover.

"I have to stop and get gas," Pete had said via cellphone. "Sorry."

But the gauge read half full. He stopped into a floral shop instead. There he picked out a superb arrangement of multicolored flowers.

"By the way," he said, handing them over inside her apartment, "this was the gas I had to get."

"Aw," she gushed. "Thank you, Pete, they're beautiful."

Ginny put the bouquet into a vase and filled it with water, spreading the arrangement to her liking. She smelled the flowers afterwards and savored their fresh scent, which would fade in time.

"Do you like Japanese food by chance?" Pete asked.

"Never tried it."

"Would you like to next weekend? I've been meaning to check out this Japanese restaurant close to where I live."

"Sure," she said enthusiastically. "I'd like that a lot."

She added that she could only do lunch, as she had to work at Godfather Italiano next weekend, both Friday and Saturday nights.

"Lunch it is then," Pete said confidently.

Ginny smiled and led her date into the living room, where he sat on the maroon sofa. He admired the scenery from here, namely Ginny's amazing ass in those tight jeans of hers. Pete could think of no better movie preview than to watch her turn on the TV and insert a DVD. Damn, she looked good. And felt good as she snuggled next to him on the sofa.

Pete threw his arm around her as they watched the movie, a drama. He stroked her arm and shoulder the whole time. She did not flinch once. In fact, she did the same to him, but to his knee and leg. Something was indeed happening here. Whatever it was he liked it. This romance was unlike any other. Pete had never felt so relaxed around a woman—or with himself. No worry. No second-guessing. No negativity whatsoever. He was simply enjoying this girl's company.

After the movie he and Ginny chatted on the balcony. They spotted a few people loitering outside the building across the street.

"I hope this doesn't turn into a bad neighborhood," she said, "because I'll pack up and move in no time."

Rather impulsive, Pete thought. She had mentioned something similar earlier: that she would quit and find another part-time job in no time if it got to be too strenuous.

"So," he said, "want me to go down there and kick some butt?"

Ginny's brown eyes twinkled in flirtation.

"I'm sure you could with those muscles."

Muscles? She must need glasses, Pete said to himself. He was no Alistair Brundidge. Still, who was he to question the compliment?

"Come here," he said, taking Ginny into his arms. "You're pretty hot yourself, you know that?"

They kissed gently. No open mouths. Pete felt it too soon for that. Although he liked this girl, he still could not read her intentions. He wasn't about to fall prey to another love-him-and-leave-him type. But if he did he knew he could handle it.

At least he hoped he could.

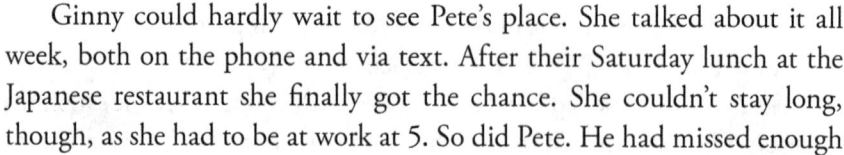

Ginny could hardly wait to see Pete's place. She talked about it all week, both on the phone and via text. After their Saturday lunch at the Japanese restaurant she finally got the chance. She couldn't stay long, though, as she had to be at work at 5. So did Pete. He had missed enough hours at the cinema already—but with a really good excuse. Dating Ginny was well worth it. So was visiting Corinne in New York, of course.

He had gone without living room furniture all winter and spring. He finally bought some after Margaret Goldberg offered him a contract. No more saving up for query-letter and return postage—and agency sign-on fees. Pete learned early that a small fortune came attached to this kind of representation. Therefore, he made certain to save every penny. Now, thanks to Margaret, he no longer had to scrimp to pay for all that postage. Or her contract fee, which was fairly reasonable. At long last he could afford to buy a few things to liven up his new home.

And just in time for Ginny's first visit. She liked what she saw: the sofa, coffee table, lamps, entertainment center, wall pictures, even the plants.

"This place is awesome."

"Why thank you," he said, wrapping his arms around her waist from behind. "Glad you like it."

He planted a moist, hot kiss on her neck. As he did this, Ginny closed her eyes. Her skin warmed. Pete could tell it was a welcome surprise. She turned around afterwards and gazed lustfully into his eyes. Though she spoke no words, she said she was ready. She had waited for his sexual touch long enough. Pete was more than ready to comply. He cupped her perfect ass into his throbbing hands and pulled her pulsating body into his. Their arms ran all over each other. They kissed hungrily, passionately.

"Oh, Pete," Ginny said, relishing the feel of his mouth on her feverish neck, "your kisses are soooo intoxicating."

Intoxicating? Part of him wanted to laugh when he heard this. But his libido overpowered this urge and made him continue.

After a few more minutes she pulled away.

"What is it?" he asked.

"Make love to me."

So he did—gladly—though it wasn't exactly love. Ginny was the second woman to share his bed, after Mary Ann Tolliver back in high school. But this time was different. With Mary Ann there was an emotional attachment. Not with Ginny. Not yet at least. Pete surprised himself. Usually he had to have very strong, very intense feelings before being this intimate with a woman. There was intensity, all right, but not in his heart.

And probably not in Ginny's either. They simply enjoyed an afternoon of sexual healing.

And he was fine with this … for now.

42

The pair got together often and not just on weekends. Sometimes they had sex; sometimes they just caressed one another. Pete had never gone through so many condoms. But he enjoyed every moment. Ginny did, too, apparently. She said, "I like you," "I want you," and "I need you" all the time. But never "I love you." She didn't utter the three words her partner began longing to hear.

Damn, it was happening again. He fought hard to stay put inside his "in like" shell, but the more visits he and Ginny had the more it cracked. Insulating himself against the harsh realities of love outside had grown increasingly difficult. Yet somehow he stuck to his vow: it was up to the woman to declare her feelings—first. Only then would he allow his shell to fully open. After they became an official couple he would introduce her to his mother.

Pete wondered if this were the reason he hadn't met any of her relatives, either. Maybe she, like him, wanted to make sure they were in a committed relationship before introducing him. After all, they never did go over to her brother's house like she once suggested.

Ginny needed a hint, Pete concluded, a little push in the love direction. But what exactly and how should he present it?

He wished Corinne were around to offer advice. She would know what to do. But he dared not ask, not now, not after her big revelation in New York. After that visit he never mentioned anything about Ginny or dating. And she never asked. Both had agreed, silently, that this subject was off limits. Still, it was okay for Corinne to talk about Alistair. Pete honestly didn't mind, though he wished she would find some other guy to date.

They talked about him late that night on the phone, the first Friday in August.

"So are you happy?" he asked.

She hesitated before answering.

"Yes, I think I am."

"Think?"

"We're just dating right now."

It was still too soon to know, she explained. But to herself she said something else. Although she may be dating Alistair, he did not hold her heart in the palm of his hand. It still belonged to someone else—and Pete knew it. Yes, he had to know that her heart belonged to him, he just had to. That was why he brought up Alistair tonight: to toss it back into the ring for him to catch.

Then reality returned...

Why, damn it, why doesn't Pete want it himself? Why can't he love me?

Because he was still dating that Ginny girl, she realized. They could be an item by now. He very well could have found genuine happiness with her. Corinne did not want to know this. She refused to go there and ask him. Her heart would split in two if this news were confirmed.

She couldn't take much more of this—any more of this, on second thought.

I've got to get over this and move on. I've got to, damn it. I can't keep doing this to myself. It's been more than a year now. The sooner I let go the better off I'll be. I've got to force myself to think of him as nothing more than just a friend. I've got to for my own peace of mind ... and for Alistair. I can't keep doing this to him. I can't keep pushing him away, keeping him at a distance. He really wants to be in a serious relationship with me, and I should let him. I should just go for it and take a chance. I have to let go of this crazy dream of Pete and me once and for all ... it's never going to happen.

Be strong, she told herself.

Though she had vowed not to bring up the Ginny subject, she now realized how necessary it was. Only then could she truly move on with her life.

"Listen, Pete," she said, "I want you to know that you can talk to me about anything, okay?"

"I know that."

"Anything," she stressed, "including your relationship with Ginny."

Silence permeated the other end of the phone line.

"It's okay, really."

"You're cool with this?"

Corinne answered with a firm, resolute "Yes." Her tone made Pete believe it. Finally, she was putting homecoming night behind her. Those feelings she had then—and at The Piccadilly

six weeks ago—must have begun to wade. Perhaps now they could truly be best friends again. No more hiding. He could be totally open and honest. No need to walk on eggshells anymore. Talking with her about Ginny would no longer hurt her feelings.

"So," Corinne said, "are *you* happy?"

This time Pete hesitated before answering with a "Yes, I think I am."

"Think?"

The two friends shared a laugh over this script reversal. They soon got back to business.

"Corinne, I really need your advice on something."

"Just like back in the college days, huh?"

"You got it."

"I'm all ears."

And with that, their bond strengthened once again. This was the kind of laidback talk they had always shared, before things got crazy. Pete was glad to be rid of this awkward tension. He prayed it was gone for good this time.

"I need to give Ginny some sort of hint, you know?" he said. "I want her to know that I'm ready for us to commit to each other."

Corinne summoned all her strength. She needed every ounce to get through this, to keep her heart intact.

"I got it," she said, succeeding. "Give her a photo. Not a digital one. Something she can frame or put in her wallet. Pardon the pun, but she should get the picture."

"Yes!" Pete exclaimed. "That's it, that's perfect."

"Hope it works."

"I do, too. Thanks, Corinne, thank you very much."

"You're welcome."

And he was. She was glad to help him ... and herself. Now she was ready, truly ready, to explore other avenues, namely Alistair Brundidge. Though she did not love him, she was willing to see if she could.

Whatever the future had in store was anybody's guess, but Corinne would soon find out.

"Night, Pete," she said.

"Good night ... and thanks again."

"Bye."

As soon as she hung up she smiled proudly. The power of the mind indeed works wonders. She then thought of Alistair. Clutching her bed pillows, she imagined how comforting his strong masculine touch would be at this very moment. That magnificent body of his, those muscles, fingering through his dark curly hair ... being with him would feel really good right now. And she needed to feel good. She needed comfort. She needed to forget about everything and everybody, especially Pete. It was time to escape the world, albeit temporarily, and Alistair would jump at the chance to journey with her.

Suddenly, her phone rang. It was Alistair. She answered it right away.

"Hello?"

"Hello, gorgeous," he said, lounging in his own bed above the pub. "I just wanted to say goodnight before turning in."

"You did, did you?"

Corinne's voice had become sultry, which Alistair liked.

"I certainly did," he said, following her sexy lead.

"What a coincidence, I was just thinking about you."

"Well, I think about you all the time."

Corinne sat up.

"Well, then," she said, "why don't you come over and say goodnight properly?"

Alistair had trouble believing what he just heard.

"Sorry?"

"I know it's late, but I'd like to see you ... I need to see you ... right now, tonight."

"I'm on my way."

He had waited ages for this moment.

Living only four blocks away it wouldn't be long before he arrived. Corinne wanted to freshen up beforehand. She got out of bed, slipped on a light-pink silky negligee, and sprayed on her best perfume at the mirror-topped vanity. After fixing her hair just so, she gazed at her reflection.

"What the hell am I doing?" she asked herself.

She was about to give herself to a man who adored and treasured her—and a gorgeous man at that. She was the envy of single women all over Manhattan. Some would give anything to be in her place right now. So why the sudden hesitation? What could be more beautiful than being with a dashingly handsome man who loved her?

A tear bubbled out of her eye as she realized the answer.

Being with a man I loved, too, that's what.

43

Ginny rested her head on the sturdy shoulder next to her. She and Pete had just finished making love on a steamy Saturday afternoon, the first one in August. She would soon leave as usual. But not before receiving a surprise from her lover.

Pete's free arm stretched into the nightstand drawer next to his bed. He took out a wallet-size photo of himself.

"What are you doing?"

"Here," he answered, handing over the gift, "I'd like you to have this. That is, if you want it. It's okay if you don't."

Her eyes lit up like Fourth-of-July sparklers.

"No, no, I do want it," she said joyously. "I only wish I had one to give you, but I will as soon as I can."

"Cool."

Corinne was right! Ginny indeed "got the picture."

And she got out of bed, too. So did Pete. Time was whizzing by. Both had to work the 5-to-close shift at their respective part-time employers.

After dressing themselves they headed to the front door.

"See you soon," said Pete.

Ginny smiled and kissed her lover goodbye—long and gentle, but firm, just like after their first movie date. She then headed downstairs to her car.

Pete, meanwhile, approached the living room window. Peering outside, he watched his special lady friend drive away. It was then he received the strangest feeling: that whatever he had with her was over. He did not know why he had this feeling or where it came from. It was powerful, though, too powerful to shake off.

My mind's playing tricks on me, that's all.

But it wasn't all. Ginny didn't text him that day, or Sunday and Monday. She never called either. Pete had left two voicemail messages; they were not returned. He wondered what was wrong.

He sent a text message to her on Tuesday. It was time to make plans to get together, he wrote. To his relief she replied. But her message really surprised him. She wrote that she was very busy and that she was going to Point Pleasant Beach with her friends for the weekend.

Well, so much for couldn't bear another weekend going by without seeing me.

Her text also differed in tone. It read more like a business letter than a note from a girlfriend. It contained no Xs or Os, no emoji, no personal touches at all. However, she mentioned that she would touch base once she got back.

Unfortunately, she did no such thing.

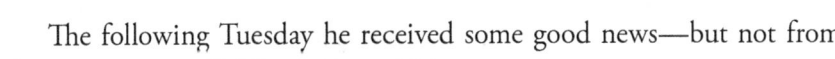

The following Tuesday he received some good news—but not from Ginny. Margaret Goldberg phoned him at work.

"Hi, sweetheart."

No need to announce her name. That smoky hoarse voice from Brooklyn could only be one person.

"Hi, Margaret," said Pete, "nice to hear from you."

"Oh, sweetheart, you're going to think it more than nice when you hear what I'm about to say." After a rough cough she excused herself and continued. "Are you familiar with FarHold?"

FarHold?! Pete's heart accelerated. His brown eyes bloomed in exhilaration.

"Yes, I am familiar," he replied. "That's a pretty big publishing house."

"It certainly is, sweetheart," said Margaret, about to burst with fabulous news, "and they would like to publish a book called *But I'll Never Be Lonely.*"

Her client was spellbound. He could hardly believe his ears.

"Wow, this is amazing!" he said, trying to keep his emotions under control, but failing miserably. "Thank you, Margaret, thank you so much!"

"You're so welcome, sweetheart," she said, most sincerely. "Oh, I'm so happy for you. Congratulations."

"I couldn't do this without you, you know."

"Oh, listen to you," she said, deflecting the praise. "Anyway, I'll be in touch with all the details later, okay?"

"Sure, anything you say."

Margaret chuckled at this, his childlike excitement, and then hung up.

Pete told his family and friends all about what just transpired. Not wanting to bother his mother at work, he left a voicemail message on her landline phone at home. He did the same with Corinne, who had been extremely supportive throughout this whole process. She never lost faith in him or his work. In fact, she believed this magical day would happen more than he ever did. She knew he could do it, she just knew it. She always said his novel rocked and that it would get published one day. Now, at long last, the prediction was coming true.

Pete would have to wait until tomorrow to tell Vito. He was out of the office today. It sure was quiet around here whenever he was out. But tomorrow the office would come alive with that classic phrase "you're one of the good ones, man." Pete owed his boss a huge thank-you as well. After all, it was he who encouraged him to write the novel in the first place. And how could he forget Carla's support? She, too, was bound to be pleased.

Pete wanted so much to share this exciting news with Ginny, but she was nowhere to be found ... until that Friday. He received another businesslike text from her. After reading it he decided not to reply. Now she would wait even longer to learn of his novel's acceptance. That is, of course, if she even cared. Ginny had written that she had to fly to Los Angeles on a weeklong business trip and would touch base again as soon as she returned.

Again, she did no such thing.

That's it. I've had it.

Pete was furious. He had to find out what was up with this girl once and for all. All this not knowing was doing his head in.

It was the fourth Tuesday of August, more than three weeks since he last saw her or heard her voice. Playing by her cowardly rules, he communicated via text message. In it he asked how her business trip was and that they needed *to talk*. As he typed it that evening, he thought of all they had done together: the movie dates, that special walk around the lake, discussing their life's dreams, and naturally, their many intimate moments. Was this it then? Was this how the relationship was supposed to end? Why? What did he do?

He did not find out. Her last text messages, received soon after Pete sent his, read as follows:

Hi, Pete. I did have a nice business trip, thank you.

After a few seconds the second part arrived:

In the last week I have had time to reflect on things, and I don't think we are a good match after all.

And then, in conclusion:

I did have a nice time getting to know you, and I wish you the best. Ginny

Finally, a sense of closure. He wanted to write just that in his reply—among other things. Like how he didn't think they were a good match either. Not when a woman cowers behind a mobile phone to do her dirty work. Not when she lacks the courage to tell him things straight to his face. Even a damn phone call would have sufficed. But no, she couldn't extend that simple courtesy.

She had accepted his photo with such energy, such enthusiasm. Her whole face beamed like a cluster of stars. She even pledged to give him a picture in return. Was this all a ruse? If she didn't want it, then she just should have said so. Why the dishonesty, the insincerity? Why did she lead him on? Why did she keep him waiting for three excruciatingly long weeks?

Because she's a tease!!!

Pete wanted to write that in his reply, too. And that she needed a nose job. But after a moment he calmed himself. No way would he stoop that low.

Flashes of the past began circulating in his mind. He suddenly remembered things that made him realize this breakup was inevitable. She certainly had an impulsive streak. Talk of quitting her part-time job and moving to another apartment "in no time" proved this. So did her sudden halt of text messages and phone calls—after his "see you soon," the last day he saw her as it turned out. She never actually said she wanted to get together again, did she? She just planted that long kiss—that goodbye-for-good kiss—and left.

His mind hadn't played tricks on him that day after all. That feeling by the living room window was real. It was over, truly over, between them.

Pete would never ignore this feeling again. He would listen attentively the next time something nudged in his gut. He could save himself a lot of aggravation. And that was what all this was—aggravation. Pete didn't get too upset over this breakup. His heart needed no re-gluing. Its pieces hadn't shattered; they were firmly intact. No tears, no crying, no nothing. He would pull himself together in no time. In fact, he was doing it now. Yes, he said to himself, this breakup was a good thing. Now he could move on to someone else, someone sincere in her words and actions, someone who says what she means and means what she says. He owed himself this much at least!

Pete's final text to Ginny was gracious, though she probably did not deserve the kind tone. It was also brief. He simply wrote that he was sorry she felt the way she did, that he enjoyed the time they spent together, and that he wished her the best as well. He then pressed the Send icon.

And that was it. Ginger "Ginny" Leeds was now out of his life.

Or was she?

Really, he was fine. There was nothing at all to worry about. Pete kept telling Corinne this, but she could not shake the concern ringing in her ears. The sound had sprung instinctively as details of Ginny's actions emerged. It died down, however, when she realized her friend was handling this breakup differently. She didn't have to run out into the rain and practically carry him home like she did before. Not this time. A new, confident, stronger Pete had seized control of his emotions. His voice did not quiver, not once, on the phone tonight. Corinne was impressed.

"You seem to be dealing with this really well," she said.

"Thanks, but I saw this breakup coming weeks ago. I just wish she had dropped her axe then. She could've saved me a lot of aggravation."

At least now he was able to move on and look forward to the future. Corinne understood this all too well. Once she realized Pete would only be her friend, a heavy weight lifted from her heart. The pain magically went away, just like Alistair said it would. She felt secure again. Finally, her good ole self had returned.

Pete was glad—and relieved. No more guilt about not returning her romantic feelings. Still, he wasn't too crazy about Alistair and her as a steady couple. He never forgot how the slick Englishman tricked him at The Piccadilly pub. But Corinne seemed happy with him, that was the important thing. And if she was happy, then Pete believed he should feel the same.

No matter how difficult it was.

45

September started off much better than August had ended. The reason: his novel had entered final publication stages, book production and distribution. The galley's appearance was nearly perfect. The publisher's editorial changes added up to a little more than a dozen. Signing off on the galley, therefore, took no time at all.

FarHold was now working on its press release, which also required author approval. Pete could hardly wait to read it. In the meantime he filled out his novel's dedication page:

For all the guys out there who give it their all to find the woman of their dreams and keep tripping on the way… just remember that no matter what happens, you'll never be lonely.

This was a real pleasure to write, as were the two acknowledgment pages at the end.

To my mother Janice, words can't begin to express how thankful I am to be your son. All the sacrifices you made will never be forgotten. Neither will your love and support. You're the best, and I love you. Same goes for you, Aunt Rae. It's easy to know why you're Mom's best friend. Thanks to both of you for raising and caring for me all my life … and continuing to do so.

Corinne Aldrich, my "little sister" who found me at college … and who fast became my best friend. Even though you told me the book rocks, I beg to differ. You, my friend, rock! What would I do without your friendship, your support, your encouragement? I don't ever want to find out. Thanks for being there, for being you.

He mentioned a few others, with splashes of humor.

Vito Caparelli, the best boss anyone could ask for. Dude, I'll never forget the day you called me into your office and encouraged me to pursue my dream. Now look at the result! How cool is that, man? You're not only my boss, you're my friend. Thanks for everything, bud. And to your lovely wife Carla (yes, lovely), thanks for allowing your husband to read the weekend away with my novel ... and for reading it yourself afterwards. I'm glad you left my perfectly combed hair in place!

My extraordinary agent, Margaret Goldberg ... Oh, sweetheart, I'm glad you took a chance on me. Oh, sweetheart, how your phone calls make my day. And did I mention, sweetheart, how much of a sweetheart you are? Thanks for absolutely everything you've done, all your hard work and devotion, to make this dream of mine come true. You truly made this process fun and memorable ... Thanks again, sweetheart.

He thanked a few more people—friends, coworkers at both the cinema and *Jersey News Central*, and the FarHold Publishing staff.

Pete owed himself a thank you as well. He had put a lot of work into this writing project. He really did labor hard this past year. But all that endless typing, the query letters, envelopes, stamps—the dozens of dollars spent at the post office—were worthwhile. More so, he believed. FarHold Publishing was huge. The renowned company published books all over the world. And his would be added to that prized list ... and very soon, September 30th to be exact.

Two weeks beforehand review copies were sent to various magazines and newspapers, along with the approved—and impressive—press release. Their write-ups could come out any time before the 30th. Pete kept his fingers crossed, hoping they would be positive.

To his sheer joy they were.

One Chicago newspaper wrote, "Webb's first novel is hopefully not his last." Another paper, in Seattle, used words like "fresh," "imaginative," and "highly emotional" to describe his story. One in Atlanta wrote how "unique" it was to read a story about "a young man's quest for true love ending tragically yet triumphantly." A magazine book reviewer all the way in Sydney, Australia, described the work as "a lovely piece of modern literature."

Even newspapers in New York City liked it. "Possibly the feel-good book of the year," stated one reviewer. "We need more stories like this," wrote another, "one that makes us realize just how strong we human beings are."

A Canadian magazine had this to say: "You will find it difficult to put down Webb's debut novel as he describes, in shameful detail, the twofaced nature of some people ... and that not all men are the heartbreakers in relationships. There is a valuable lesson to learn in this book, suitable for people of all ages."

Pete liked this assessment most. But he believed a magazine based in Denver had the best conclusion: "Beware, your eyes are bound to get stuck to this Webb!"

As the reviews came in, so did the people at work. His cubicle, not the copy room, had become the new office hotspot. How kind of them, Pete thought, to drop by and wish him great success. They didn't have to do that. But when they did he thanked them all heartily. He did the same with their emails.

Little did he realize that this was only the beginning…

His congratulatory messages surged after September 30th, the day *But I'll Never Be Lonely* went on sale. And not just from people he knew. Nearly every day after work Pete came home to discover a full email inbox. FarHold Publishing and Margaret Goldberg forwarded all kinds of messages from the public. Many came from men like him, ones who could truly relate to the main character's plight. Parker West, they wrote, was a lot like them. They, too, had jumped over all sorts of hurdles to find true love—and got burned for it. But in the end these experiences had made them stronger, more confident people.

Pete was amazed. The familiar tune had also chimed in his ears, especially after The Tease event back in August.

These young men mentioned something else noteworthy: that his novel was unique, a rarity. Not a lot of stories existed about the guy being the one to get dumped. Usually it was the other way around. Funny, Pete recalled Vito and Carla saying the exact same thing.

Gratitude and appreciation also flowed within the public's messages. Having a book out there that describes what some men go through in relationships—that it wasn't always the man's fault—was a welcome change, they wrote. Sometimes women broke hearts, too. And not in the most gentle manner, either. Most readers concluded that Bethany Spikes was the most ruthless. She had absolutely no compassion, especially after saying how a nice working-class guy like Parker could never meet her standards.

Pete quite agreed.

If only they knew just how much!

The new author responded to every email forwarded to him, thanking each reader wholeheartedly. It was the least he could do to pay them back for their touching compliments. This was a time-consuming process. Pete spent several hours on his replies but didn't mind in the slightest.

He also enjoyed reading reviews of his book on various Internet sites. Virtually all of them glowed in praise, accompanied by either four or five stars—not including the online trolls, of course, whose lives were so empty they had nothing better else to do than disparage everything about *But I'll Never Be Lonely*.

Word got out fast. News of the novel—and the author who kindly responded to his fans—spread across the media like laser beams. Several television, radio and newspaper personalities requested interviews. Pete gladly granted them. He had no choice in the matter anyway, per his contract with FarHold. A couple of fan pages devoted to his work, and him, soon popped up in the social media world. Pete resisted establishing an official Website or social media page but realized he may have to change his view and eventually create one—if FarHold didn't do so first, that is.

His popularity soared. By the end of October the polite young man on the top-floor apartment who pretty much kept to himself had a name. *Jersey News Central* became a familiar newspaper outside the Garden State as much as inside. And the cute face on the book jacket generated a number of female admirers—Ginger "Ginny" Leeds among them.

The pretty brunette phoned the first Saturday afternoon of November. Her ex-lover, resting in bed before his shift at the cinema, thought he was seeing things when the name Ginny Leeds appeared on his mobile phone's caller ID. He blinked rapidly, just in case he was dreaming. But the name did not fizzle away. It was indeed The Tease. He didn't want to spoil his relaxing afternoon by speaking to her, but his curiosity got the better of him.

Pete let out a deep breath, reached over to the nightstand, and picked up the phone.

"Yes, what is it?"

He was in no mood to exchange pleasantries.

Ginny noted his cool tone right away. She knew she had better get to the point—fast.

"Hi, Pete," she said timidly. "I just wanted to call and congratulate you on your novel."

"Okay, thanks."

A tense pause followed.

"So," Ginny uttered, anxious to end it, "how have you been?"

"Just swell, peachy, couldn't be better."

His words reeked of sarcasm.

"Listen, Pete, I think I was wrong to end things between us like I did."

Damn right you were. And you're realizing this now, huh?

Ginny continued: "Do you think we can get together sometime to talk about it, maybe later today?"

"Sorry, I have to work."

"You do?"

She sounded surprised. Surely he could more than afford to quit his part-time job at the cinema. Pete picked up on this. He knew where she was heading. With fame came fortune. Usually, that is. It would in his case, just not right now—and not that much. Book profits diverted to both his publisher and agent. Naturally, Uncle Sam took his hefty cut as well.

Only afterwards could the new author reap in the fortunate fruits of his labor, however small they were.

Although his first residual paycheck had not yet arrived, Ginny definitely wanted a piece of it. This much he knew. He also knew she would be in for a big disappointment.

"So when can I see you?" she asked.

"I'm not sure I want to see you."

"Please, Pete," said Ginny. "Please, I really want to see you. Just name the time and day, and I'll be there."

He loved hearing her beg and plead like this.

"Can we get together tomorrow?" she pressed. "Please?"

"I'm busy."

He planned to take his mother and "aunt" out for Sunday brunch, he explained. It had been way too long since he last saw them. And next weekend was out because he was heading to Miami for a mini-vacation, which he desperately needed. Crushed between two jobs, book promotions, and a constantly full email inbox lay an exhausted 24-year-old man. So Dr. Webb ordered some good old-fashioned rest and relaxation.

"In a beach-view room at a five-star hotel," he added, on purpose.

"Where, the Galloway Towers?"

Yeah, right.

"No," he corrected her, "someplace even nicer, The Palatial."

Ginny was intrigued. Her brown eyes dazzled in starry dollar signs. Things must be looking up for her ex. They had never done anything this extravagant when they were dating. Perhaps not, but he had planned to. Four luxurious nights on a Florida beach was definitely down the relationship road. But Ginny wanted out too soon. She escaped onto the detour and kept driving wherever it took her. She now sought the onramp. However, Pete wasn't the least bit eager for her re-entry.

He had stashed away extra cash for this trip since the summer. Regardless of how things turned out with Ginny, he was going to Florida. And next weekend, as it turned out. What perfect timing, too. Not only would he get some much-needed R&R at a classy resort, he could rub Ginny's ugly nose in it at the same time.

He was so glad she called today.

"I love the water, the beach," she said.

"Do you now?"

"I sure do. Hey, why don't I join you? This way we could spend some quality time together."

Man, this just gets even better.

"I could apologize to you properly."

Pete sneered at this last line. Although it carried a seductive flavor, he no longer desired the taste. The thought of being with Ginny Leeds staled into nothingness the day of her infamous text messages ending their relationship.

He wasn't going to play any more of her games. Those days were over.

Or were they?

Pete decided to play just one more hand—only he would deal. Like Brandi, it was time for The Tease to be on the receiving end of a mind game.

And it would cost her plenty.

"Sure, we can meet there," he said nonchalantly. "It's a free country; I can't stop you."

Nor could he stop himself from grinning.

46

Janice Webb welcomed her youngest son with warm open arms. Her home always felt complete whenever her Peter visited. So did Woodlake Square. Somehow the neighborhood of chipped brick townhouses got a little brighter, just like her spirits.

Rae quite agreed.

"So where's my hug?" she said, her smile outlined in exceedingly dark lipstick. "Don't I get one, too?"

"Of course," said Pete.

Her close, tight embrace surprised him. Usually air hugs sufficed. Then he realized something. Aunt Rae's long blue dress, the same color as her shoes and purse, was made of denim. There was no danger of heavy wrinkling.

"So are you two ready to go?"

The women did not answer. Instead, they turned to each other.

"Honey," Rae said with a mysterious smile, "can you believe there's a famous author in your house right now?"

Janice returned the gesture as she answered, "No, I certainly can't. And he looks just like my baby boy."

"The one whose diapers I changed, right?"

"Yes, that's him."

"Who would've thought?"

Pete blushed in embarrassment.

"Thanks," he said good-humoredly, "thanks a lot."

The two ladies giggled and collected their coats. Before exiting, Janice stared lovingly into her son's eyes, which looked just like hers.

"Peter," she said, "I just want you to know I am so, so proud of you."

"Thanks, Mom."

During this mother-son exchange, two eavesdroppers lurked from upstairs. Belinda elbowed Adam's ribs, a gesture that carried a clear message: there she goes again. Janice couldn't help herself. She always told Pete how proud she was of him. But never did she say this to her eldest son—obviously not her favorite.

"I can hardly wait to hear the latest on your book," said Rae, her hazel eyes flickering in celebrity excitement. "You better tell us all about it."

Pete smiled in amusement. Aunt Rae just had to know everything, he said to himself. But this was okay. Woodlake Square was her turf.

"Your mother and I are your biggest fans, you know," she said on the way out.

"We sure are," said Janice, who followed.

Pete smiled and shut the front door. As soon as it closed, Adam's green eyes boiled into acid pools of envy.

"I hate you!" he yelled to his author-brother, who was out of hearing range. "I hate you! I hate you!! I hate you!!!"

His hand clinched into a fist, which he used to thump open his bedroom door.

Belinda, most pleased, followed.

47

Vito's brown eyes flashed wide open as Pete entered his office Friday morning. The copyeditor was not supposed to work today. His flight to Miami left from Philadelphia at 2 o'clock this afternoon. He was to take the day off, the whole day off. For Christ's sake he owed it to himself. The guy had never taken a vacation since coming to *JNC* nearly a year and a half ago. He was definitely one of the good ones.

"Man, what are you doing here today?" asked Vito, shaking his head.

"I just wanted to double-check that the entertainment articles for our weekend edition were good to go, that's all."

"They are," the managing editor assured, "and you should be, too. Stop worrying already. Everything's under control here, okay?"

"Well, is there anything else I can do before I—"

"No!"

Pete chuckled, as did his boss.

"Actually, have a seat, dude."

Now that his prized subordinate was here, Vito had something he wanted to discuss—but not before guzzling down some steamy hot coffee.

"Listen, my man," he said afterwards, "I wanted to let you know that we love having you here. You're one of my best employees."

"Thank you."

"But I know that you're making quite a name for yourself out there."

And he was. The name Peter Michael Webb was fast becoming a well-known writer. There would come a time when another job offer, a better one, would come his way. Vito urged his young friend to accept it when it arrived.

"I'm serious, bud," he added. "There's a world outside *Jersey News Central* you know. Bigger and better opportunities lay outside these walls, and they're coming your way. Mark my words."

Pete had never really considered this. He was happy here at *JNC* and honestly believed that his novel's popularity was a one-time thing. Like all new products the success of *But I'll Never Be Lonely* would die down eventually. The flood of emails into his inbox would recede. In time he would be lucky to receive a fan-mail letter a month.

"Thanks, Vito," he said, appreciating the prediction nonetheless.

"Now for the other thing I wanted to talk to you about…"

"Sure, what is it?"

Vito sipped more coffee before answering.

"Carla and I ran into Ginny at Godfather Italiano last night. Is it true she's joining you in Florida?"

Yes, it is, but not the way you mean.

"I know this is a personal question, that it's none of my business," Vito continued, "so just tell me to back off if I'm being—"

"No, it's okay," said Pete. "I like that you look out for me, like the older brother I wish I had."

Vito relaxed after hearing this. He had always felt responsible, at least somewhat, for how things turned out with Ginny. After all, he was the one who encouraged the pursuit of the hot waitress. To hear their brotherly bond confirmed came as quite a relief.

"Thanks, dude," he said. "I appreciate you saying that. And for the record Carla and I both consider you family."

"Well, it's an honor to be related to the Caparellis."

Vito, truly amazed, shook his head.

"Man, are you for real?" he said. "I tell you, I have never in my life met someone as cool as you. You're so damn modest. When it comes to compliments you either bounce them back or downgrade them."

"Well, I'm no angel."

"There you go again!"

The two men shared a laugh over this. Afterwards, Vito told his young friend to be careful in Florida. Ginny had broken his heart once already.

"I just don't want to see you get hurt all over again, that's all."

"Oh, don't worry, I won't," Pete said with a splash of devilishness. "I've got everything under control."

The Palatial more than lived up to its title. As Pete's taxi approached, the hotel's silver exterior glistened majestically underneath Miami's royal sun. It also created the most serene contrast against the blue Atlantic Ocean across the road. Palm trees, flowers, and other tropical plant life flourished all around the hotel property. This place was a paradise, especially this time of year. While cool and chilly in the U.S. northeast and mid-Atlantic, the southern part of the Sunshine State was warm and pleasant.

When the taxi pulled into the lobby entrance, a uniformed bellboy arrived and opened the passenger door.

"Hello, sir," he said, "and welcome to The Palatial."

"Thank you," said Pete, impressed by the five-star greeting.

He took a whiff of some salty beach air as he hopped outside. It was most invigorating. As was the constant sea breeze on which it drifted.

He then paid the driver and went to the trunk to retrieve his luggage.

The bellboy beat him to it.

"Allow me, sir."

Pete stood back as the hotel employee took out his suitcase and placed it onto a shiny silver rack. He had never experienced such service. This was part of the reason he wanted to stay here: to live the high life, if only for a few days.

"This way, sir," the bellboy said, wheeling the rack inside the lobby.

A wave of cool air conditioning crashed on Pete's face as he entered. But he hardly noticed. Instead, the hotel's interior seized his attention. Its décor thrived in various tints of silver, gray, black and white. The floor was made of black marble, whereas shades of gray enveloped the furniture and front desk. Silver and white consumed the walls. The colors dominated both their woodwork and abstract paintings. And with glimmering crystal chandeliers hanging overhead, The Palatial had truly become palatial.

"Hello, sir, how are you today?" said the 40ish front desk clerk, sporting a flawlessly trimmed goatee.

"Fine, thanks," said Pete, "and yourself?"

"Very well, thank you, Mr. Webb."

"I'm here to check in. My name is—"

Wait a minute. How did he know my name?

"We've been expecting you, Mr. Webb, and we hope you enjoy your stay here at The Palatial."

"Thank you," said a mystified Pete. "But I've never been here before—never been to Florida actually—so how did you know who I was? Have we met before?"

"No, sir, we haven't," the clerk said, concealing his amusement.

He recognized him from the *But I'll Never Be Lonely* book cover.

"I just finished reading it, sir. I must say I thoroughly enjoyed it."

Pete was stunned. The last thing in the world he expected down here—more than a thousand miles away—was to run into a fan of his work. Then again, he received mail from people all around the country … and beyond.

Still, he was surprised.

"Thank you," he said, most grateful for the compliment. "Thank you very much. I appreciate that."

The clerk smiled and handed over Mr. Webb's plastic card-like room key.

"You're in room 745," he said, "which has one of our best views."

And it did.

When Pete pulled opened the heavy silver curtains, the magnificent Atlantic Ocean appeared. A peace rushed over him instantly. The scene of wave after wave crashing inland made him forget about life.

This was just what he needed. And while sunbathing on that awesome beach tomorrow he could forget even more. But now it was time to hop in the shower, and after that, relax—on that huge king-sized bed. Like everything else in the room, it followed a mostly silver color scheme, accented with blacks, whites and grays. This room, this entire plush hotel, was unlike anything he had ever seen.

After his rest it was off for a late-evening dinner alone. But tomorrow he would have company by the name of Ginny Leeds.

Romance, however, was the farthest thing from his mind.

―――●●―――

The Tease arrived Saturday evening at 8 o'clock. Right on schedule. Pete was ready for her, ready to conclude this sham of a relationship once and for all. When she knocked on his door he did not immediately answer it. She deserved to stew just a little while longer. Only after the third impatient knock did he rise out of bed and lumber toward her. He certainly took his sweet time.

Ginny did her best to rid the edgy frustration from her face as Pete opened the door. And not just because of his tardiness. Though looking more tanned, his sloppy appearance was most unflattering. Both his white tank top and beige cotton shorts contained more wrinkles than Florida peaches. His hair was also different. With all its ruffles it looked anything but perfect. This was most unlike him.

"Hi," she said with a seemingly cheerful smile.

She would never dream of questioning his tardiness or appearance, not after those cowardly texts back in August.

And Pete knew it.

"Hello."

His reply was stoic. No excitement resided in it, though she looked really hot in that strapless red blouse.

Ginny entered the ritzy room and dropped her suitcase in stunned amazement. Like Pete, she couldn't believe her eyes. What a room. Everything was fantastic, from the ocean view to the carpeting, furniture and wall decorations.

"Wow," she said, "this is really nice."

"Thank you."

"You know what else is nice?" she asked, throwing her arms around his neck. "It's being here with you."

"Is it?"

Ginny nodded seductively, kissed his cheek, and pressed her body against his. Pete, on the other hand, gently tapped her back. Being this close to her almost ruined his appetite.

"So," he said, pulling away, "ready for some room service?"

Room service? She liked the sound of that, just not right now.

As Pete rushed to the phone to order dinner, Ginny grabbed his wrist.

"Why the rush?" she asked. "Dinner can wait, you know … I can't."

She clutched his other wrist and yanked them both around her waist, forcing their bodies to brush against one another's. She then kissed him.

Pete pulled away, yet again.

"Not so fast," he said.

"What's the problem?"

She wasn't expecting this, his standoffishness. Was he still hurt? Probably so. But after tonight his pain would go away. He would melt right back into her arms just like he used to. His hard-to-get act would end soon enough. Then they could be a proper couple, more than what they were before, much more. Peter Michael Webb wasn't just another good-looking guy. He was an author who was getting more and more famous … and wealthy. Staying here in this majestic hotel proved this. Indeed he was quite a catch. And when he landed back in her embrace she couldn't drop him. No letting go this time. She had to hold him tighter than anything she ever held before.

Pete yawned suddenly.

"Sorry," he said.

It had been a tiring day. Soaking in the sun on the beach was to blame. All he wanted to do was hop in the shower and crash into bed. Room service could wait. He would have a big Sunday breakfast instead.

Ginny understood … all too well. This was all part of the act. But she knew the reason behind it: to spend even more time in bed.

"That's fine," she said, smiling flirtatiously. "Whatever you want to do is fine with me."

Pete replied with an indifferent, apathetic, "Okay."

He then headed to the bathroom, locking the door behind him. It was the only way to keep out any Ginny intruders.

But she had another plan up her sleeve.

When the shower water turned on, she dimmed the room's lights. She then removed her clothes—all of them—and hopped into the luxurious king-sized bed. Lounging on the silvery comforter, Ginny awaited her royal host. She could hardly wait to see the expression on his face when he spotted her naked voluptuous body. He was in for quite a surprise.

So was she.

Ginny tingled all over as the shower water turned off. It wouldn't be long before their two bodies joined as one.

A towel-dry Pete exited the bathroom wearing denim shorts and a white t-shirt. He immediately noticed the room's lights had been dimmed—and a nude ex-lady friend. She looked incredibly sexy, just as he remembered. It took all his strength to stick to his plan. Considering the open invitation sprawled on his bed, this was no easy task.

"I've missed you," Ginny said sultrily. She then reached out for him. "Let me show you just how much."

Pete was right to don denim shorts. They hid his erection best, especially in this dimly lit room.

"No," he told her dispassionately, "I don't think so."

"What!"

Ginny was stunned, much to Pete's enjoyment.

"No," he reiterated.

"But…"

"But what?"

"But I flew down here to see you."

"And if you recall, I said I wasn't sure that I wanted to see you."

Ginny grew more and more perplexed. He couldn't be turning her down. He couldn't possibly.

But he was—flat.

"I told you it was a free country, that I couldn't stop you from doing what you like," Pete continued, straight faced. "What part of that didn't you understand?"

Ginny's confusion mounted even more.

"But we made plans to do things together," she said.

Her ex corrected her.

"No," he said, "*you* made those plans, not me."

"You mean we're not here to try and get back together?"

This was the moment for which Pete had been waiting so long, since that string of text messages at the end of August. The time had come to throw those gutless, spineless words back in her face.

He savored every moment as he delivered them: "In the last week, I have had time to reflect on things, and I don't think we are a good match after all. I did have a nice time getting to know you, and I wish you the best."

Ginny's jaw sagged in utter humiliation. So did her breasts, which were no longer aroused.

Pete loved the sight.

"By the way," he said, "you're in my bed." And with a triumphant glare added, "Get out."

Not just out of his bed, but his life—for good this time.

Ginny Leeds understood these words all too clearly ... she was duped! Her scheme to woo him back had backfired. And she paid a hefty price for her mistake. This Miami trip required chopping off a sizeable chunk from her savings account. Now that she was here there was no way to replenish it. Pete obviously knew what he was doing, she concluded. He had no intention of resuming their affair, their relationship. He had no intention of splurging his newly found wealth on her. He just wanted to disgrace her, which he did with sickening success. Her own medicine, the one marked Tease on the bottle, indeed had a nasty taste.

An infuriated Ginny stormed off the bed and breezed on her clothes, saying absolutely nothing the entire time. She then snatched her suitcase. As she left the room she slammed the door fiercely behind her. She very well could have broken it, Pete thought. But the expression on her face—the embarrassment, outrage, rejection—would have made the expense worth every penny.

The victorious ex-lover collapsed into bed laughing vigorously. Finally, he got even with The Tease. And it felt damn good, too.

He sure was enjoying this swanky Miami vacation.

Little did he know that another posh hotel visit lay just ahead ... in New York, where a number of surprises awaited *him*.

49

Surely she was kidding. She just had to be. Margaret did not just say that. The phone line at work must be acting funny, Pete thought. But no, she was serious. He indeed heard his agent correctly: he had just been nominated for a major American Writer Award. The category: Favorite Fiction Writer–Young Adult. He couldn't believe it.

"Well, believe it, sweetheart," Margaret said happily.

Pete paused in stunned silence. He kept asking himself how this could happen.

"Sweetheart, are you there?"

"Yes, I'm here," her client answered, snapping out of his daze. "Sorry."

"Forget about it," Margaret assured. "Now before we—" She coughed slightly. "Excuse me. As I was saying, before we get to the ceremonial details, I'm sure you're wondering why this is happening in the first place."

He certainly was.

Margaret explained, through smoke-strained vocal chords, that September 30th marked the last day new books could be considered for the award. Released on that day, *But I'll Never Be Lonely* was indeed qualified.

"Now for the ceremony here in New York," she continued after clearing her throat. "It's in exactly 15 days, the first Saturday in December. I know this is short notice, but can you make it, sweetheart?"

"Can I make it? You bet!" Pete exclaimed joyfully.

"Oh, I'm so glad," said Margaret, adding that he should be there, that this was a big moment to cherish.

The nominee agreed.

"I suppose I'll have to get cracking on booking my train ticket," he said.

"Train ticket?"

Margaret laughed, which turned into a rough cough. Pete sensed her lungs could explode any second. But they remained intact.

"Oh, sweetheart," she said. "Oh, how you amuse me so."

She explained that a limousine would pick up him and five guests for a personal drive to and from midtown Manhattan. There they would stay overnight at the highly acclaimed Galloway Hotel Towers overlooking Central Park.

No, not the Galloway Hotel Towers. Why there, why does it have to be there?

The ceremony would be held in the downstairs banquet hall, Margaret added, as would the nominee book signings after Sunday brunch.

Pete would just as soon go to some seedy motel than the prestigious headquarters of Todd's family's legacy. But he had no choice in the matter.

"Okay, great," he said through a wall of gritted teeth. "I can't wait."

He could, though, he really could.

Nevertheless there were a couple of positives about this excursion into New York. One, he could see his best friend again. That is, of course, if Corinne had no plans that weekend. With Alistair Brundidge slithering around, he wondered if she could escape his snaky squeeze for a while. Pete certainly hoped so. He really wanted her there. Of the five guests allowed to accompany him she ranked at the top of the list.

And two, he could finally meet Margaret Goldberg in person. To his delight she would be attending the ceremony as well. Pete had been curious about the face behind that gravelly Brooklyn voice for a long time, ever since her initial summer phone call. But soon, at long last, his curiosity would end.

So far the table of eight comprised of author, literary agent, and hopefully Corinne. His publicist from FarHold Publishing, Harry Perkins, would also be there. Four more to go... Pete knew exactly who to invite: Mom, Aunt Rae, Vito and Carla. Perfect.

"I'm so looking forward to this, sweetheart," said Margaret. "I hope you win that award. Oh, I just hope you do. You so deserve it. Such a sweet young man you are."

Pete, amused by this last line, cracked a grin.

Don't think Ginny would agree!

Still, he thanked his agent for the compliment and passing on this terrific news.

Now it was his turn. But first he took a moment to reflect. After hanging up the phone he leaned back in his desk chair and gazed at the white ceiling tiles above his cubicle. Everything was happening so fast ... too fast actually. These past few months have been a whirlwind. He only just finished his novel in May. Since then he had landed an agent, a publisher, and a nomination for Favorite Fiction Writer–Young Adult. The pace at which all this was happening was surreal. His life certainly had changed in the last six months.

And in December, next month, it would change even more.

50

This was incredible. Unbelievable, more like it. It was the most awesome white limousine he'd ever seen. Never in his wildest dreams did he expect to ride in one. But here he was, doing just that. Gliding away from the Ewing apartment complex, it was off to grace Woodlake Square—which needed every bit of elegance it could get.

The plush limo was definitely out of place here, even more so than Todd's red sports car two summers ago. At least its red color had meshed, somewhat, with the townhouses' chipped brick exterior. Aside from the hovering clouds there was nothing in the Square to reflect the brilliant allure of the white limousine.

Not until Janice Webb exited her home.

With a gleaming smile she approached wearing a long ashen dress with matching high-heeled shoes. Pete remembered them well. His mother only wore them—and her faux pearl necklace, which she also displayed—on special occasions. What an honor, he thought, that she decided to put these on tonight. This evening must mean a lot to her as well.

An unbuttoned overcoat kept her plenty warm this December afternoon, though there was plenty of heat inside the limo.

"Hi, son," she said as the driver opened the door.

With a warm embrace Pete said hello in return. He then wondered where Aunt Rae was.

"She is coming, isn't she?"

"Oh, she sure is," said Janice. "You know what she's like when it comes to something like this."

Indeed he did. When Todd Galloway had dropped by, Aunt Rae was all too eager to welcome the celebrity guest into the Square. Now there was another one to greet ... sort of. There was a bonus this time. She was a guest of honor for an awards ceremony in one of the country's most glamorous hotspots: Manhattan. Attending this event was undoubtedly a dream come true for her, too.

Five minutes after 3 o'clock Rae Jacobson opened her front door. Fashionably late, the Webbs concluded. They got such a kick out of her, though. Her slow waltz to the pristine limousine was especially entertaining. Pete shook his head. Not just because of her grand entry outside—one she hoped many neighbors would witness—but because of all that bright pink. If she wanted to be noticed, which she unquestionably did, then she succeeded. That flashy pink blotted her entire outfit, from her shawl and two-piece suit to her purse and shoes. Even her jewelry was pink. And when she got closer, Pete and Janice noticed the same rosy shade in her lipstick and eye shadow. The only thing not pink was her freshly dyed jet-black hair. Not a single strand could move from all that tornado-proof hairspray.

"Hello there," a star-struck Rae said to the driver, who held open the door. "Why thank you, kind sir."

She relished every moment of this royal treatment, and would again and again throughout this whole weekend.

"Sorry I'm a little late," she said inside the limo. "I couldn't find a thing to wear."

That'll be the day!

"Not a problem, Aunt Rae," said Pete, concealing his amusement. "I'm just glad you're here." And with a glance to his mother, added, "Both of you."

They wouldn't have missed this for the world. Neither would the Caparellis, who were to be picked up next in Princeton.

Then it was off to New York, where an unforgettable night awaited.

51

There it was, the Galloway Hotel Towers: two enormous structures, connected by a mezzanine, overlooking the picturesque Central Park from the south. As the driver pulled outside the front lobby, Pete recalled his recent trip to The Palatial in Miami. Only then he approached in a taxi. This time it was in a fancy white limousine. Like The Palatial, however, hotel staff here bestowed a friendly professional welcome. They also scurried to the trunk to collect their guests' belongings.

Now, off to check in.

"Look, he's here!"

Maybe not, on second thought. When Pete turned his head toward the voice on the sidewalk, he noticed about a dozen young ladies approaching. All were holding copies of his novel. And all were downright gorgeous.

"You're so cute," one said.

"I really enjoyed your book, Mr. Webb," said another. "Can you sign my copy?"

Yet another asked, "May I take a selfie with you?"

Pete could hardly believe his ears. All these compliments! Nor could he get over the sight surrounding him: beautiful girls wanting to see him, wanting their picture taken with him. Was this some sort of dream? With all that had happened these past six months it was a logical question. But like then the answer was no. He was indeed wide awake.

So was Vito.

"Need some help, bud?" he offered, gladly.

Perhaps a little too gladly.

His petite wife Carla interrupted with an edgy, "I think he's handling everything just fine by himself, dear."

"We should find out for sure just in case."

God, did he want to. But as he left to "help" his friend welcome the hot young babes, a claw-like hand clutched his wrist.

"Freeze, Caparelli!"

Carla meant business, and Vito knew it. He had better not take one more step.

Man, Pete's one lucky dude.

His mother thought the same. She got a kick out of seeing her baby boy surrounded like that, talking to fans of his book, signing autographs and posing for selfies as if he were a movie star.

Now that he had found success professionally it was time for him to do the same romantically. Janice wondered if any of those pretty girls could be the one for her Peter. Then she remembered Corinne. She seemed so smitten with him at his graduation. Of course, that was more than a year ago. Things could have changed by now. Still, she was his best friend. And she was due here this evening. Maybe there was still a chance.

"Thanks again for all your support," Pete said to his fans. "It meant a lot that you came here to wish me well tonight."

And with a wave goodbye the nominee headed into the hotel. His honored guests followed. Three luxurious rooms had been reserved, each adjacent to one another. Pete would have his own room, but Janice and Rae had to share, as did Vito and Carla. Corinne, already a City resident, did not require one. She could have spent the night for free if she wanted, of course, but Alistair wanted to take her out after the ceremony. She also could have transported herself over to the Galloway, but Pete had insisted she enjoy the five-star limo ride. Okay, she told him, but she probably couldn't get there until the ceremony started at 8. She and Alistair had made dinner plans as well. Pete was fine with this. As long as his best friend was seated at the guest table, that was all that mattered. He really wanted her there when they announced his nomination for Favorite Fiction Writer–Young Adult.

First things first: check in, collect room keys, and freshen up before the awards dinner and ceremony.

Gold trim bordered the majestic, sparkling, perfectly polished wooden front desk. So did something else—some*one* else.

My God, it can't be.

But it was. The lean and lofty Todd Galloway himself. Though a remote possibility, Pete honestly believed he would not run into his former friend here. Surely the heir to the Galloway fortune didn't have to labor behind the front desk in a uniform. He could work at any hotel he wanted, any office he wanted.

Apparently not.

Damn. No way out of this. He had to go up there. He had to check in and collect everyone's room keys ... from Todd. He could do it, though. He knew he could. The new, confident, stronger Peter Michael Webb could handle just about anything. Nevertheless, this was going to be interesting.

Todd's smile faded when his pale-blue eyes met Pete's approaching dark-brown ones. Suddenly, the memory of their last encounter surfaced. He had driven quite a distance to Woodlake Square that hot summer day. Only Pete didn't want to salvage their friendship. In fact, he wanted nothing more to do with him. That harsh door slam, that last gesture, pretty much said it all. Todd hadn't seen or heard from him since that defining day. But Pete saw him, and the lowly Miss Sparks, at Corinne's graduation. Unlike then, however, he now had to exchange words.

So did Todd.

"Yes, sir," he said, "can I help you?"

His tone, his whole mannerism, was strictly professional.

Pete's was, too.

"We're here to check in, three reserved rooms ... I believe you know the name."

He certainly did. The tension between them was so thick—and so obvious—not even dynamite could blast through it. The Caparellis looked on in puzzlement, but Janice and Rae knew exactly why it existed. They were just as stunned as Pete to see his former friend behind the front desk.

"Here you are, sir," said Todd, handing over the three room keys, continuing his rigid formal tone. "We hope you enjoy your stay. Thank you for choosing Galloway Hotel Towers."

I didn't!

"Thank you," said Pete, "*sir.*"

That last word, peppered in bitterness, conveyed his scorn. Absolutely nothing had changed. He still held much resentment. The things Todd and Brandi did more than a year and a half ago remained unforgettable. He had no regrets, though. Ironically, if it weren't for their misdeeds his novel would not have featured the loathsome, but popular, Bethany Spikes character. In fact, there probably wouldn't even be a *But I'll Never Be Lonely*.

He certainly wouldn't be here in this hotel right now. But he was. He was nominated for Favorite Fiction Writer–Young Adult. Not bad for someone having been raised in a slum. Make that a real slum.

It was time to focus on this massive achievement. And be happy.

52

Glitz and glamour consumed the banquet hall. Hotel staff, in spotless maroon uniforms, looked as spiffy as the guests on whom they waited. Gold chandeliers hung overhead as they strode the floor delivering dinners and picking up dishes afterwards. A brightly-lit elongated stage lay in front of all the tables. In the center, a wooden podium—perfectly polished like the front desk outside.

Only seven sat at the Webb table of eight. Corinne had not yet arrived. Pete hoped she would appear shortly. The 8 o'clock hour was fast approaching. He did not want her to miss one second of the ceremony. Only his best friend could occupy the empty seat to his right.

To his left sat Margaret Goldberg. Meeting his literary agent in person was such a treat. Her appearance was exactly how he had imagined: an older woman, medium weight, rather short, and sporting a frosted bouffant hairstyle. To his surprise, however, he experienced some unusual sniffles. Must be the waterfall of perfume dousing her mauve plaid outfit, he thought—an outfit that, without a doubt, had earlier reeked of tobacco. Pete wondered if she could sit through a long awards ceremony without popping outside for a smoke. Probably not, but that was okay. Margaret would ensure her presence during her client's nomination. That was the important thing.

"Oh, sweetheart," she said, her scratchy voice broadcasting live in front of him, "you're just as charming in person as you are on the phone."

"Thank you, Margaret," said Pete. "So are you."

And he meant it.

"Oh, listen to you," she said, laughing her trademark laugh: high-pitched and hoarse—and followed by a cough.

This time, however, the laugh was accompanied by a hand wave, one from a very limp wrist. Pete figured the gesture had been there all along, though this was the first time he could actually see it.

Harry Perkins sat on the other side of Margaret. When *But I'll Never Be Lonely* became a surprise hit, FarHold had assigned one of its best publicists. Tonight was especially important that he be here, considering their client's prestigious nomination.

But Harry's mind drifted away from his work. The tall, bearded, somewhat stocky 61-year-old man couldn't resist stealing glances across the table. There was something about her, the lovely lady next to the woman in all that God-awful pink. Janice was her name, he recalled, the young author's mother. But no wedding ring adorned her left hand. There was no sign of a husband or boyfriend, just that flamboyant friend of hers. For some reason Janice attracted him like a magnet. She may have had a few extra lines on her face, but she was still nice looking. That ashen dress of hers revealed a very trim figure. Harry figured she worked out regularly. She worked out, all right, but not at a gym. Decades of hard labor had formed that tone body—and, unfortunately, those facial wrinkles. Still, Harry liked what he saw. More so, what he heard. Janice had this sweetness about her. It was sincere, pleasant, and ever present in her smile. She seemed quite secure within herself, too. He noted these traits during their introduction … traits that made him want to learn more about her.

Suddenly, the houselights dimmed. It was 8 p.m. The ceremony was about to begin. But where was Corinne? Pete glanced at the banquet hall entrance hoping to find out. It was too dark to see anyone but the tables of people surrounding him.

He then rose.

"Will you all excuse me for a moment?"

His honored guests were stunned. Surely he did not want to leave now, just when the ceremony was getting underway. The reason must be really important.

It certainly was.

"Are you all right, Peter?" asked Janice.

"I'm fine, Mom, thanks," he assured. "I just want to call Corinne and see what's keeping her. I hope she's okay."

"Don't worry, I am," Corinne said, appearing directly behind him.

Pete spun around and embraced her right away—and closely, which kind of surprised her.

"I'm so glad you're here."

Corinne smiled.

"Wouldn't miss this for anything," she said, patting his back.

They held each other a little while longer. For some reason Pete did not want to let her go. Part of him wondered why.

So did his guests around the table. Rae's thickened black eyebrows arched in curiosity, as did Janice's natural ones. Vito's arched as well. Unlike the ladies, however, a dropped jaw had accompanied his gesture.

This is Corinne??? This is the girl who made that pass at you last year? The one you just wanted to be friends with?

He couldn't believe it. Not this girl, not her, not this knockout. She looked like a storybook princess in that periwinkle silk gown with matching diamond earrings and necklace. And that body!

Pete, my man, you're crazy to have let this chick go. Jesus, what a babe! Dude, if I weren't married, I'd—

"Close your mouth, dear," whispered his wife.

Carla's command sent Vito back on the train to Reality Station, with no stops in between.

"Sorry," he said awkwardly. "I think I need some water."

As he reached for the pitcher and poured himself a tall cool glass, Pete finally unglued himself from his best friend. Corinne was relieved. The feelings she had fought long and hard to suppress had tried to escape their maximum-security prison. They may have succeeded had that embrace lasted any longer. This could not happen, not now and not ever. Those feelings had been sentenced to life behind bars—with no chance of parole.

She sat down quickly, much faster than Pete did.

"So nice to see you again, Corinne," Janice whispered, flashing a warm smile.

"Nice to see you, too, Mrs. Webb."

It was too late to greet the rest of the guests individually. The emcee was already onstage.

"Welcome, everyone, to the 34th Annual American Writer Awards," she announced.

Everyone applauded.

As the emcee continued her greeting and ran down a list of tonight's various awards, Pete's mind began to wander. It drifted someplace it had never traveled… Corinne looked beautiful tonight, so incredibly beautiful. More so than at last year's homecoming. Pete felt as if he were meeting her for the first time. But he had met her. He had seen her before, plenty of times. Just not like this. Not this stunningly gorgeous. And here she was, next to him, supporting him, cheering him on like always. Like best friends should.

Right, we're best friends. So why didn't I want to let her go earlier? What made me hug her like that?

Pete's brain searched for answers. He was happy to see her; that much was obvious. He was glad she could be here on this special night. But that embrace… it was so tight, and it lingered for what seemed an eternity. It certainly lasted much longer than any friendly gesture. And it felt really good. Something was happening.

Before he could figure out what it was, enormous cheers erupted from his table. Thunderous applause surrounded him. It took a moment for his mind to return and figure out what had happened: he won. Yes, Peter Michael Webb had just been awarded Favorite Fiction Writer–Young Adult. And he missed it; he missed the whole announcement.

Margaret gently squeezed his shoulder.

"Go ahead, sweetheart," she said into his ear. "Go on up there and collect your award. You'll be okay."

She must have thought he was too nervous. Shocked was more like it. And in more ways than one, considering where his mind had ventured.

Pete rose from his chair slowly, taking time to grasp the reality of the situation. He honestly did not expect to win this award. He had absolutely no speech prepared. But he had to go onstage and pretend he did.

There was something he had to do first, though.

Almost instinctively, Pete turned to Corinne and took her hands into his. He then bent down and kissed her cheek.

"You're the best," he said afterwards, softly into her ear.

Corinne felt her heart racing.

Why did he say that? And why did he hug me the way he did when I first got here?

She reflected on these questions as Pete approached the stage. He certainly was acting a little differently tonight.

Tonight! Of course, it's because of tonight. His feelings haven't changed for me. He's just ecstatic because of the awards ceremony, that's all. Corinne, girl, you never should've gone there. What would Alistair say? I'm with him now, and I had better remember this. He's the one who loves me, not Pete ... well, not in the same way.

The applause and cheers intensified as author Peter Michael Webb collected his trophy. Vito stood up and blew a variety of loud whistles through his fingers. Carla stood proudly beside him, and was soon joined by the others at the table.

"Wow," Pete said into the microphone, savoring this moment of a lifetime. "I know this sounds very cliché, but I really never expected this to happen ... but it has!"

Once again, applause and cheers.

"There are so many people to thank," the newly crowned author continued, "especially every single person at my table."

More applause.

"I thank and love you all," said Pete. "Without your encouragement and support I definitely wouldn't be here right now."

Vito shook his head as if to say, "There you go again." His young friend just couldn't help himself, even now during this moment of triumph. His modesty never ceased to amaze.

"This has been quite a year for me," Pete continued. "So many things have happened. But I got through them, and I have you all to thank: Harry Perkins, the best publicist I never asked for; Margaret Goldberg, the best agent I did ask for; Vito and Carla, who tell me I'm part of their family; Aunt Rae, who's always been there for me and for my mother. Which leads me to you, Mom... You've always told me how proud you were of me, but I'm the one who's proud, proud to be your son."

That did it. Tears of joy streamed out of Janice's watery eyes. She could no longer hold them in. Harry wished he were sitting closer so he could throw a comforting arm around her. Maybe in time he could.

"And finally, Corinne Aldrich..."

Pete paused. He just couldn't help but stare at her, his best friend, his absolutely stunning best friend. He was viewing her under a whole new light—a pretty hot one. She was so beautiful.

What in the world is happening to me?

He honestly didn't know. But he had better wrap up this unscripted speech so he could find out.

"Corinne," he began again, carefully choosing his words, "you're so important to me. I don't think I've ever met anyone who's stood by me the way you have. I only hope that I've done the same for you."

Corinne nodded, and with a proud smile. The combination clearly told him that of course he had.

"Thanks for being here tonight," Pete concluded.

And with a glance around the banquet hall, said, "Thank you everyone. Thanks to people everywhere who read my novel and sent me such kind messages. I'm so honored. I will always cherish this moment. Thank you. Thank you so much."

The audience again applauded, with Vito clapping loudest.

Someone else was clapping, too.

But Brandi Sparks did not want to be seen. Not right now, that is. She made sure to stand in the back corner, where it was darkest.

53

As much as Pete wanted to join his honored guests huddled in the lobby, he had to stay behind. It was time to pose for photographs and field questions from the press. He prayed it wouldn't last long. He wanted to talk to Corinne before she left. She was due to leave shortly after the ceremony.

She was all he thought about as he smiled into the flashbulbs and answered the media's questions. Why? Was it because she had never looked so beautiful before? Or has she always been this way and this was the first time he actually noticed?

But she's my best friend!

Exactly! This was why last year's homecoming night was so awkward ... and why tonight was, too.

This is crazy, this is just insane.

Indeed it was.

I shouldn't be thinking of her this way.

Maybe not, but he was.

"Thank you, Mr. Webb," said a reporter, the last to throw a question.

"Thank you," said Pete.

And not just for their coverage. Now that this Q&A session was over, he could finally talk to Corinne and figure out just what the hell was going on here.

He whizzed past the flock of media, breezed open the banquet hall doors, and entered the main lobby—where he froze instantly.

Why is he here?

It was none other than the smarmy muscle man himself, Alistair

Brundidge. There he was, mingling with the Webb guests of honor as if he were one of them. But he was not invited—on purpose. Pete remembered all too well what happened here in New York this past summer. He never forgot how that suave Englishman wormed his way into Corinne's heart ... and how he ate away at the core of her strongest friendship.

As Alistair spread his magical charm, Carla Caparelli became spellbound. Her mouth hung open in utter astonishment. This 20-something man—tanned, chiseled, and with thick dark hair flowing in curls—was the most gorgeous male specimen she had ever laid eyes on. And that dreamy British accent...

"Close your mouth, dear," Vito whispered, gladly echoing his wife's command just hours ago.

Carla shuddered.

Her husband grinned.

"Oh, honeybunch," he said, "how about a glass of water?"

She needed a pitcher actually ... with lots of ice.

Pete could use one as well—to douse the flames of jealousy. Why did they exist? And why were they burning so fiercely?

He noticed the nearby men's room and ducked into it. At the sink he turned on the cold water and splashed some into his face. After turning it off he looked up and stared directly into the mirror. Calm down, he told his reflection, just relax. There was no use getting worked up like this. Remember, this was the new Peter Michael Webb, strong and confident. He could handle anything now.

Including this? He had to try.

Pete took a deep breath, held his head up high, and exited the men's room.

No.

Corinne was leaving. She and Alistair were passing through the lobby doors leading outside.

Don't go.

She stopped suddenly, as if she heard the thought. She then stole a glance over her shoulder. She just had to see her best friend one last time before heading out—if he were there, of course. To her great surprise he was. Corinne smiled. Although a bit of a distance away, Pete caught the expression. It sparkled just like her blue eyes. He smiled in return.

Their gaze lasted only a few seconds, but it seemed much longer. It was a profound, powerful moment. Corinne did not want to go; Pete wanted her to stay. His smile also said thank you from the bottom of his heart. Having her here tonight meant the world to him.

Corinne soon vanished from sight, led by the tug of Alistair's hand. Pete heaved a long sigh. Although no words were voiced, what had just transpired spoke volumes. Still, perhaps it was best she left when she did. Maybe this was a sign not to bring up these feelings jumbling within. The timing must not have been right.

Seeking a distraction he approached the rest of his guests.

"Hey, guys," he said.

All turned to this year's award winner.

"Having a good time?"

"No," said Rae, "a fabulous time."

Pete chuckled. His "aunt" certainly was enjoying herself here in posh Manhattan, a galaxy away from gloomy Woodlake Square.

"But," she added with a yawn, "I think I'm going to head up to bed now."

Harry Perkins was thrilled. Now he could talk to Janice—alone. The Caparellis were also ready to turn in for the night. But not because they were tired. The image of that oh-so-fine British hunk flashed continuously in Carla's mind … and only her husband could relieve this "tension."

Vito, on cloud nine, was all too eager to oblige.

"Pete, my man," he said, "we couldn't be happier for you. But if you don't mind, Carla and I are going to follow Rae's lead and head upstairs."

"Not a problem."

Vito winked, threw his arm around his wife's waist, and hurried into the elevator, passing Rae Jacobson on the way.

Meanwhile, Pete's remaining guests bid their good nights.

"Oh, sweetheart," Margaret began, "I couldn't be happier for you."

"Well, this couldn't have happened without you."

Margaret took out a tissue and dabbed her moistening eyes.

"Oh, I have to go now or I'll be no good," she said, overwhelmed by her client's praise.

Plus she needed a cigarette. Badly. It had been at least three hours since she last took a drag. A record, Pete thought, perhaps even a miracle.

Margaret had fought her nicotine urges all during the awards ceremony. She wanted to be there for this sweet young man, to offer her utmost support. Pete sensed this and was truly grateful. For her to stay put for so long—without even one cigarette—he must have meant a lot to her.

Author and agent embraced.

"Bye, sweetheart," said the latter.

"Thanks again, Margaret," her client said heartily, "for everything."

She looked at him one last time, uttered an emotional "oh" while flinging a limp wrist, and left the hotel.

Pete felt like following her. Although nippy, a refreshing walk outside would do him some good. Tonight's events were a lot to take in, least of which his coronation as Favorite Fiction Writer–Young Adult. He could deal with this just fine. But not the other thing, not what was stirring inside. Make that *who*.

"I think I'm going to take a walk."

"Oh, son, please be careful," said Janice, her maternal instinct kicking in. "And don't forget your gloves."

Pete shook his head and laughed. Here he was, nearly 25 years old, being told to do things like a child heading off to school.

"And if I promise to be a good boy, can I have a lollipop?" he said playfully. "Please? Please, please, please?"

Janice laughed this time, which made Harry all the more eager to ask her out. How, though? When? It would be awkward with Pete still here. And how would he feel about his publicist taking his mother out on a date? That is, of course, if the lovely lady would do him the honor.

Harry was about to ask Janice for a moment of her time when Pete mentioned needing to collect his coat upstairs. Perfect, Harry thought—but too soon.

"I'll come with you," said Janice.

"Okay," said Pete, who then shook hands with his publicist. "Good night, Harry, and thanks again for everything."

"You're very welcome."

And he was. His client was a fine young man, very humble and polite. Qualities, he believed, passed on by his gracious mother.

Janice also shook his hand.

"It was nice to meet you, Mr. Perkins," she said.

"Please, call me Harry."

"Okay … Harry."

This was it, the moment he had been waiting for all evening: to make his move.

"Uh, Janice … may I have a quick word with you?"

She looked surprised.

"It won't take long, I promise."

"Uh … okay, sure."

She had no idea what he wanted to talk to her about, but the reason, whatever it was, must be important.

"Peter," Janice said, facing her son, "I'll just see you tomorrow, okay?"

"Sure, Mom," he answered. "No problem."

Still, he felt a little awkward leaving the scene. Entering the elevator, Pete wondered what Harry could possibly want with his mother. He was a decent man, though, definitely safe enough to leave alone with her. There really was nothing to worry about.

With this reassurance the elevator doors slid closed.

"Shall we?" Harry said, pointing to two plush maroon chairs.

They had very high backs. Only a marble coffee table separated them. Situated by the far wall, the three furniture pieces created a quaint semiprivate area, away from all the main-lobby traffic.

"So," Harry began, rubbing his salt-and-pepper beard, "I'm glad we have this chance to talk … just the two of us."

This made Janice smile a little.

"But I know it's getting late," he continued, "and I don't want to keep you too long."

"It's okay."

"What I'm wondering is…"

"Yes?"

Harry looked up at the ceiling, rolled his eyes, and sighed.

"Oh, hell," he said, "I've never been very good at this."

"Good at what?"

Harry met Janice's gaze when he replied, "This… Would you like to have dinner with me sometime?"

Janice turned red as a stalk of rhubarb. This was the last thing she expected tonight. She never really viewed herself as attractive anymore, not since falling prey to accelerated aging. She was 49 but could easily pass for 60 or older—Harry's age probably, she thought. He may be a touch on the heavy side, but he was still a good-looking man. Especially in that smart blue suit! She liked his deep bass voice as well. There was something intriguing about it.

But why on earth would someone like him ask out someone like me?

Janice was no Manhattan socialite. Far from it. Besides, the two of them lived in different states, albeit neighboring ones. They were just too different. He lived the high life, and she the hard life. He drove the fancy cars, and she the junkyard specials. Plus she worked two jobs. She had no time for romance. Making sure her bills got paid was her top priority—after her two sons, of course.

She certainly sacrificed a lot of extra dough by coming to New York tonight. Saturdays at the bar were best for collecting tips. But she had to be here right now. She had to support her Peter. This evening meant everything to him.

"I'm very flattered, Harry," said Janice, "but I live all the way in Woodlake Square, New Jersey."

"That's not a problem for me."

"And I work *a lot*," she added. "Sunday is my only day off of the week."

"Then Sunday it is," said Harry. "Not tomorrow, of course, so how about next weekend?"

Persistent, wasn't he? Yet charming. Somehow Janice didn't mind that he had trouble taking no for an answer.

"Tell you what," Harry said, handing over his business card, "take this and give me a call sometime if you like. You're really interesting, and I'd enjoy getting to know you better."

Janice slipped his card into her purse and smiled politely.

"Hey," Harry added softly, "no pressure, okay?"

She nodded.

"Good night," said her suitor, who then walked away.

"Harry?"

He paused and turned around.

"Yes, Janice?"

Her smile expanded.

"Next Sunday sounds wonderful."

54

Pete exited the elevator wearing a heavy black coat and, per Mommy's request, gloves. He glimpsed at the front desk as he passed by. Todd Galloway was back, he noted, and busy assisting guests. The twofaced jerk must be working a long shift, maybe even a double. Pete just hoped that by the time he got back from his walk Todd would be off duty. Seeing that disloyal face first thing upon returning would fever his body all over again.

As he dashed toward the front lobby doors, a voice to the right prevented him from leaving the hotel.

"Hello, Pete," she said.

His legs locked. As did his jaw. He knew that voice. He would know it anywhere. Such feminine soother could only come from one mouth.

Pete's eyes shifted unhurriedly to the right, where they verified what he knew to be true.

Jesus Christ, it's her. It's really her.

He dreaded using the Lord's name in vain, but Brandi Sparks, like the devil, drove him to it.

"I've been meaning to talk to you," she said, "for quite a while now, too."

He uttered no response. All he could do was stand in place and stare. The amount of emotions flooding his psyche right now could crush the world's tallest, most fortified dam. Although close to two years had passed since the defining "standards" moment—and having just been crowned Favorite Fiction Writer–Young Adult because of it—Pete was at a loss for words.

"You probably have nothing to say to me, I'm sure," said Brandi.

You got that right!

"But if I could please just have a few minutes of your time…"

You don't deserve it!

True, but he relented anyway. Perhaps if he revisited the Brandi chapter of his life—one last time—this book could finally close for good.

Pete knew tonight would be memorable, but not this memorable.

Ironically, they sat on the very maroon chairs where Harry had just asked out Janice. Unlike his publicist, however, Pete would do nothing of the sort with the lowly Miss Sparks. This conversation would be short and sweet. Well, maybe not sweet, but it would definitely be short. He really needed that brisk walk outside now.

"So what is it?" he asked, voicing his first words since their encounter.

Brandi took a deep breath before answering, all the while twirling the crimps in her sandy-blond hair.

"I just wanted to say I'm sorry," she said. "I never realized how much I hurt you until I read your book." And with saddened brown eyes, added, "I think I know that Bethany Spikes character pretty well."

You sure do!

She reached across the coffee table and took Pete's gloved hands into her bare ones. He wanted to whisk them away but fought the urge.

"Can you ever forgive me?"

What? Never did he expect to hear those words from her, not from the high-and-mighty Queen of Standards. But he did. She indeed apologized. And she seemed sincere. But was she? Had she changed since the college days? Did she really mean what she just said? He had no idea. And it was all Brandi's fault. Her word meant nothing. She could very well be sincere; then again, she may not.

He could forgive her, though. But he could never forget.

"I appreciate you saying this," Pete began, "but Brandi… you know that I can't take your word at face value. You appear to be genuinely sorry, but I've been fooled by your appearances before."

She nodded guiltily.

"Like the time when we met on the stairwell outside the cafeteria. Remember that? I was alone, and you were with all your friends from prayer group. And in front of them you kept thanking me for the chocolates and the poem."

His tone then turned angry.

"But less than 18 hours beforehand you and Todd were all over each other ... and mocking me ... making fun of my car, where I grew up. How do you think that made me feel, huh?"

Brandi lowered her head in shame.

"So how in the world am I supposed to believe one word that comes out of your mouth now?"

Silence.

"The simple truth is I can't," said Pete, his voice relaxing. "But... I can forgive you nonetheless."

Brandi looked up at him.

"You can?"

He nodded.

"Not many people would do that," she said.

True. But he was glad he did. No more lingering bitterness. Let it lie in the past. That was where it belonged. This did not mean, however, that he and Brandi could be close again. Or even friendly. But civil would do quite nicely. And one day—maybe, just maybe—he and Todd could be civil to one another as well.

Did he really just think that? Why, yes, he did. Wow, how liberating. Amazing what can happen by letting go of past resentments. Toward people who sought forgiveness, of course. A category his brother Adam could never belong.

"So," said Pete, "life treating you well?"

Brandi wasn't at all upbeat when she answered, "I suppose."

"You don't sound convinced."

"Well..."

She looked over her shoulder and found many women at the front desk, beautiful exotic women. They seemed to enjoy cavorting around her filthy rich boyfriend ... who did nothing to send them away.

Brandi refaced Pete, again with saddened brown eyes.

"I got myself into a fine mess, didn't I?" she said, fighting back tears.

"Looks like it."

He could tell she wanted to let out a good cry, that she needed a good old-fashioned hug. Pete decided to swallow his pride and offer one. He rose with open arms.

"Oh, Pete."

Brandi collapsed into his comforting embrace and sobbed away.

Unbeknownst to them, Corinne reentered the hotel lobby from outside. She had sneaked away from Alistair and their friends at a nearby nightclub. She needed to see Pete again, if only for a few minutes. They hardly had any time to talk or catch up. And she would be gone all day tomorrow visiting family in Long Island.

Plus the other reasons… That long embrace, the words he said and the way he said them, their parting glance. Against her better judgment she had to find out if they were more than just friendly gestures.

She soon regretted her decision.

Corinne stared in shock, almost horror, at Pete hugging another girl. And not just any girl, Brandi Sparks! The very woman who had turned his life upside down, who said he could never meet her standards, who slept with Todd Galloway when they were dating!

Oh, God.

Corinne turned away. Her stomach's intactness depended on it.

Why do I keep doing this to myself?!

Her eyes began to water. She had to get out of here—now—before she made an even bigger fool of herself.

Corinne tore through the main entrance as if the hotel were on fire.

Only she was the one burning up inside.

55

Unbelievable, simply unbelievable. The month of December kept turning up surprise after surprise after surprise. And it wasn't even Christmas! That was next week. Apparently, though, Santa decided to deliver a couple of special gifts early this year. With help from a devoted elf, that is.

First, Margaret announced that first-quarter sales were through the roof. *But I'll Never Be Lonely* had trickled into top-10 bestseller lists almost everywhere, even reaching number one in some instances. This meant beaucoup bucks! Her client's residuals would arrive soon after the new year, after the official quarterly data had been configured. His first check, she told him, would be well worth the wait.

Pete was stunned. So much so he almost dropped the phone. Luckily he was at work. The office phone here had a sturdy cord attached.

"This sometimes happens, sweetheart," said Margaret, "when authors win awards."

"No complaints here!"

Margaret laughed, but coughed soon afterwards. She then delivered her second announcement, which came as an even greater shock.

A new soap opera was in development. Unlike most in America, this one would depict the lives of ordinary working-class people. Characters in *Community Spirit* would work real jobs and face real problems. None would own corporations, live in mansions, or have servants at their beck and call. They would not own the fanciest cars and clothes money could buy. Nor would everyone have perfect bodies—or hair and makeup, especially first thing in the morning.

Actors were to be cast who resembled ordinary people, whose faces contained no plastic. And they had to be able to act. Talent must trump appearance. Actors of all ages and backgrounds were needed. The soap's most prominent storylines wouldn't all focus on the young or one particular ethnicity.

Despite a fair amount of children and elderly, most characters in this drama series would be of working age—holding jobs such as laborers, store clerks, drivers, mechanics, bartenders, and others that defined the working class. They would all live in the same neighborhood, one with nearly identical homes. Set interiors would have a "lived-in" look: children's toys scattered on the floors; dishes piled in racks next to sinks; magnets, photos, and other personal decorations on refrigerators; handmade blankets covering old comfy sofas. The list went on.

No retconning, children aging by a decade in a subsequent episode, or over-the-top plots in *Community Spirit* either. Characters would never discover secret underground cities, time travel, or turn into vampires. No one would be held hostage as their alien twin took their place. Instead, people would endure struggles such as unemployment, delinquency, marital woes, substance abuse, physical and mental illness—all with a sense of realism. No sugarcoating the issues with political correctness. Tough love, soul-searching, saying what needed to be said, doing the right thing no matter how difficult the situation ... this was where the heart of this drama series lay.

By diving into the human heart—and by creating a realistic working-class neighborhood, one with an overwhelming sense of togetherness—the show would be something to which blue-collar Americans could relate.

Pete was intrigued, but he had no idea why Margaret brought this to his attention. So he asked.

"Because, sweetheart," she began, "the show wants you to join their writing team."

"Me?"

"That's right."

"Why?"

The reasons were clear. Just not to Pete. The award-winning author had no clue just how much of an impact his debut novel had made. It certainly was enough to impress television series developers in New York. Margaret said they enjoyed his description of Parker West's working-class background as much as the character's plight and journey of self-discovery. These vivid, illustrative details had seized their attention.

"So, sweetheart, are you interested?"

"Yes, I am," said Pete, "very much."

Writing for a TV show was a dream job. The series sounded very promising, too. There really was nothing like it on American television today, not in the soap opera sense. Woodlake Squares just did not exist.

Woodlake Square! That's it! That's what this show reminds me of.

No wonder he was intrigued.

Pete accepted the job offer on the spot. Not only was it an excellent opportunity to expand his literary horizon, he could live closer to Corinne. He would have to wait until March, though. That was when the script's first drafts were to be written. This left ample time to find a place and make the big move to the Big Apple. Exciting!

Even if the series did not catch on and ended prematurely, he would have plenty of money to live on. Aside from his initial novel's royalties, FarHold would soon offer him a new six-figure book deal. The publisher would actually pay him first, before he wrote a single word. That was how confident they were in Peter Michael Webb's work. And after that book—whatever it would be about—was published, residuals from that novel would roll in, too. Wild. He never dreamed something like this could happen to him, to some nobody from Woodlake Square. But his name meant something now.

"Thanks for everything, Margaret," Pete said, "as always."

"You're so welcome. Oh, I couldn't be happier for you. I'll be in touch, okay?"

"Okay."

"Bye, sweetheart."

"Bye."

Pete hung up the phone, leaned back in his chair, and released a breath of exhilaration. Writing for an actual TV series! What an incredible opportunity. He could hardly wait to share this news … except with Vito. Telling him, the best boss anyone could ask for, was going to be tough.

But he had said to accept a better job offer if one came along. Well, it did. And it was time to let him know.

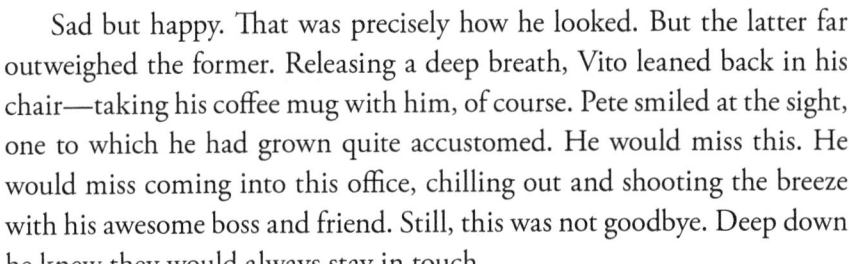

Sad but happy. That was precisely how he looked. But the latter far outweighed the former. Releasing a deep breath, Vito leaned back in his chair—taking his coffee mug with him, of course. Pete smiled at the sight, one to which he had grown quite accustomed. He would miss this. He would miss coming into this office, chilling out and shooting the breeze with his awesome boss and friend. Still, this was not goodbye. Deep down he knew they would always stay in touch.

So did Vito.

"Well, my man, what can I say," he said, sipping his coffee, "I knew this moment would come sooner or later. I always knew bigger and better things would come knocking on your door. It was only a matter of time."

"Well, it's not until March," said Pete. "We've got a couple more months."

"Not soon enough, I bet."

"What do you mean?"

Vito grinned. Mysteriously, so did his eyebrows.

"Are you sure that's the only reason you're moving to New York?" he asked.

Pete knew what he was getting at.

"Well…"

"I knew it!" Vito exclaimed, leaning forward. "You like Corinne, don't you?"

He sure did. He just never said it before. Well, not in that way.

"Dude, she is such a babe. And I'm not talking just in looks. She's a baby doll, a real sweetheart. Warm, friendly, down to earth, fantastic sense of humor … and even though she's with that British guy, I think she still has a thing for you."

"What makes you think that?" Pete asked, the urgency for an answer drifting in his voice.

"Just a feeling, bud, that's all," said Vito. "I could be wrong you know. Hell, Carla tells me I'm wrong all the time. Anyway, just so you know, I'm really happy for you. But I'm also going to miss the hell out of you. This office won't be same without you, bud."

Vito rose from his chair, walked around the desk, and embraced his special employee.

"I love you like a brother, man."

Hearing this, Pete forgot all about his situation with Corinne. He, too, loved Vito like a brother—and actually wished they were, considering his real one. Adam never did the things his boss had done for him. He never looked out for his best interests, offered support, or made him feel like a lifetime friend. Basically he never treated him like a human being. But Vito did. And Pete would miss him immensely.

To return the favor, to thank his boss for absolutely everything he had done, he uttered one sentence: "You're one of the good ones, man."

That pretty much said it all.

And for Vito it meant the world to hear it.

56

The time to tell Mom had arrived. It was Saturday, almost 1 p.m. Pete wanted to catch her before she went upstairs to nap. She had an eight-hour shift at the bar ahead of her. They usually called one another on Sundays, but Mom had plans tomorrow, special plans. She and his publicist, Harry Perkins, were to go out on their first date. Pete definitely didn't want to interrupt their time together. He secretly hoped something would develop between them, something unique and magical. Not necessarily right away, of course, but no complaints if it did. Harry was a really great guy; he would treat Mom well. There was no doubt about it.

Pete also wanted to ask her an important question: to move with him to New York. She could live at his home, wherever that may be, and would no longer have to labor such long hard hours at the restaurant and bar. He felt it the least he could do to pay her back for all she had done for him—all her sacrifices to ensure he had a roof over his head, clothes on his back, and food on the table. Pete had always dreamed of alleviating her hardship one day. Now, at long last, he could.

But Janice declined.

"Thank you, Peter, I appreciate that," she said to him on the kitchen phone, "but I just can't up and leave. Your brother needs me."

He certainly did. He needed her to keep working so he could carry on his pathetic life of boozing and sleeping off hangovers—with that no-good pig, Belinda Price.

"By the way," Janice continued, "Adam has a job interview Monday morning, this time at a car dealership. Say a prayer he gets it."

Pete wanted to ask if he in fact had an interview. And if he did, would he attend. Instead he uttered an "okay." No sense in getting into the Adam mess. It would only upset her.

"Thank you again, son, for the kind offer," said Janice. "But Woodlake Square is my home. My life is here, my friends are here. My God, can you imagine Aunt Rae's reaction?"

She would be very supportive, Pete thought, but very upset as well.

"Plus my jobs—"

"But Mom, that's my point. You've worked hard all your life. You've done so much for me when I was growing up. Can't you just let me repay you, now that I can?"

"Peter, you don't have to pay me back."

"I know I don't have to, I want to."

Janice smiled. Her baby boy was so compassionate, so caring and generous. He always worried about her. But she was fine. She was okay all through his childhood, and she would be okay now through his adulthood.

"Thanks, son, but I'm going to pass," she said. "Besides, if I were to move in with you, I'd be giving up something very important: my independence. What I have may not be worth much, but knowing that I worked hard to earn it is."

Pete lay silently on his couch as he absorbed his mother's words, especially that last sentence. It indeed spoke volumes.

"You're right, Mom, you would be losing your independence," he said afterwards. "I can't take that away from you. Anyway, I better let you go so you can get some rest."

"Okay, Peter. Congratulations again on your incredible job offer."

"Thanks, Mom. And have a great time with Harry tomorrow."

"I hope to."

Janice paused a moment then bid her son goodbye.

Pete, on the sofa, set his cellular on the nearby coffee table, then gazed at the ceiling. Here he was on a Saturday afternoon with nothing to do. It had been ages since he last had a day like this, a whole day off. Ordinarily he would be getting ready to work his shift at the cinema. But he had quit that part-time job, one he'd held since he was 16 years old. Sunday was his last day. He no longer needed it. His salary at *Jersey News Central*, which had increased again after his one year of service, was enough to make ends meet. And with book royalties arriving shortly he would have even more dough rolling in.

But there was more to life than money.

Pete turned his head to the phone on the coffee table. He contemplated picking it up and calling Corinne. They hadn't spoken since last week's awards ceremony. There was too much unfinished business between them, especially after their parting glance in the hotel lobby. They had texted this week, but nothing serious was stated. Just the basic chitchat stuff: Hi, how are you? How's work this week? What's the weather like where you are? Everything but what they both felt that night.

Pete sighed. Part of him wanted to call and talk to her, to share the conflict stirring inside. After all, she was his best friend. He could always come to her about anything.

Even about this?

He answered the question by turning away and pulling the throw blanket over him. By napping away the afternoon he had found an escape route. But it was only temporary. Sooner or later he would have to face the situation.

Not today, though.

But a lot sooner than he ever imagined.

57

Ever the gentleman, Harry Perkins walked his date to her doorstep. It was just about 10 o'clock this cold dark Sunday night. Janice did not expect to be out this late. She had to be at work in eight hours. But she didn't mind the inconvenience. Quite the contrary, she welcomed the change of routine. Moreover, she welcomed this charming man into her life.

The pair got to know each other rather well this evening. Janice learned that Harry was a widower. His wife had passed away five years ago from a heart attack. It was the saddest time of his life, he had said, and for his children, two daughters and two sons, all in their 30s. But he was ready to date again, to meet someone new. And Janice was the loveliest woman he'd met in quite some time.

Harry discovered she had two grownup kids. Of course, he already knew Pete, her youngest. But he didn't know her other son … the dependent one.

Janice preferred to keep it that way, at least for now. Maybe she could introduce Adam later, after he had landed a decent job—the one at the car dealership, she hoped. Maybe then the time would be right.

For now it was time to just enjoy each other's company, which they thoroughly did. They never ran out of words the entire four hours they had spent together—during the drive to the restaurant in Mount Holly; through dinner, dessert and coffee; back to Woodlake Square; and now at the doorstep.

Neither was ready for the date to end, but it had to.

"I had a wonderful time tonight," said Harry, his deep voice adding the perfect flavor to the romantic air between them, "and I'd very much like to see you again."

Janice smiled sweetly.

"I'd like that, Harry," she said. "I'd like that a lot."

He wanted to kiss her right then and there, but he stopped himself. He glanced at the door instead, touching the Christmas wreath that hung on it.

"A shame this isn't mistletoe," he said.

"Oh?"

"Uh-huh."

"And why's that?"

Harry turned to her as he answered, "Because if it were, I could do this…"

The bearded man kissed her tenderly, which Janice enjoyed, proven by the magical spell of silence that followed.

"Good night, Janice," Harry said afterwards.

"Good night."

Both shared a smile then went their separate ways, Harry to his car and Janice into her townhouse.

Her smile never left her face.

Rae, who was sorting laundry on the sofa, noticed it as soon as she came through the door.

"Well, well, well," she said excitedly, a big smile of her own ever present, "looks like somebody had a nice time tonight."

She certainly did.

And Rae couldn't wait to hear all about it.

She had volunteered to do the Webb's laundry today so that her friend could spend as much time with Harry as possible. Janice appreciated this wholeheartedly. Strange, though, that it took all this time to wash, dry and fold everything. Then again, Rae probably planned it this way. She just had to know how the date with Harry went—as soon as it ended.

But Janice, blissful as a schoolgirl, was happy to indulge her.

"I had the best time tonight," she said. "It was wonderful, everything was absolutely wonderful."

Rae's hazel eyes dazzled with anticipation.

"And???"

"And..."

Janice hung up her wool coat in the closet before answering. As she did this, Rae noticed she had worn her sapphire-blue evening dress. A little dark, she thought, but still a nice choice. Harry must have been very impressed.

"And he kissed me," Janice answered, finally, and with the broadest smile.

Rae's mouth dropped to the floor.

"He did?" she said. "Oh, honey, that's so—"

Approaching footsteps from upstairs interrupted them. They were loud and obnoxious, as if trying to disrupt the pleasant moment on purpose. Proudly attached to the pounding feet was none other than Belinda Price, a smirking Belinda Price. She had on blue jeans with an extra-large black sweater, dark enough to hide—almost—her unflattering chubby physique. Her bleached frizzy hair was spiked with lots of gel.

Adam followed closely behind her. He was dressed similarly, wearing jeans and a long-sleeved button-down black shirt. His hair also contained way too much gel—and spiked in every direction imaginable.

A couple of freaks, they were, the pair of them.

As they arrived downstairs Belinda looked Janice straight in the eye.

She then asked, in all crudeness, "Get lucky, huh?"

Her boyfriend's mother, too appalled for words, did not reply. But Rae Jacobson sure as hell did—in the form of an enraged glare, which transmitted a silent reminder of her warning earlier in the year: *You better start treating Janice with some respect around here. This is HER house, not yours. Stop making trouble for her. Stop deepening the rift between her and her son. Stop pitting them against each other. You had better remember this, or you'll have me to deal with all over again. Got it?*

Maybe then she did. Not anymore.

Thanks to Belinda the tension in the living room had risen fast. A desperate Janice changed the subject ... which made matters worse.

"So, Adam," she said, "excited about tomorrow's interview at the car dealership?"

"Yeah, sure, uh-huh," he answered.

"So what color suit did you end up buying?"

"Uh… gray."

"Well, can I see it?"

"It's upstairs in my closet, Mom," said Adam, quickly adding that he and Belinda were on their way out.

Janice stopped them as they attempted to pass. She sensed something fishy.

"I'd like to see your suit, Adam," she said, eyeing him with razor-sharp skepticism, "you know, the one you were to buy with *my money*."

"Can't it wait, Mom? Belinda and I are—"

"Sticking around for a while."

Belinda rolled her eyes.

"No, we're leaving," Adam reiterated, sternly, "now."

At 28 he certainly wasn't going to be told what to do by his mother, especially in front of his girlfriend.

Oh, yes, he would! Janice had been fooled by his deception one-too-many times. No more.

You better not be lying to me, Adam, not this time. You better not skip this interview … if you even have one.

She hated to doubt his word, but what choice did she have? He had deceived her in the past, and he could very well do the same again … and without one ounce of guilt. She could no longer allow herself to be taken in by his lies and manipulations.

As Adam opened the front door Janice said, "Okay, then you won't mind if I go upstairs and have a look myself."

He stopped immediately. He then shut the door in a fit of temper, his sea-green eyes seething in resentment.

"What the hell is your damn problem, Mom?! Why are you such a nagging pain in the ass?!"

Janice was shocked. She had heard his harsh tone spew out of his mouth before, to Peter, but never to her personally.

Rae was shocked, too, but livid more than anything.

"Adam, don't you dare speak to her like that!" she said in defense of her best friend.

"I'll say whatever the hell I want to say."

"Not to me you won't."

"I think I just did."

Belinda could take no more. Highly amused, she cackled away. Janice was furious. This young woman had caused so many problems so many times, including now. She knew exactly what she was doing. She enjoyed, actually enjoyed, turning people against one another. She was certainly good at it—and good at getting away with it, too. Under Adam's eyes, that is. Not Janice's.

"Shut up, Belinda," she said. "Shut up now!"

Her son's girlfriend stopped her piggish laugh—but not because she was told to. She had a little something to share herself. It was high time Adam's pussy-tight mommy got a reality check. She turned to her boyfriend first.

"So you want to know what your mother's problem is, huh?" she said, referring to his earlier question, before the Square's gossip queen so rudely interrupted him, "because I know. I know exactly what her problem is."

Belinda faced Janice to conclude: "She needs a good lay."

What did she just say?!?!

Janice indeed heard the words, loud and clear. She just couldn't believe Belinda had the audacity to voice them. Neither could Rae.

Shockingly, Belinda had even more to say.

"Too bad that guy left," she began. "You sure as hell need a good lay tonight."

Janice froze.

But Rae was having none of this.

"How dare you!!!" she yelled into Belinda's round pudgy face. "I warned you what would happen if you caused Janice any more grief: you'd have me to deal with. Well, missy, the time has come for you to get yours."

Sweat glistened on Rae's makeup-covered forehead as she spat her words. But she didn't care. She was fired up like never before.

Janice, on the other hand, stood eerily calm.

"Don't Rae," she said quietly. "I can handle this."

Belinda laughed yet again—but stopped suddenly. Her cheek swelled. She then found herself staring at the carpeted floor. Slowly she realized what just happened: Mrs. Webb had slapped her—hard.

A rage had seized control. Janice could no longer contain it. It bore inside her the day Belinda Price entered her house, her life. For years it had been fighting to break free. Only now did she let it out.

And did she ever...

"You bitch! You troublemaker bitch!!!" she screeched, grabbing Belinda's short spiky hair. "You get out of here, understand?! You get the hell out of my house, out of my life, and don't you ever come back! Got it?!"

Belinda was in too much pain to answer verbally. Janice's fixed, unyielding grip was excruciating. Uttering a response would only intensify the throbbing on top of her head. Screaming would, too, which was what she wanted to do most, and so badly. But standing there at the mercy of Mrs. Webb was all she could do. She had no choice but to soak in the agonizing stinging and soreness.

With her free hand Janice flung open the front door. She then shoved Belinda out. Not only by lobbing her head forward, but with a swift kick to her fat, blubbery rear end.

She had no idea where she got the strength to do what she just did. Or the flexibility, considering she was wearing an evening dress.

Neither did Rae—or Adam, to whom Janice now turned.

"You get out of my house, too," she said to her freeloading son.

"What!"

"You heard me: get out! I've had it with your lies. I've had it with you doing absolutely nothing while I work two jobs day and night. I've had it with you."

"You don't mean that."

"Yes, I do! I can't take it anymore! I can't take *you*. You stood there and said nothing the whole time Belinda insulted me. You never once defended me. You're just like her, Adam. You're both garbage. And what do you do with garbage? You throw it out."

Adam glared at his mother.

"Fine," he hissed, stretching out the word for all its bitter worth.

He approached the threshold, then stopped and spun around. There was more to say.

"Take one last look, Mom, because this is the last time you'll ever see me."

Janice paused. This was it. This was really it this time. But it was something she had to do. And it was long overdue.

"Get...out," she said.

Well, if that's how you want it...

Adam smirked one last time.

"Go…to…"

Before he could finish, Janice ran to the door, and with all her might pushed her son outside.

"Get out of here now!!!" she screamed. "And don't you come back, either!"

She then slammed the door.

Rae approached cautiously. She had never seen her friend this angry, this incensed. Never did she think this day would come. But it did. Janice had finally had enough. She actually threw Adam out of the house—and Belinda. It sure did Rae's heart good to see that lousy piece of trash get what was coming to her.

Now, though, it was time to be supportive.

"Janice, honey, are you all right?"

She paused before answering, waiting for her breathing to return to normal. What an evening. The euphoric mood she was in at dinner had taken a drastic turn at home … her home. Yes, this was her home, all hers. No more Belinda. The troublemaker bitch was gone. So was Adam. And this was a good thing.

"Yes, Rae, I'm fine," Janice said, realizing just how true it was. "As a matter of fact I've never felt better in my whole life."

58

Rae Jacobson had graciously offered to spend the night. She didn't want to leave her best friend alone. Not after everything that happened. Janice needed her now more than ever. Yet she was strong, perhaps the strongest Rae had ever seen. She had amazing energy last night, enough to pack up all of Adam's things and haul them to the curb outside. If he picked them up, fine. If not, that was fine, too. Belinda's belongings deserved even worse treatment. They went straight into a trash bag, a pretty big one considering the size of her clothing. Instead of taking it out to the curb Janice tossed it into the dumpster. She didn't stop until everything, every last trace of Adam and Belinda, was erased from her home.

To foil any plans they had to return, she had an on-call locksmith drop by. She was taking no chances. Adam and Belinda were not coming back. No way. Changing the locks to the front and back doors was the only way to guarantee this. That and getting a home security system installed. Janice wanted this done as soon as possible. She didn't care about its cost. No estimates were necessary. Just get here fast. The company obliged and would arrive tomorrow afternoon at 4.

It was 3:30 a.m. by the time the locksmith left. He had issued three new keys. Janice gave one to Rae and kept the other two, one of which would go to Peter.

She then went to bed. Needless to say, she was not going into work tomorrow.

Make that today.

The Webb matriarch slept until 1 o'clock in the afternoon. As she lumbered down the stairs she noticed Rae seated on the sofa watching TV.

"Good morning, Janice," she said, "or should I say, good afternoon."

Either. Now that the Adam/Belinda problem was solved, the day was good no matter what the time was.

Janice dressed very casually today. She had on black jeans and a pink-and-gray checkered flannel shirt over top. Clearly the outfit did not compare to Rae's lime-green pants and blouse, which she had packed and brought over late last night, along with her makeup bag, hairspray, toothbrush, and other toiletries.

"Honey, did you sleep all right?"

"Yes, thank you, I did," Janice answered, sitting on the chair beside the sofa.

Rae had a fresh pot of tea made, which sat in a tray on the coffee table. She poured her friend a nice hot cup.

"Here you are."

"Thanks."

Rae turned off the television and asked if Janice heard the phone ring a couple of hours ago. She heard no such thing. In fact, she slept so soundly that only an earthquake could have woken her.

"So who was it?"

"Harry."

Rae explained that he had planned to leave a voicemail message. And when she got home from work she would have a nice little surprise waiting for her. But Harry was the one surprised, and not just because Rae picked up the phone. It was what she told him, what all went on last night after the dinner date.

"I hope you don't mind that I told him," said Rae. "I didn't want to wake you, and I didn't want to lie as to why I was here."

Janice sighed.

"I probably scared him away," she said cynically.

"No, honey, not at all," Rae assured. "He was actually very concerned about you."

"He was?"

Before Rae could nod a reply someone knocked at the front door. The two women glanced at each other, wondering who it could be. It was entirely possible that Adam and Belinda wanted back in. That, of course, was out of the question.

"I'll answer it," said Rae, who rose off the sofa. "Don't worry, honey. Before those two get through that door, they'll have to get through me first."

She opened the curtain next to the door to see who it was.

"Well, I'll be."

"Who is it, Rae?"

She opened the door instead of answering verbally. It was Harry!

"Hello, Rae," he said, "nice to see you again."

He recognized her right away, only this time she wore too much God-awful lime green versus God-awful pink.

"Come in, Harry."

"Thank you."

Janice put down her teacup and rose anxiously. She looked a wreck. Her outfit was definitely not appropriate for greeting guests, especially someone she had just started to date. But there was no time to run upstairs and change.

Still, she was happy to see him.

"Hi, Harry."

"Janice."

"You'll have to pardon my appearance," she said. "If I'd known you were coming over, I would've put on something a little more halfway decent."

Harry, dressed in a sharp brown suit, no doubt the best money could buy, couldn't have cared less what she wore. Her well-being was what concerned him. Besides, she was attractive no matter what she had on.

"Don't worry about it, don't even give it a second thought," the bearded man said. "In fact, I'm the one who should be asking you to pardon my appearance. After all, I'm the one who showed up unexpectedly on your doorstep."

Yes, he did, but Janice didn't mind, not in the slightest.

Neither did Rae, who excused herself.

"I think I'm going to head home now," she said, collecting her overnight bag from inside the closet. "I've got a million things to do."

Not exactly true. She just wanted to leave the two lovebirds alone for a while.

"Nice to see you again, Harry."

"Same here," he said.

He shook her hand, grateful for the support she lent to his lady friend.

Janice saw Rae to the door. There, she embraced the woman she long considered a sister, thanking her wholeheartedly for everything.

"You're my best friend," she added, "and I love you."

"I love you, too," said Rae. "Remember, I'm just across the street if you need me."

Yes, she was, thank goodness.

Their embrace ended, though Rae had something else to say, something important her dear friend needed to know.

"Honey, always remember that you did the right thing."

Yes, I did, didn't I?

The thought produced a proud, appreciative smile on Janice's face, after which she said, "I'll call you later."

"You better."

Rae's eyes twinkled as she said this. She wanted to know all about Harry's surprise visit.

Janice shook her head in amusement.

Same ole Rae, she'll never change.

Nor did she want her to.

After closing the door, and locking it, Janice turned to her guest.

"May I offer you something, Harry? A snack? Something to drink? I have some juice in the fridge, there's a pot of tea on the coffee table, and—"

He placed his finger gently on her lips.

"I didn't come here for refreshments," he said. "I came because I wanted to make sure you were all right."

How sweet. This man—this charming, thoughtful man—left his job in the middle of the day to come down here and see to her well-being. The commute couldn't have been easy. It took a lot of time just to reach the New Jersey Turnpike. Zigzagging around the stampede of Manhattan vehicles was no simple task. Then, of course, there was the drive down the Turnpike itself, to Exit 7A halfway down the state. Plus all the tolls!

He just did this last night.

And he did it again, not even 24 hours later. For her.

"I can't believe you came all this way, again, just for me," Janice said, deeply touched.

"I would've driven a thousand miles if I had to."

His words brought her to near tears.

"Really?" she said to him, her voice about to crack.

Harry kissed her forehead, smiled, and assured her with a tender, "Absolutely."

Wow, I must really mean a lot to him.

She did ... and he was starting to mean a lot to her as well.

Janice displayed both a fond and grateful smile. She would have got through this ordeal just fine by herself, or with Rae, but having Harry here made it a little easier.

He smiled in return but also opened his arms. Janice happily fell into them. She had no idea if any relationship would blossom with this man. But him showing up here, holding her, comforting her, was a sure step in that direction.

"Thank you, Harry," she said. "I'm really glad you're here."

"So am I."

In more ways than she probably knew.

But was only just beginning to find out.

59

Later that Monday, across the Hudson, another relationship was about to go a step farther. Alistair Brundidge had been waiting a long time for this moment, since the day he first met the lovely and charming Corinne more than a year ago. She was his girlfriend now, steady girlfriend. They had been an item since the summer. He desperately wanted the relationship to continue, to flourish. But in exactly 12 days, New Year's Eve, his visa would expire. He had to leave the country and return to his native Britain.

And he wanted Corinne there with him.

Outside her condominium door Alistair released a deep breath. Tonight was the night. He wanted everything to be perfect. His appearance certainly was, as always. He wore a white button-down dress shirt, crisp non-faded blue jeans, and a beige suit jacket overtop. His brown shoes had just been polished. As was the dialogue he had prepared.

He knocked on her door gently.

"Corinne, love, it's me."

"Coming," he heard.

She opened the door, smiled, and kissed him.

"Come on in," she said, ushering him inside. "Dinner is just about ready."

She prepared an Italian meal for them, eggplant parmesan. She also fixed a salad, complete with homemade creamy Italian dressing.

She looked incredible this evening in that sexy lavender dress.

And Alistair knew just the thing to add to it.

After putting the dinner dishes into the dishwasher and turning it on, the couple headed to the comfy cream-colored sofa in the living room. With soft music playing in the background, they relaxed in each other's arms, sharing occasional kisses and joining of hands. Eventually Corinne rested her head on the broad shoulder behind her. Her eyes soon closed.

Alistair gazed upon her. He ran his fingers through her fine brown hair, savoring the feel of its softness.

The moment was ideal. It was time to do what he came over to do.

He reached into his suit-jacket pocket and pulled out a small box. He then released his second deep breath of the evening, this one silently.

"Corinne?"

"Yes?"

"Can I ask you something?"

"Sure."

"Will you… will you marry me?"

What!

Her eyes popped open as if she heard a gunshot in her sleep. She removed her head from Alistair's shoulder and faced him with a look of great surprise.

"You know I'll be leaving for London shortly," he said.

"Yeah, but … but we … we already discussed this."

True, they had. Alistair was to go home for at least a month. To reconnect with life and loved ones back in the U.K., to see if good ole Blighty was really where he wanted to live. It was, of course, but he also had a loved one here, right beside him.

Corinne realized this. Still, she wanted to give their relationship some space. She wanted Alistair to be absolutely sure that she was the woman he truly desired.

He *was* absolutely sure. And not only about his feelings for Corinne. He was sure he didn't want to leave her alone … with Pete. The famous author would be moving to New York soon, which would only lead to trouble. Alistair had enough hurdles to jump just to get Corinne to date him seriously. Hell, to take him seriously. But with Pete frequenting the City to look for flats, with him about to live in such close proximity… No, he couldn't allow it. He couldn't allow her so-called best friend on campus to stir any second thoughts inside her head. Or worse, steal her away.

"Come with me," he said to her, opening the small box, revealing a diamond engagement ring. "Marry me, Corinne."

She was speechless. The ring was the most gorgeous thing she had ever seen. An enormous diamond sat atop a shiny gold band, both of which sparkled in captivating brilliance.

"Alistair," she said, regaining the ability to speak, "I… I don't know what to say."

"How about, yes?"

Corinne bounced off the sofa.

"What about my family, my job?" she said, and with stretched-out arms, added, "This place?"

Alistair reassured her calmly.

"Your family can pop over anytime, they're always welcome," he said. "London is a mere six or seven-hour flight from New York. It's not that bad, really."

He was right about that. Now, onto the others…

"I just can't quit my job on the spot and pack up this place."

"You won't have to," said Alistair, explaining that while she finished these last two weeks of work he could pack her belongings himself.

"That's not the point," Corinne said. "This is my home. I don't want to sell it."

"You don't have to," he said. "This is New York. There are millions of people who would love to rent this place … including, soon enough, your famous author friend Peter Michael Webb."

Corinne turned away.

Why did he say that? Why did he have to bring up his name?

Because Alistair knew she would miss him terribly. He wanted Pete out of her life—their lives—once and for all. There was no better way to accomplish this than whisking her out of the country.

Startled by the thought, Corinne walked around the sofa to the window. She stood next to the teal curtain and peeked outside. An array of Christmas lights and other décor hung somewhere on virtually every building in sight. People below strode a little more slowly than usual. No doubt to take in this seasonal wonderland. Some of these passersby walked hand in hand, which made Corinne think of Pete … and how he would never do such a thing. But Alistair would and had. He was the one who wanted to do these things with her, who wanted her.

Why doesn't Pete? Why, damn it, why?

She already knew the answer. In fact, she always knew: he just wasn't into her physically; they could never be more than just friends. What more evidence did she need than what she walked in on at the Galloway Hotel Towers?

Brandi… The vision of that girl in Pete's arms flashed like paparazzi cameras. How could he? After everything she had put him through, how could he hold her like that? Caress her?

I should be the one. Me. Not Brandi Sparks.

But this wasn't the case, was it?

Corinne could not, for the life of her, figure out why. And did she ever try to figure it out. No more. Enough already. She could not, and would not, live like this. She had made up her mind to forget about Pete, in the romantic sense, last summer. Once she invited Alistair into her bed that was it. And it worked … until the night of the awards ceremony. The things he said, the way he stared at her, embraced her. She never should have gone. She should have stayed away that night. Still, she went.

She had to erase that evening from her mind. Damn it, she had to. There was only one way.

This time Corinne took a deep breath. She knew what she had to do now. She had to leave, move away from New York before Pete's arrival in March. She couldn't bear to see him with Brandi, or any other woman, again.

Alistair approached from behind.

"Corinne?"

"Yes?"

"Will you look at me, please?"

She faced him, though it was extremely difficult. She so wanted to cry right now.

"You mean everything to me," Alistair said, falling to one knee. "I know I can make you happy, even happier than you've made me."

Corinne managed to crack a smile, which Alistair took as a good sign.

"So will you?" he asked again, slipping the ring onto her finger, adding the perfect decoration to her lavender dress. "Will you marry me?"

She paused a moment. She told herself over and over that this was the right thing to do. This was her ticket to safety, literally. Moving to England, an ocean away, was the best way to be free of this heartache for good.

"Yes," she said, finally. "Yes, I will marry you."

It worked! Everything I said worked! She agreed!

To be sure, he said, "You will?"

Corinne nodded.

Alistair rose to his feet in utter euphoria. He swept his new fiancée into his muscular arms, lifted her, and spun in a circle.

"I'm the luckiest bloke in the world," he said, realizing his longtime dream had just come true. "I love you so, so much."

Corinne could not reciprocate. Not yet anyway. She believed she would, though, in time.

God, she hoped so.

60

Yet again Pete found himself heading to New York City, this time the night before New Year's Eve. Better now than tomorrow, as Times Square would be brimming with people. So would the trains heading into Manhattan for the annual spectacle. Still, this Friday evening's train was quite crowded. No doubt people wanted to get to the City beforehand. Hotels in the area had been booked for weeks, if not months, in advance.

New Year celebrations were the last thing on Pete's mind tonight. As he gazed out the window, he reflected on last week's two extraordinary events. He was so proud of his mother. She finally kicked Adam—and his pig of a girlfriend—out of the house. She hadn't heard from them since, and she seemed fine with this, she really did. With those two not around, Christmas dinner in Woodlake Square was a real pleasure this year. The table contained surrounding chairs for only Mom and himself … and Harry. How great to have him there. He and Mom were hitting it off really well. Their relationship seemed to be blooming into something very special.

Arriving at Penn Station ended this particular trip down Memory Lane. Pete got out of the train and headed outside, where he hopped into a taxi. He soon ventured on another trip down Memory Lane. There was another extraordinary event that happened: Corinne deciding to leave for England with Alistair. He would never forget the day he found out, her phone call the Tuesday night before Christmas.

It was not the present he hoped to receive from her.

"Hey, it's me," she said.

It was the first time they had spoken since the awards ceremony. Pete couldn't help but feel a little awkward.

"Hi, Corinne, how are you?"

"Well… I've got some news."

She then told him how Alistair proposed—and that she accepted. Pete, seated on his couch, was stunned into immobilization.

This can't be happening; it just can't be.

Sure enough it was. She must really be happy, he thought. She must really love Alistair. For her to move across the Atlantic—to leave her home, job, family and friends, including himself—this British guy must mean the world to her.

And I thought I did.

He desperately wanted to say this out loud but couldn't voice the words. He was not about to upset her happiness. Pete had only one choice in the matter: accept her decision. But damn, was it hard. He wanted to ask her about what went on between them at the awards ceremony—if she, like him, felt anything magical. He must have been wrong. Corinne obviously felt nothing more than just friendship that night. Plus she accepted Alistair's marriage proposal. What more of an answer did he need than this? The matter was over. No sense in asking her now.

It was too late anyway. Here he was, a week and a half later, in a taxi on the way to The Piccadilly in the Upper West Side. It was where Corinne and Alistair chose to have their going-away party.

Going away? Yes, she was leaving. Not just the City, not just the state, but the country—tomorrow, New Year's Eve.

It was hard to believe: Corinne, an ocean away. They had gone through so much together. He would never forget all her support, especially during his tenure at Stepney Green. She helped him ease a lot of heartache. Dana, Liz, Brandi… he never could have got through the pain they inflicted without her. She was even supportive when Ginny dumped him.

Then there was the book, his prized debut novel. Corinne chose to read it instead of going off somewhere to celebrate Senior Week. Her faith in his writing abilities was unshakable. She always said his book would "rock," even before she read a single word. She knew he would find an agent. She knew that agent would find a publisher. And she knew *But I'll Never Be Lonely* would be a hit. How cool was this?

Pete had always dreamed of having a great girl on his side, someone to share his life's dreams, someone whose loyalty knew no bounds.

This girl was Corinne Aldrich. And he was in love with her.

If only he had realized this sooner…

The taxi arrived outside the pub. Pete opened the door and paid the cabbie. He then faced The Piccadilly entrance and let out a deep breath. This was going to be difficult, this whole evening.

He was ready, yet not ready.

Ready to face her, but not ready to say goodbye.

61

Corinne's family and friends crowded The Piccadilly's small banquet room in the rear of the pub. When Pete walked in, her circle of friends was complete. He looked incredibly handsome tonight. Hanging up his long black wool coat revealed dark-gray pants, a white dress shirt, a light-gray suit jacket, and black shoes. His short brown hair, like always, was combed and gelled to perfection.

Corinne sat at a corner table, the one with a Union Jack draped behind it. Where she was going, she would be seeing a lot of those flags, a different kind of red, white and blue. Portraits of the Royal Family, past and present, hung proudly on the adjacent stone walls. Beneath them rested thick wooden tables, filled to capacity tonight with guests of Mr. and soon-to-be Mrs. Alistair Brundidge.

The latter wore a casual yet dressy outfit, off-white slacks and a diamond-blue blouse. Her below-the-shoulder brown hair had a brilliant shimmer to it, even in this dimly lit banquet room. Something was missing from her smile, though. Pete could not figure out what it was. He knew this woman too well not to have noticed. Her smile seemed strained, like something she felt obligated to do.

Oh, heck, who was he kidding? Himself probably. Pete just wanted to think this, to believe this. He had never met a person more true to herself, aside from his mother, than Corinne Aldrich. She was genuinely happy. She had to be or else this going-away party wouldn't be happening, would it?

Suddenly, she tilted her head. Her best friend on campus had arrived! He was here, really here. At last!

That special sparkle in her smile had returned.

Pete noticed the change right away and smiled back.

They were so happy to see each other ... yet so sad, as this was the last time their eyes would meet. For a long, long time.

He wanted her. Yes, damn it, he wanted Corinne. She was more than his best friend now. That smile of hers, that beautiful smile attached to that beautiful woman with a beautiful heart... He wanted all of it, all of her.

But she was leaving ... tomorrow! True, but she was here now. And so was he. Maybe it wasn't too late after all. Maybe if they talked she would change her mind and stay. Pete had promised himself he would do no such thing. He would not do anything to upset Corinne or her plans. But this was a promise he had to break.

Or was it?

What am I going to do?

A slap on Pete's shoulder interrupted his thinking.

"Hello, mate."

Alistair said this with a broad, smug smile. He had won the hand of the lovely and charming Corinne Aldrich. He was the victor, not Pete. That was the message he wanted conveyed to her former love—which was received loud and clear.

"Congratulations," Pete said, forcing out the word. "You must be very proud."

Indeed he was, but still insecure when it came to this particular friend of his fiancée's.

"I'm really glad you're here," Alistair began.

Yeah, right.

"There are people dying to meet you, mate, big fans of your novel. Come, let's introduce you."

"Sure, but..."

What about Corinne? He wanted to say hello—and more—to her. Alistair probably knew this, which was why he led him to the other guests. He wanted to keep him busy for a while ... for as long as possible actually.

Pete was too much of a gentleman to excuse himself prematurely. He accepted the praise and compliments on his book graciously. He took his time answering their questions and talking to them about whatever topics they happened to bring up. Still, the minutes were fading fast. They turned into hours. Each one that went by meant less time for Corinne. Damn it, this was exactly what Alistair wanted to happen.

It was almost midnight. People were beginning to say their goodbyes, some of them tearful, and head home. Pete had to do the same. His train back to New Jersey was to leave in a little more than an hour. No more interruptions. He had to speak with Corinne—now.

He approached her table taking slow baby steps, savoring every moment of the beautiful woman—inside and out—seated before him.

"Hi, Pete," Corinne said softly.

She smiled that special smile, the one that contained the sparkle. Her Mediterranean blue eyes got a little brighter, too.

"Hi, Corinne … Gosh, I can't believe this is it."

Neither could she.

"Well, it is," said Alistair, snaking into the seat next to her.

He eyed his nemesis sharply. No one was going to take away his precious Corinne. He would make damn sure of that.

Pete paid him no mind.

"I'm going to miss you," he said to his best friend—and soulmate. "I'm going to miss you so much."

His eyes began to water, but still he continued.

"How do you say goodbye to someone who's always been there for me, who's always…"

Pete paused. This farewell speech was getting more and more difficult. He really thought he could handle this. He had prepared for this moment ever since he found out she was leaving. But that was before he learned what true love was, before realizing that Corinne defined it.

"I just wish…"

"What, Pete, what do you wish?"

"I wish… I wish we had more time, that's all."

No way did he want that guy to overhear.

Corinne sensed this and offered a suggestion.

"Why don't you come to the airport tomorrow?" she said. "A few people will be there to see us off. I'd love it if you came, too."

"I'd like that," said Pete. "I'd like that a lot."

Corinne smiled. She then turned to Alistair and asked him to write down their itinerary.

"And while you're doing that," she added, "I'll wait with Pete outside for the taxi. Just meet us there when you're done, okay?"

Alistair, not at all pleased, nodded his reply.

Voicing it would have revealed his objectionable scorn.

Alone at last. No Brundidge bloke. It was just he and Corinne, the way it used to be ... the way it ought to be. Pete had something really important to tell her. When he released a deep breath, a mouthful of vapor came out. It was really cold tonight. But what he was about to say would add just the right amount of warmth.

"There's someone I've been thinking a lot about," he said.

"Yes?"

"And the problem is... she's involved with someone else."

"Oh."

Corinne had no idea that she was the woman in question. As far as she knew, this was about Brandi Sparks.

And it infuriated her.

"So what should I do?"

What should you do??? How about getting over her once and for all? For Christ's sake, Pete, she's with Todd. She's probably just using you to make him jealous. Remember Dana O'Brien? Remember what happened with her? She did the same thing, only the guy she was trying to make jealous was married.

If you want to endure this again, fine. I'm not going to stand here anymore and watch you make the same mistake.

I won't put myself through this again, I just won't.

"Just go for it," Corinne said, concealing her hurt. "That's all, just go for it."

A euphoric Pete embraced her instantly, which shocked her. He held her tightly to his chest, so much that Corinne could feel the drumbeats of his heart. This clinch was just like the one at the awards ceremony, which made her wonder. Was *she* this woman he was talking about? Could it be possible?

No! I won't do this. Not again.

Too late, she already did.

Corinne closed her eyes. She savored Pete, the feel of the man she truly loved, in her arms. This could very well be the last time.

The embrace lasted a full minute, which seemed an eternity. Time stood as still as they did. Neither Pete nor Corinne seemed to mind. In fact, both wished the hug could last even longer. Forever would do just fine.

Not if Alistair had anything to say about it.

He was definitely not pleased with the sight he walked out to.

"Here you are, mate," he announced, holding a copy of the flight itinerary—and pretending not to be bothered.

Corinne broke away in haste. Hearing her fiancé's voice, realizing what he just witnessed, made her extremely uncomfortable.

"See you tomorrow," she whispered to Pete.

She then glanced awkwardly at Alistair. Unable to explain her actions, she hurried back inside the pub.

Pete's taxi arrived seconds later. Perfect. He could make his escape. The situation had become pretty intense. The embrace he and Corinne just shared said a lot. Even though it resembled the one earlier this month, there was still something different about it. Pete knew what it was: the way it *felt*. Not just physically but emotionally. His feelings were clear this time. No more confusion. Love and longing swirled throughout his entire body, down to the fingertips. And Corinne felt the same, he just knew it.

"Well, I better get going," Pete said, taking the flight information out of Alistair's hand. "Thanks for getting me a copy of this."

His rival's eyebrows arched mysteriously.

"No worries."

Pete hopped inside his taxi. As it departed he received an overwhelming feeling: he must tell Corinne how he felt about her, that he… that he loved her. Not just in the friendly sense. He was *in love* with her. This feeling, this urge to tell her, was powerful. Pete recalled a similar sensation earlier in the year, that summer day by his apartment window. Somehow he knew that whatever he had with Ginny Leeds was over. He couldn't shake that hunch then, nor could he shake what was stirring inside him now. He had promised himself never to ignore a gut feeling like this again.

Flashing a proud, determined smile, Pete pocketed Corinne's flight information. He was going to stop her from leaving. He was going to tell her exactly how he felt about her … no matter what.

Alistair, meanwhile, continued to stand outside The Piccadilly. He gazed into New York's light-polluted sky, unable to wipe the grin off his face.

He won.

It was over.

This was the last time he—or Corinne—would ever see the likes of Peter Michael Webb, the most naïve and foolishly trusting person he'd ever met.

62

Each time this happened, falling in love, Pete found himself in the dugout, dejected and humiliated. He should have thought the same this time as well. What a fool. When would he ever learn? There was no such thing as true love. Well, not for him. It was always like this—always. He never should have thought differently this time. But he did anyway. Why, damn it, why? It certainly would have been easier that way. He should have just focused on his writing career.

If only it were enough…

He was led to Stepney Green College for a reason, more than just to become a strong person. It was to find the love of his life. This he truly believed.

Only the love of his life wasn't Dana, Liz or Brandi. It was Corinne. All this time it was her. She knew it, too. But when she kissed him at homecoming more than a year ago he was just too confused. Romance was the last thing he needed then. It was too soon.

But now he was ready … and too late.

Pete reflected on this as he sat underneath the college's arched monument, the one made of huge earthly stones, the so-called "gateway to education excellence." He just had to come here tonight. Somehow, after everything that happened, it just seemed appropriate. The last time he was here he realized Brandi and Todd had betrayed him—and how incredibly stupid he was. He certainly had made his share of mistakes during that troubling time.

But they were nothing compared to the one he made last night. And realized just hours ago.

According to the itinerary Corinne's flight was due to leave at 10 p.m. Everyone who was coming to the airport to see her off should arrive no later than 7. Pete, however, was early, having pulled in at 6:15. Strange that he saw no sign for the U.K. airline Air Briton. He was in the right terminal, though. This section of Newark Liberty International was for flights to and from foreign countries. The United Kingdom included, of course.

Inside the airport Pete glanced around looking for something—anything—to direct him to Air Briton. But just like outside there were no signs to be found.

There was one for Skywards, however. Was there a mistake? Was her flight on this other British airline? Pete took out the itinerary and examined it once more. Again it read Air Briton not Skywards. So why was only the latter here?

He sighed in frustration. He needed to talk to Corinne—and fast. He needed to tell her how much he loved her ... and to please not go.

But where was she? To find out, Pete rushed to the uniformed agent behind the Skywards information counter. Fortunately, he didn't have to wait in line to speak with her.

"Excuse me, ma'am," he said, nearly out of breath, "I was wondering if you knew where I could find departures for Air Briton."

The lady looked puzzled.

"Sir, to my knowledge JFK Airport services that airline, not Newark."

Oh no.

"Are you sure?"

"Let's have a look," she said. "One moment, please."

The agent maneuvered her computer's mouse and typed a few keys.

"Yes, sir," she confirmed, "John F. Kennedy International Airport in Queens, New York, services Air Briton."

What!

"Is London the destination of the flight in question?"

Pete responded with a weak, downtrodden nod.

The agent glanced at the computer screen and informed the gentleman that Air Briton had daily flights to London departing at 6 p.m.

No!

Corinne's flight had taken off. He would not see her—or talk to her. She and Alistair were already in the air. Alistair! He lied! He deliberately wrote down phony information. There was no Air Briton flight out of Newark Liberty International, never had been. And it certainly didn't leave at 10 p.m.

Damn him. Pete's stomach twisted in knots of agony. He grew sick at the thought of having been played the ultimate fool. His face reddened. His breathing became irregular. Tears of despair—and anger—raged in his eyes. God help him, he wanted to strangle Alistair Brundidge with his bare hands. He was never so furious in his life. Or upset. This was his last chance to speak to Corinne, and he missed it. He couldn't even drive to JFK in Queens. No point now.

She was gone, really gone.

And there was absolutely nothing he could do about it.

Pete turned away from the counter. His whole world seemed to cave in around him. His hope, his dream, of Corinne rushing into his arms had been crushed, along with his spirit.

"I'm sorry, sir," the agent said, noticing his distress.

"Yeah, I'm sorry, too."

How could he have been so stupid? Yet again! How could he not have gone online to verify Corinne's flight information beforehand? Why, but why, did he ever believe that Alistair would write down their actual itinerary? How could he have trusted that guy? How could he be so naïve? How?! And why didn't he just text or call Corinne earlier in the day? Why?!

Slumped underneath the arch, Pete asked himself these questions over and over.

Some gateway to education excellence...

So here he was, alone again on New Year's Eve. Though strong, he didn't want to end up like Parker West from *But I'll Never Be Lonely*. Not really. Deep down he wanted more. Damn it, yes, he wanted a girlfriend, a solid relationship, a life partner, someone to love and someone to love him.

But Corinne was gone, halfway across the Atlantic by now.

She probably hated him anyway. He never came to the airport to say goodbye. There was no excuse for that.

If she only knew there was…

Pete shivered. It was getting colder out here. He turned his head to the left, toward the paved slope leading upward to the college. So many memories of that pathway: the walks, the piney air, rollerblading with Brandi, Corinne leading him back to Rockford Hall weeks later. A sheet of powdery snow lay on it now. What a sight. The college grounds were turning into a winter wonderland. He sure wished Corinne were here to witness it with him.

She was all he wanted right now, and for the rest of his life. She was the dream for which he longed. Sure, becoming a well-known author was terrific—it certainly had its perks—but true love would top this achievement, no question. No major book deal or TV writing job could compare to the feeling Corinne Aldrich produced inside his heart. She was the perfect woman for him, the one he had been searching for all his life.

And he had found her.

Then lost her.

Pete glanced at his watch. It was 11 p.m., one hour before the New Year. He wondered if he should head back home. Or should he just spend the night here, like he did nearly two years ago? But it was raining then, not snowing. He could freeze to death tonight. No chance of Corinne rescuing him like before.

Suddenly, a car pulled up. Curious, Pete turned away from the pedestrian slope and faced the open road to his right. The headlights on the car got brighter the closer it approached, the more it slowed down. Probably campus safety, Pete thought, or a cop who was going to kick him off college property. No loitering was allowed, even though he was probably the only student, current or alumni, on campus tonight.

He squinted through the falling snowflakes to get a better look. The car, which parked several feet behind his, definitely did not belong to campus safety. No Stepney Green College insignia. Maybe it was an unmarked police car. Even when the headlights flashed off, Pete couldn't make out who the driver was. But he noticed the license plate; the car was a rental.

And then the driver exited…

My God, it can't be.

Pete rose to be certain, even though his eyes did not deceive him. It really was an angel!

"Corinne?"

She was just as stunned to see him.

"Yes, it's me," she said. "What on earth are you doing here?"

"What am *I* doing here?"

She closed the car door and slowly approached the arch, the place she once found Pete in severe depression. Now, though, it was her turn to come here. It was her turn to escape the insanity bouncing off the walls of the brain. This was the craziest night of her life. And with Pete here—of all places, of all times—her night got even crazier. He was the reason behind it. He was always the reason.

She stared at him with dry puffy eyes. Obviously she had been crying her eyes out for hours.

"I can't believe it," she said. "I can't believe you're here."

"And I can't believe you're here."

Maybe so, but he was ecstatic that she was.

"I'm not dreaming, am I?" he asked her.

Corinne cracked a smile.

"Funny," she said, "I keep asking myself the same question."

Pete smiled this time. He then took her gloved hands into his.

"Well, I'm here," he said tenderly, euphorically, "and so are you. We're both here, and we're both real. This moment is real. It's not a dream."

Hearing this, Corinne flung herself into his arms. She was so exhausted, so emotionally drained. If she had any tears left to cry, she would have cried them.

Pete sensed she needed him right now. It was his turn to be strong, to hold and comfort her. It was the least he could do to return the favor, ironically underneath this very monument. Corinne certainly was there for him that stormy spring morning. Now, on this chilly winter night, he was there for her.

And he loved every minute of it. He loved holding this remarkable woman in his arms. He loved being her rock. Most importantly, he loved *her*.

"I couldn't go through with it, I just couldn't," she said in the midst of whimpers. "I couldn't get on the plane with Alistair. I can't marry him."

"Oh."

"I couldn't face my family. That's why I drove out here tonight. I needed to think, to try and clear my head. I had to get out of New York, too—it's so crazy there tonight, traffic is insane—and this was the first place I thought of."

Pete chuckled, which made Corinne pull away.

"What's so funny?" she asked.

"Nothing," he replied, "it's just that after leaving the airport this was the first place I thought of, too."

"You came to the airport?"

"Newark."

"But JFK was where—"

"I know, I know," said Pete. "Alistair gave me phony itinerary."

"He did what?!"

Corinne was furious—but not for long.

"Don't worry about it," Pete said softly. "He's gone now. It's just you and me ... the way it's meant to be."

Meant to be? She pressed her hand to her heart, which was beating faster.

"It's been a crazy night, hasn't it?" he added. "And if I told you how much I loved you, it would be even crazier."

"Yes, it—"

What! Did he just say what I thought he said?

He did ... and would again, only next time without the "if." He had waited ages for this moment. Well, not exactly, but the last 24 hours sure seemed like it. His world had come to an end at Newark Liberty International. He thought he had lost his chance to utter those three special words. But she was here now. She was here with him, not Alistair Brundidge. There was hope after all. Corinne came back, his best friend, soulmate, the woman who turned his dream into a reality. Finally, he could tell her just how much she meant to him.

"I love you," said Pete. "I love you with all my heart."

She stared at him in shock, amazement, and bliss. She could hardly believe what she just heard.

"You love me?"

He nodded, and then said, "I was going to tell you tonight at the airport. Obviously that didn't happen."

True, but telling her right here and now more than sufficed. Corinne was about to cry. New tears had miraculously—and joyously—reformed. She had waited such a long time to hear "I love you" come out of his mouth.

But she held in those tears of joy. A question remained.

"What about Brandi?"

"Brandi?"

"Yeah, Brandi Sparks," she said, turning away. "I saw you two at the Galloway, the night of the awards ceremony. You were all over each other."

Pete again chuckled.

"Sweetie," he began, "we were not all over each other, believe me."

Sweetie? She liked the sound of that.

"Brandi was going through a rough time," he continued. "She needed a little support, that's all. I haven't seen or spoken to her since. And to tell you the truth I have no desire to. I really had no idea she was even there. Or that you were even there, that you had come back." He then placed his hands on Corinne's waist, leaned into her ear, and whispered, "Jealous, were you?"

She swung around to answer him face to face.

"Jealous? Me?"

"Yes, you."

"Don't be silly, Pete," she said. "I could never be—"

He kissed her before she could finish the fib. And what a kiss: long, deep, passionate, and full of love. Corinne literally saw stars, during and afterwards.

"Yeah, I was jealous," she admitted, finally.

Pete smiled triumphantly, like a schoolboy who just outsmarted the teacher in front of the whole class. He then asked why she was so jealous.

"Because..."

Girl, just say it. He wants you to say it. It's okay now; he won't run off this time. He said he loved you, remember? He broke his cardinal rule, the one about the woman having to make the first move. He's the one who made the first move, who planted the kiss, who admitted his love. Just go for it, Corinne, everything will be all right.

Still, she took a deep breath.

"Because..." she began again, "I was jealous because I love you, Pete."

He froze. Even though he sensed how she felt deep down, hearing her say "I love you" out loud cast him under a spell. Finally, he found someone who loved him as much as he loved her. Could life get any better?

"It's the same reason why I couldn't marry Alistair," Corinne added. "How could I when I'm in love with someone else?"

She removed her gloves to stroke his face with her bare hands. Pete closed his eyes and savored the touch.

"I couldn't leave you," she whispered fondly. "You're the man I love, the one I've always loved."

She then kissed him. Their lips locked for countless minutes. The display of affection revealed so much emotion, so much relief. Both had found the love of their lives. And both admitted their love. No more confusion or miscommunication. Pete did not still love Brandi; Corinne did not really love Alistair. Pete and Corinne loved *each other*.

Their lips soon parted, but very gradually. The moment had become pretty serious. Now, though, it was time for a little humor.

"By the way," said Corinne, "what took you so long?"

"Huh?"

"Why did you wait so long to tell me that you loved me?"

"I could ask you the same question."

"But I asked first," she said playfully.

Pete hesitated before answering. He had to think of the perfect answer. It was out there, and after a few seconds he found it.

"It took me a while to realize, that's all," he began. "After all, I do have some really, really high standards."

Amused, Corinne smiled.

Pete then added, softly and lovingly, "And you're the only one who will ever meet them."

Exhilarated, the couple kissed yet again. They held each other closely, tightly. Neither could let go. Nor did they want to. Both could stay like this forever. The moment was beautiful. What they felt was beautiful. So was the snowy scenery outside the arch, which neither considered. Their undying love for one another consumed their every thought.

What a way to end the year and begin a new one.

Pete was with the woman he was meant to spend his life. At long last he found her—and before his 25th birthday in January, the midway point of his 20s. He always dreamed this would happen.

Well, it did.

Acknowledgments

I must first mention a woman by the name of Erinn Elizabeth Farver, who sadly passed away in 2008. A talented writer herself, Erinn spent numerous hours reading over my initial text way back when. She then offered detailed, very helpful suggestions. For this she has my utmost gratitude. I love and miss you, dear friend.

Karen Reinhold… You have always been supportive of my writing, and I hope you know how much I appreciate this. Your time and feedback are also most appreciated. Thanks for everything.

Sandipan Chaudhuri… Your enthusiasm for this project has far surpassed my own, and for this I am grateful. Thank you for all your support, your friendship, for being "mon frère" all these years.

Dad… Thank you for your helpful suggestions – and for coming up with the perfect title.

My other family members… Thank you for your love and support. You know who you are, and I hope you know how much I love and support you as well.

Jim Stokes, CJ Barnes, Casey Franco, and other Lettra Press personnel… Many thanks for all your assistance.

And finally, my friends, coworkers and other special people who have wished me well… Thank you for your words of encouragement, thank you for being *you*.

CPSIA information can be obtained
at www.ICGtesting.com
Printed in the USA
BVHW091311061022
648825BV00013B/314